MW00861424

THE ILLEGITIMATES™ ©

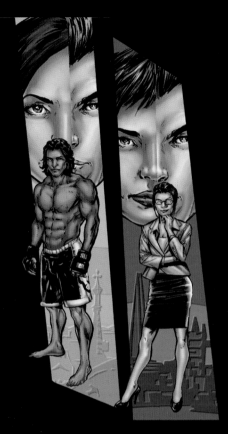

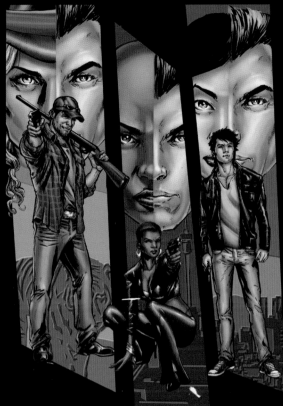

COLLECTION EDITS BY
JUSTIN EISINGER AND ALONZO SIMON

COLLECTION DESIGN BY
CHRIS MOWRY

ISBN: 978-1-63140-036-0

17 16 15 14   1 2 3 4

Ted Adams, CEO & Publisher
Greg Goldstein, President & COO
Robbie Robbins, EVP/Sr. Graphic Artist
Chris Ryall, Chief Creative Officer/Editor-in-Chief
Matthew Ruzicka, CPA, Chief Financial Officer
Alan Payne, VP of Sales
Dirk Wood, VP of Marketing
Lorelei Bunjes, VP of Digital Services
Jeff Webber, VP of Digital Publishing & Business Development

www.IDWPUBLISHING.com
IDW founded by Ted Adams, Alex Garner, Kris Oprisko, and Robbie Robbins

Facebook: **facebook.com/idwpublishing**
Twitter: **@idwpublishing**
YouTube: **youtube.com/idwpublishing**
Instagram: **instagram.com/idwpublishing**
deviantART: **idwpublishing.deviantart.com**
Pinterest: **pinterest.com/idwpublishing/idw-staff-faves**

THE ILLEGITIMATES

CREATED BY

TARAN KILLAM

WRITTEN BY

MARC ANDREYKO AND TARAN KILLAM

PENCILS BY

KEVIN SHARPE

INKS BY

DIANA GREENHALGH

ADDITIONAL INKS BY

JOHN LIVESAY

COLORS BY

PETER PANTAZIS

LETTERS BY

THOM ZAHLER

SERIES EDITS BY

SARAH GAYDOS

COVER BY

PHIL JIMENEZ

COVER COLORS BY

PETER PANTAZIS

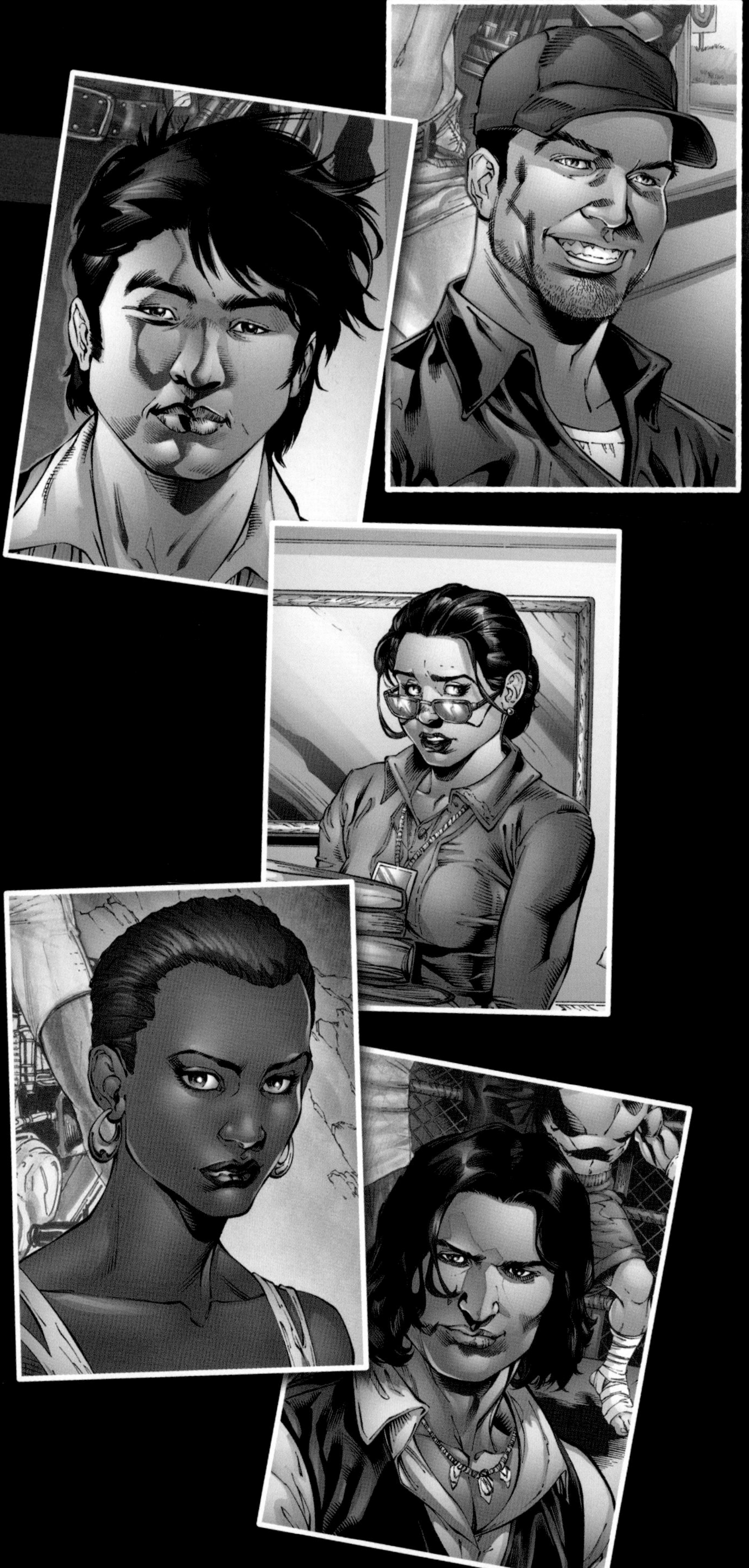

INTRODUCTION

When Taran Killam sent me the first issue of *The Illegitimates*, I dived in completely cold and was quickly won over by the mischievous premise.

I was a Bond fan growing up (who isn't?) and am unapologetically a child of the Roger Moore generation. Yes, he's certainly the silliest 007, with permanent arched eyebrows, endless gadgets and a wizard's sleeve of one liners, but I care not. Seriously, do you even need *Austin Powers* when *Octopussy* exists?

So I was immediately amused when the premise of Taran's comic opus became clear, as it revolved around one of the more questionable aspects of the international spy genre. Hard facts tell us that James Bond slept with more than fifty women in twenty three films, but what if the very dangerous spy was less than safe...

Enter Jack Steele, another veteran superspy with a taste for destruction, but seemingly a complete disregard for protection. Suppose that Steele's decades of international bed hopping had produced several illegitimate children, the secret children of a secret agent.

Then suppose that the unknowing spawn were brought together to form their own team of mercenaries.... well then you have the very entertaining tome in your very hands, *The Illegitimates*, an explosive love letter to the dad you never knew.

Please enjoy, in collected form for the first time, Taran Killam's glorious bastards.

Be safe,

Edgar Wright
June 2014

Artwork by **Kevin Sharpe**
Colors by **Peter Pantazis**

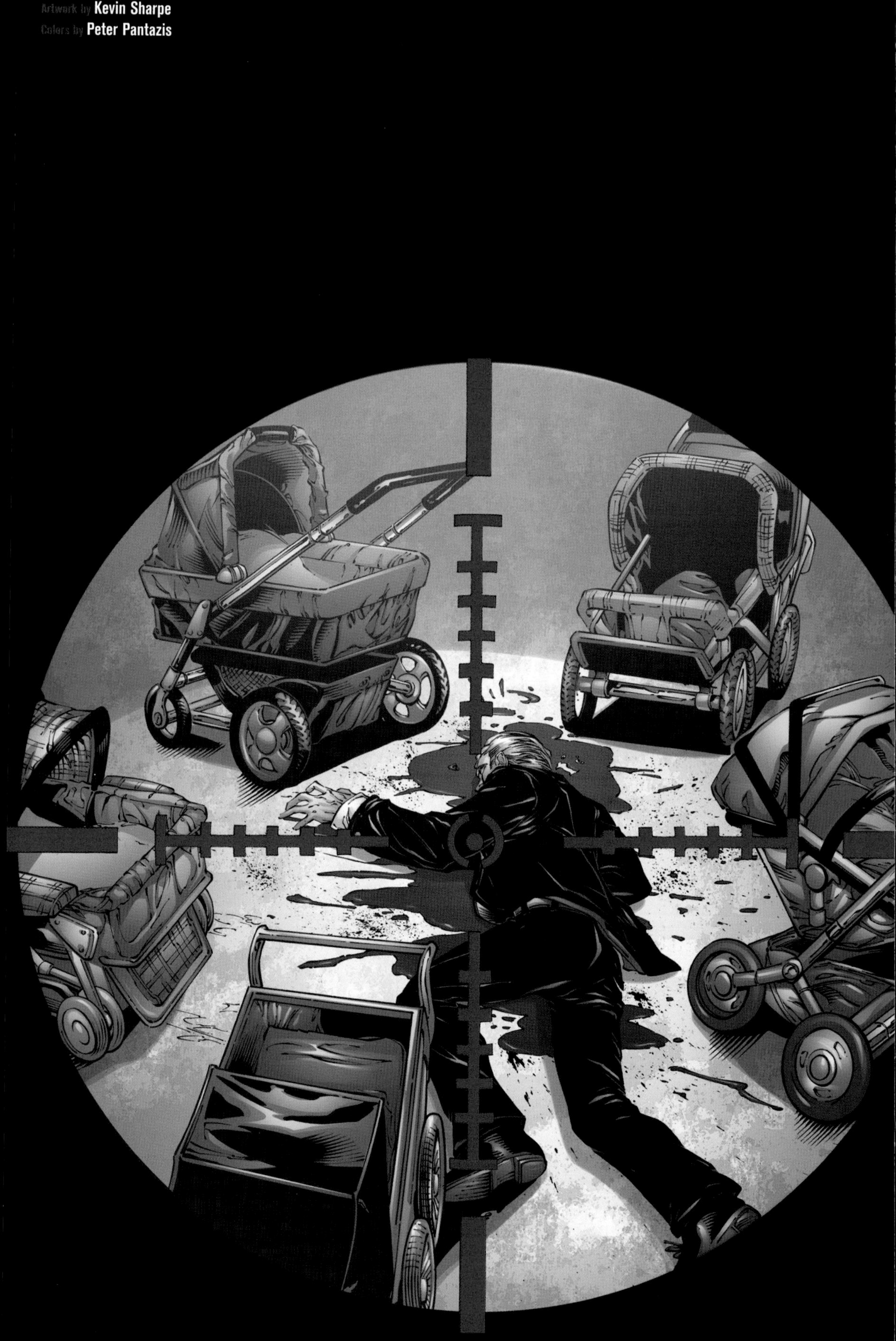

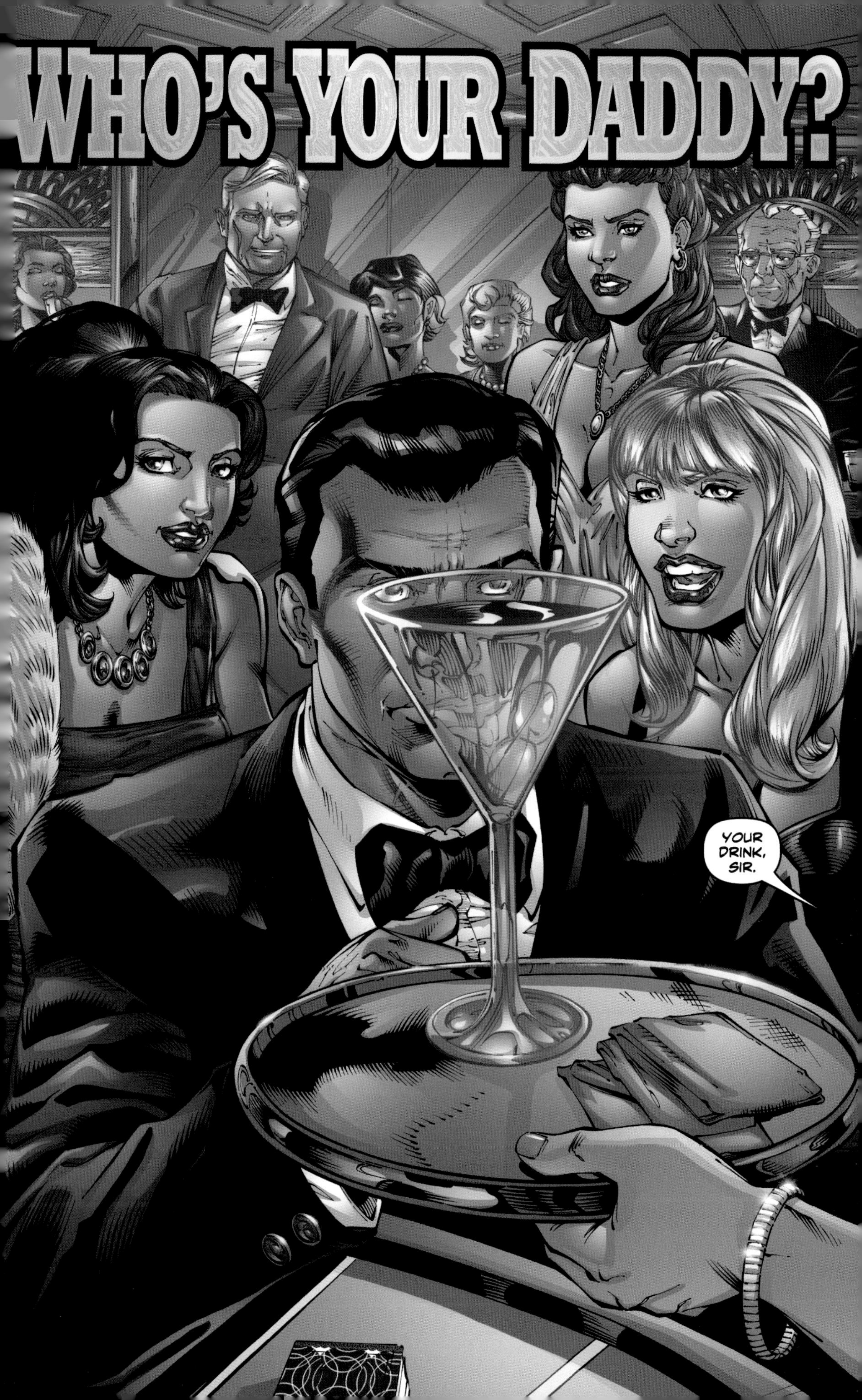
WHO'S YOUR DADDY?
YOUR DRINK, SIR.

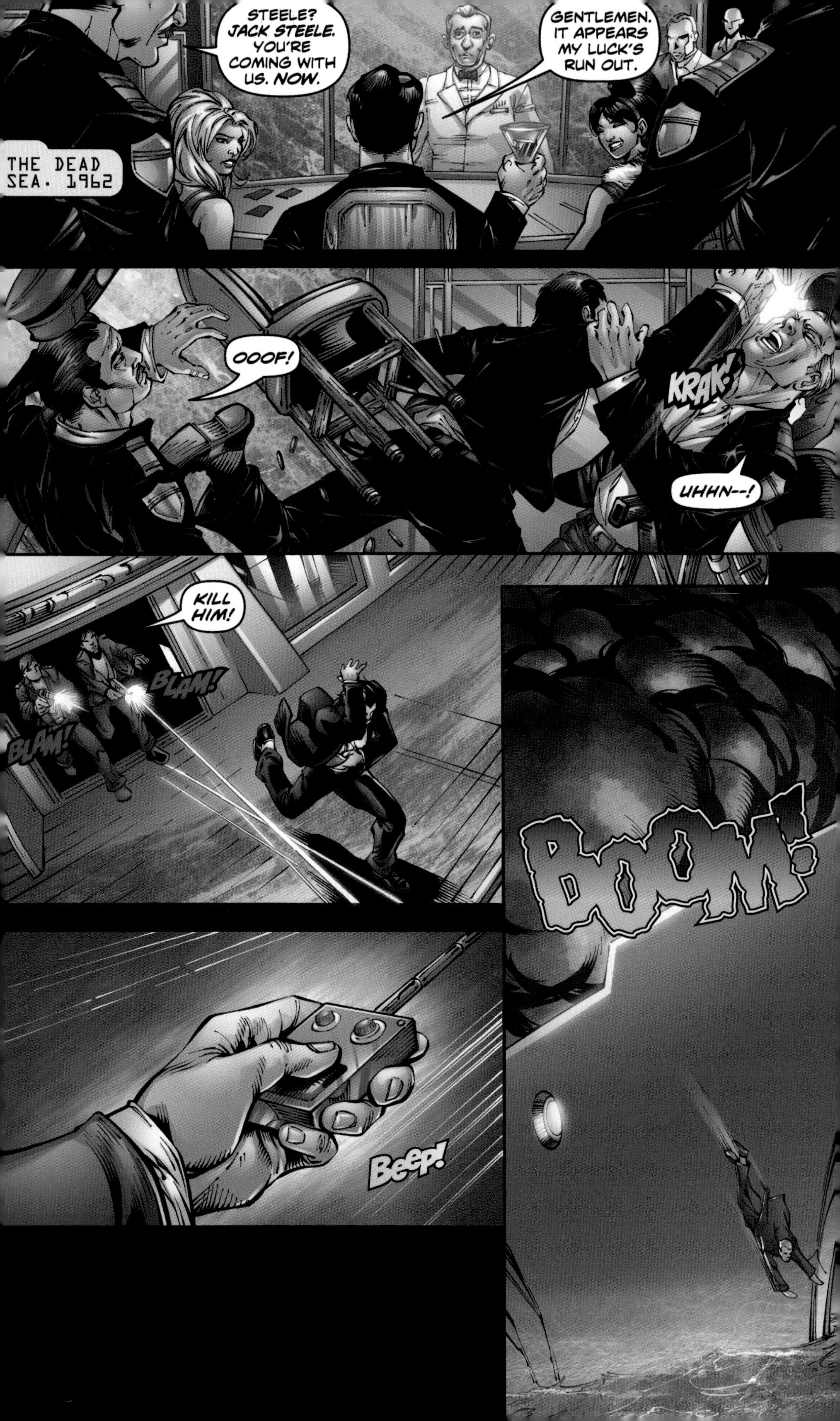
THE DEAD SEA. 1962
STEELE? JACK STEELE. YOU'RE COMING WITH US. NOW.
GENTLEMEN. IT APPEARS MY LUCK'S RUN OUT.
OOOF!
KRAK!
UHHN--!
KILL HIM!
BLAM!
BLAM!
BOOM!
Beep!

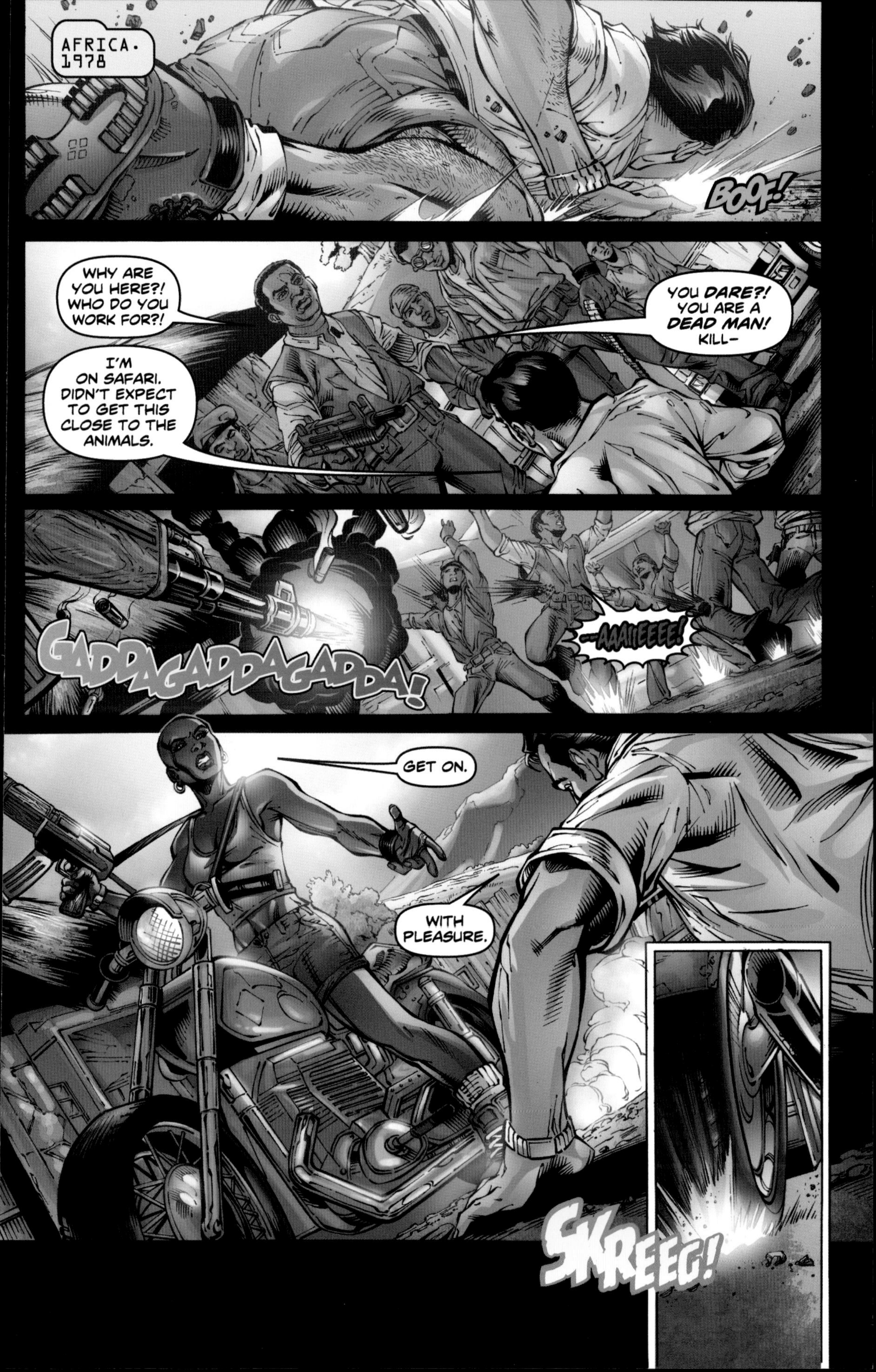
AFRICA. 1978
BOOF!
WHY ARE YOU HERE?! WHO DO YOU WORK FOR?!
I'M ON SAFARI. DIDN'T EXPECT TO GET THIS CLOSE TO THE ANIMALS.
YOU DARE?! YOU ARE A DEAD MAN! KILL-
GADDAGADDAGADDA!
--AAAIIEEEE!
GET ON.
WITH PLEASURE.
SKREEG!

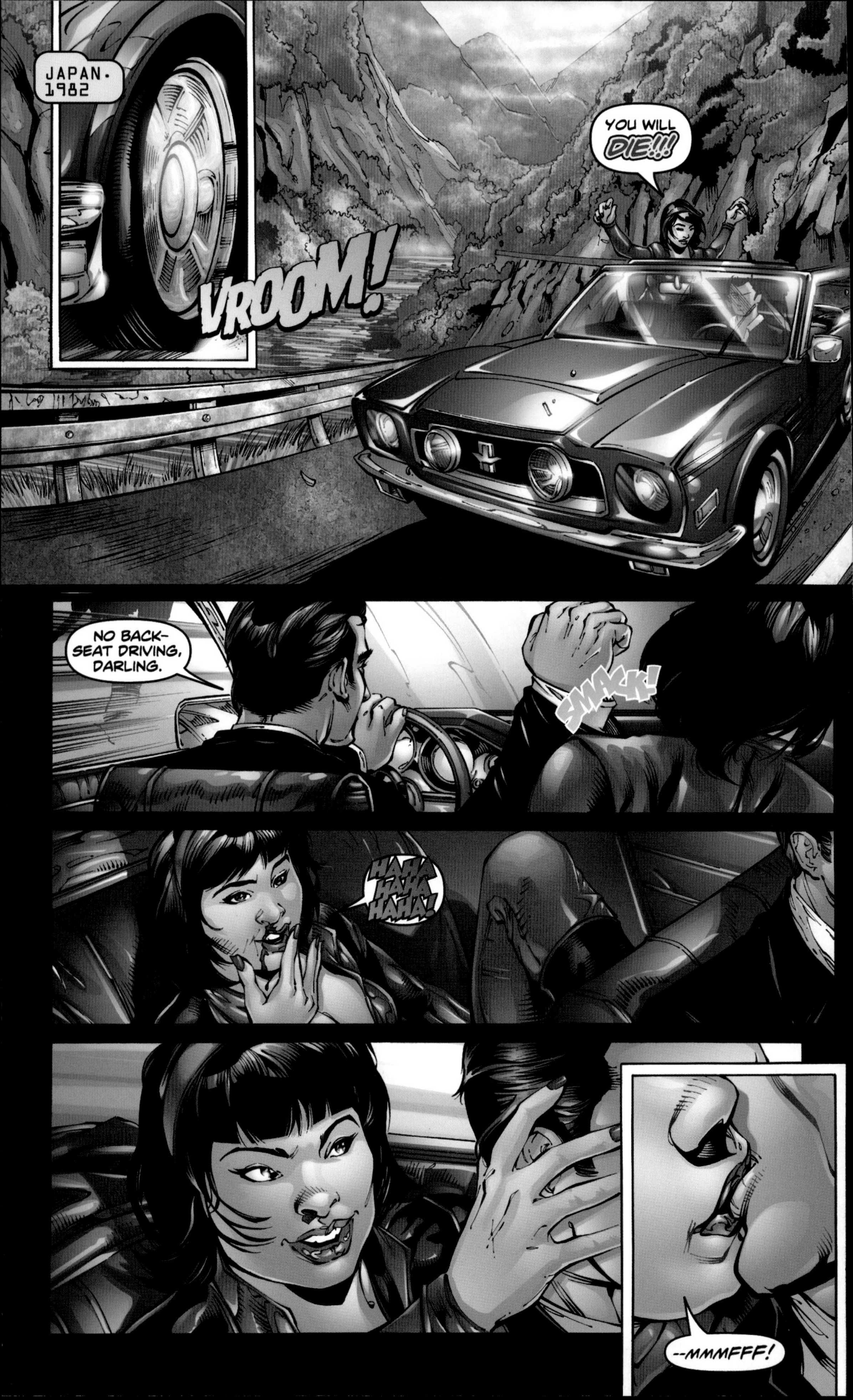
JAPAN. 1982
VROOM!
YOU WILL DIE!!!
NO BACK-SEAT DRIVING, DARLING.
SMACK!
HAHA HAHA HAHA!
--MMMFFF!

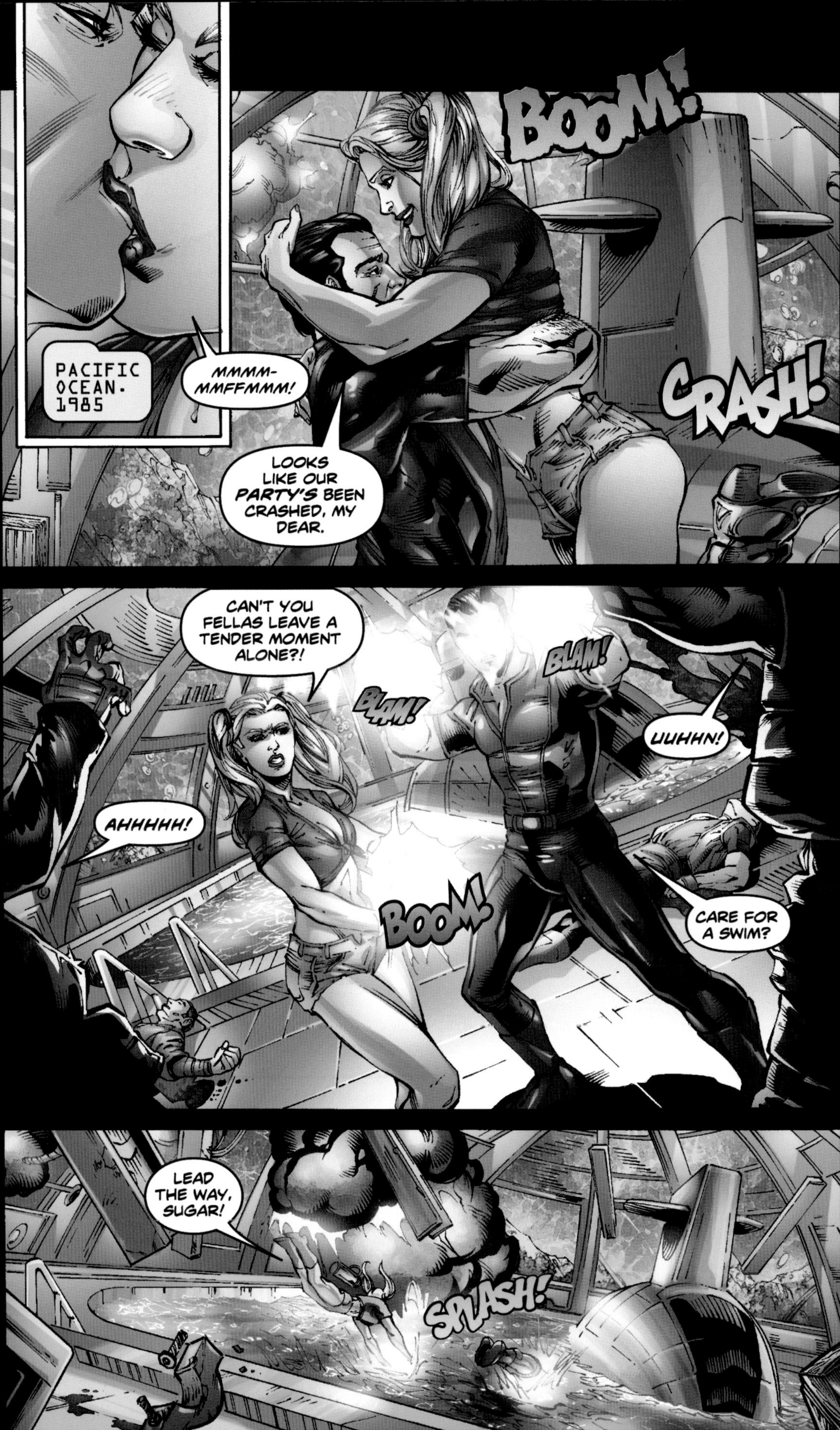
BOOM!
PACIFIC OCEAN. 1985
MMMM-MMFFMMM!
CRASH!
LOOKS LIKE OUR PARTY'S BEEN CRASHED, MY DEAR.
CAN'T YOU FELLAS LEAVE A TENDER MOMENT ALONE?!
BLAM!
BLAM!
UUHHN!
AHHHHH!
BOOM!
CARE FOR A SWIM?
LEAD THE WAY, SUGAR!
SPLASH!

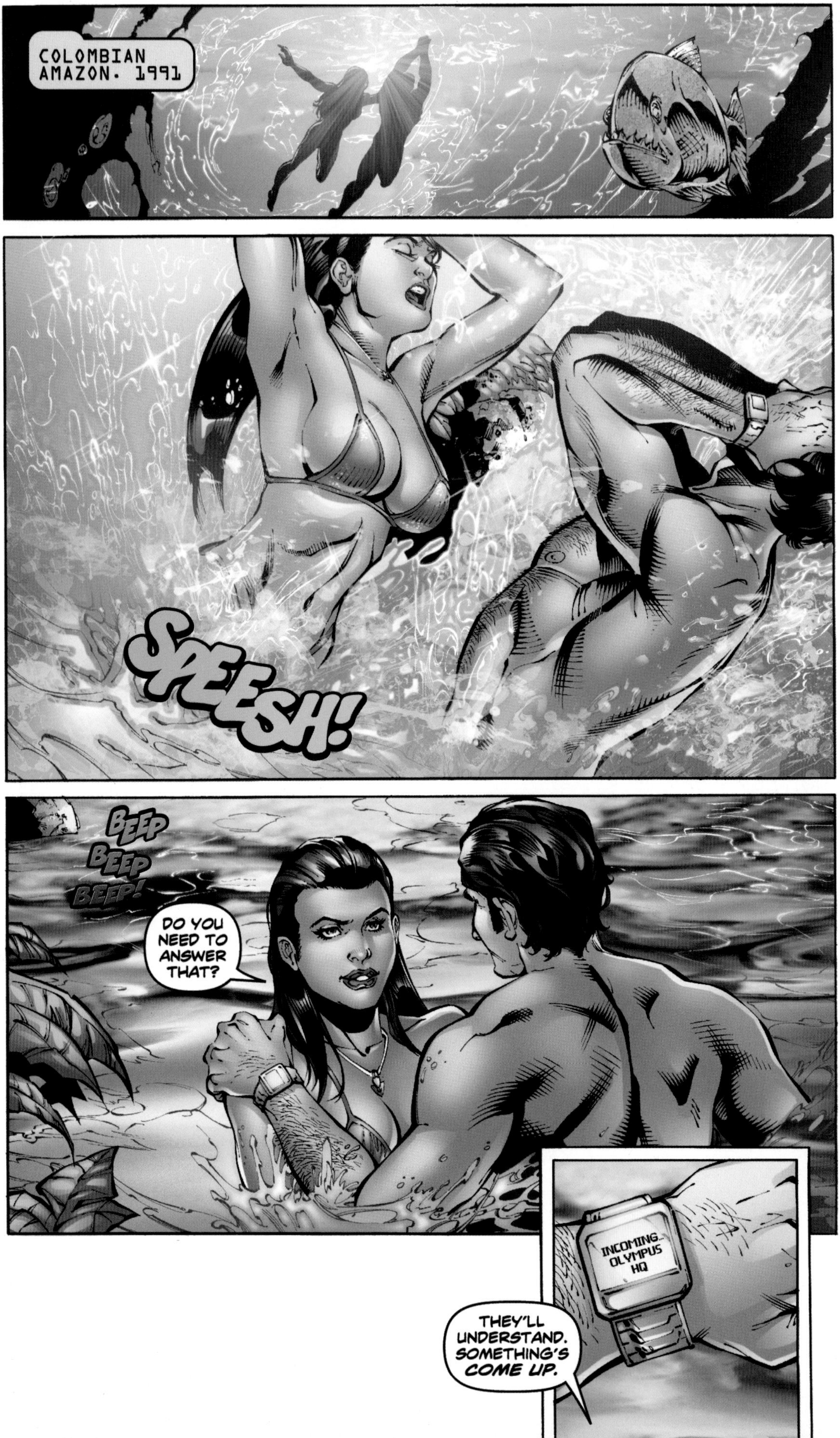
COLOMBIAN AMAZON. 1991
SPEESH!
BEEP BEEP BEEP!
DO YOU NEED TO ANSWER THAT?
INCOMING... OLYMPUS HQ
THEY'LL UNDERSTAND. SOMETHING'S COME UP.

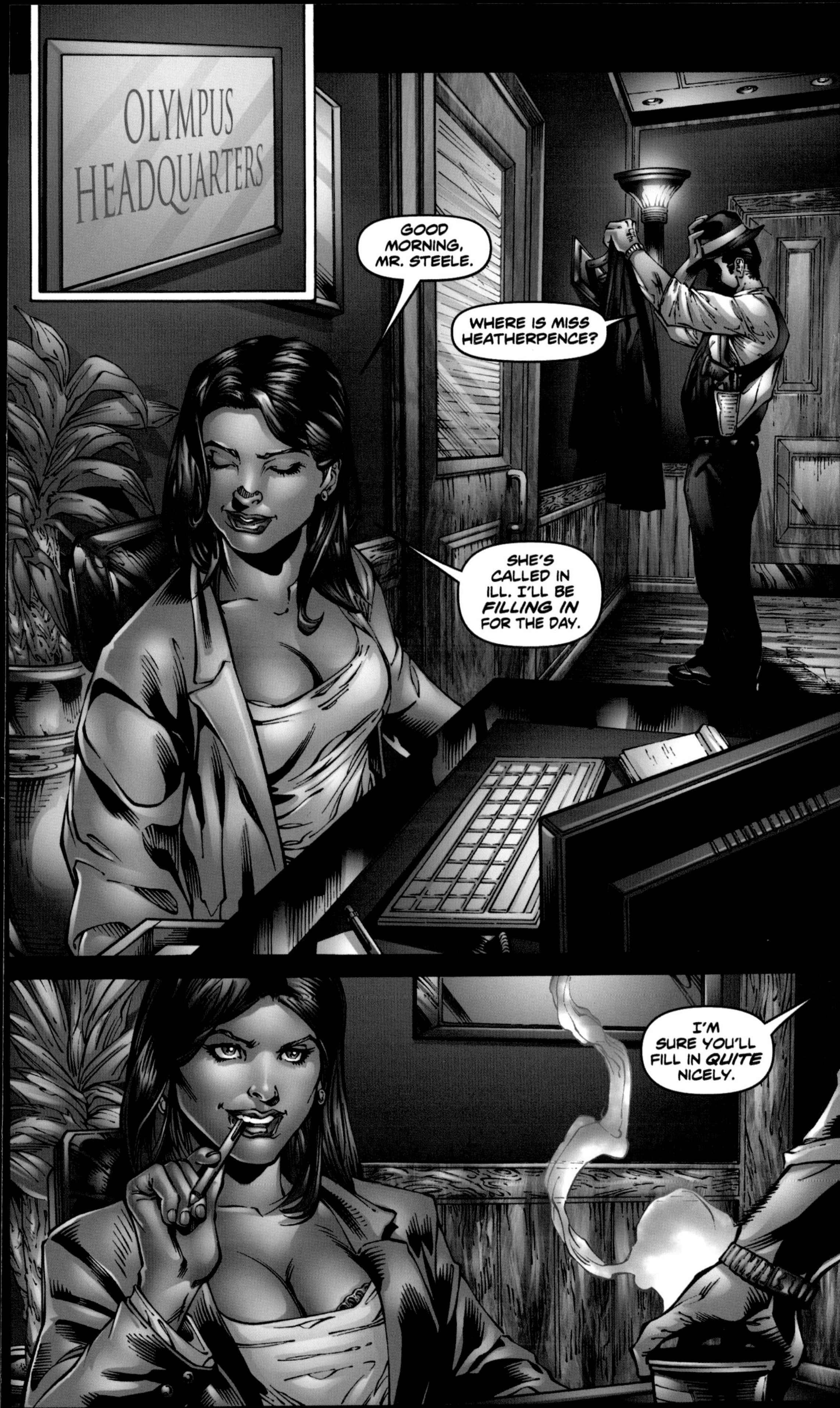
OLYMPUS HEADQUARTERS
GOOD MORNING, MR. STEELE.
WHERE IS MISS HEATHERPENCE?
SHE'S CALLED IN ILL. I'LL BE *FILLING IN* FOR THE DAY.
I'M SURE YOU'LL FILL IN *QUITE* NICELY.

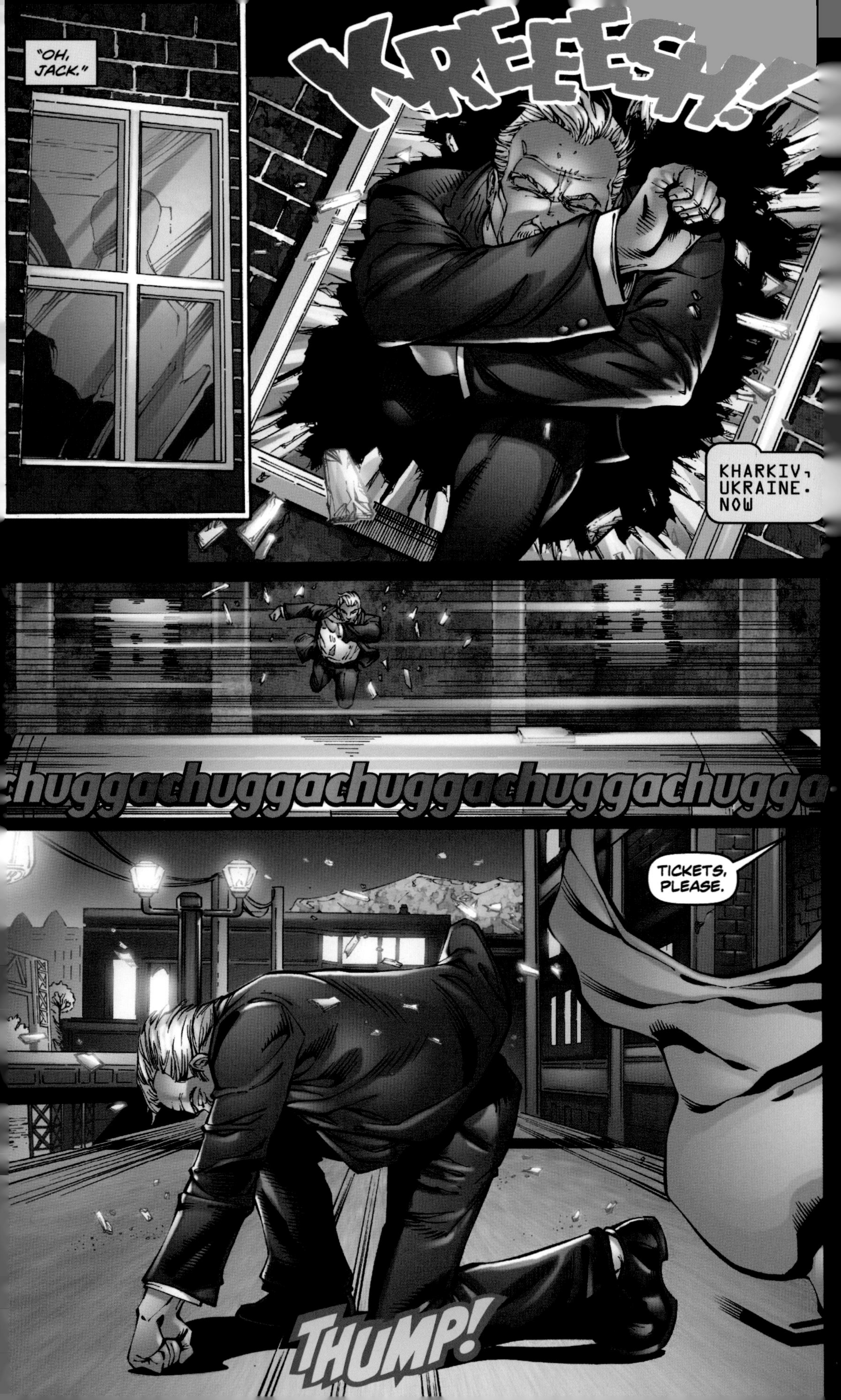
"OH, JACK."
KREEESH!!
KHARKIV, UKRAINE. NOW
chuggachuggachuggachugga
TICKETS, PLEASE.
THUMP!

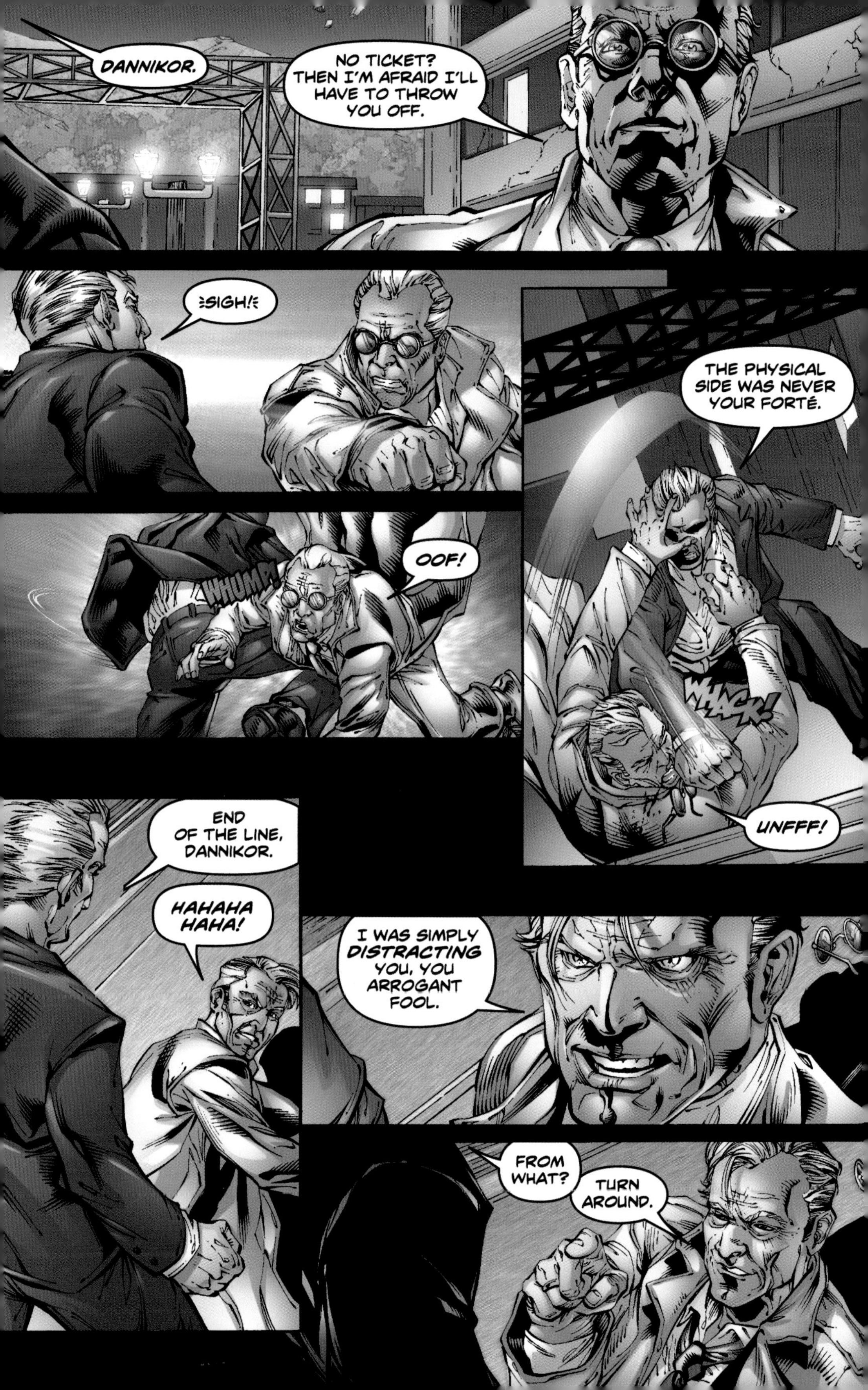
DANNIKOR.
NO TICKET? THEN I'M AFRAID I'LL HAVE TO THROW YOU OFF.
SIGH!
THE PHYSICAL SIDE WAS NEVER YOUR FORTÉ.
WHUMP!
OOF!
WHACK!
UNFFF!
END OF THE LINE, DANNIKOR.
HAHAHA HAHA!
I WAS SIMPLY DISTRACTING YOU, YOU ARROGANT FOOL.
FROM WHAT?
TURN AROUND.

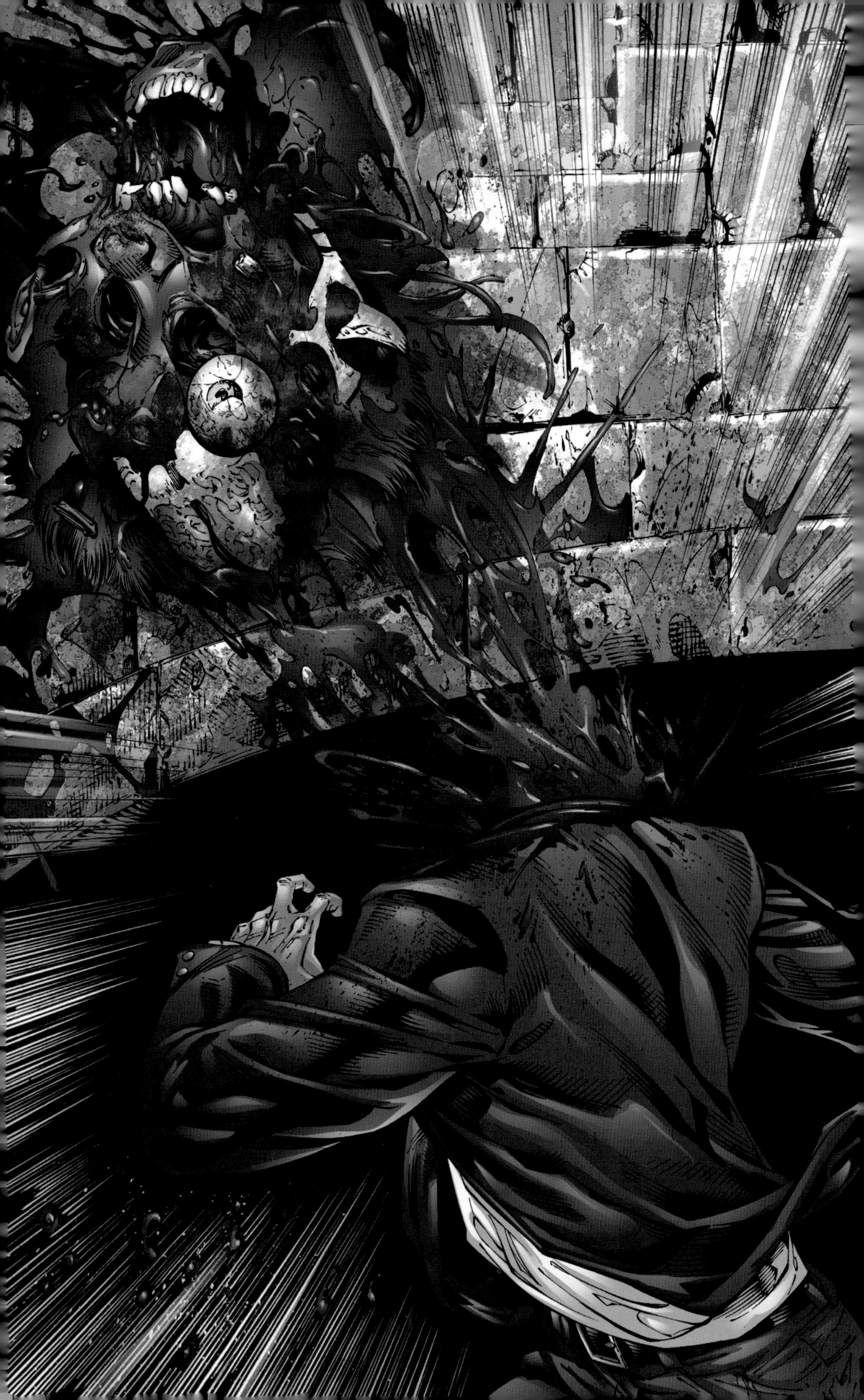

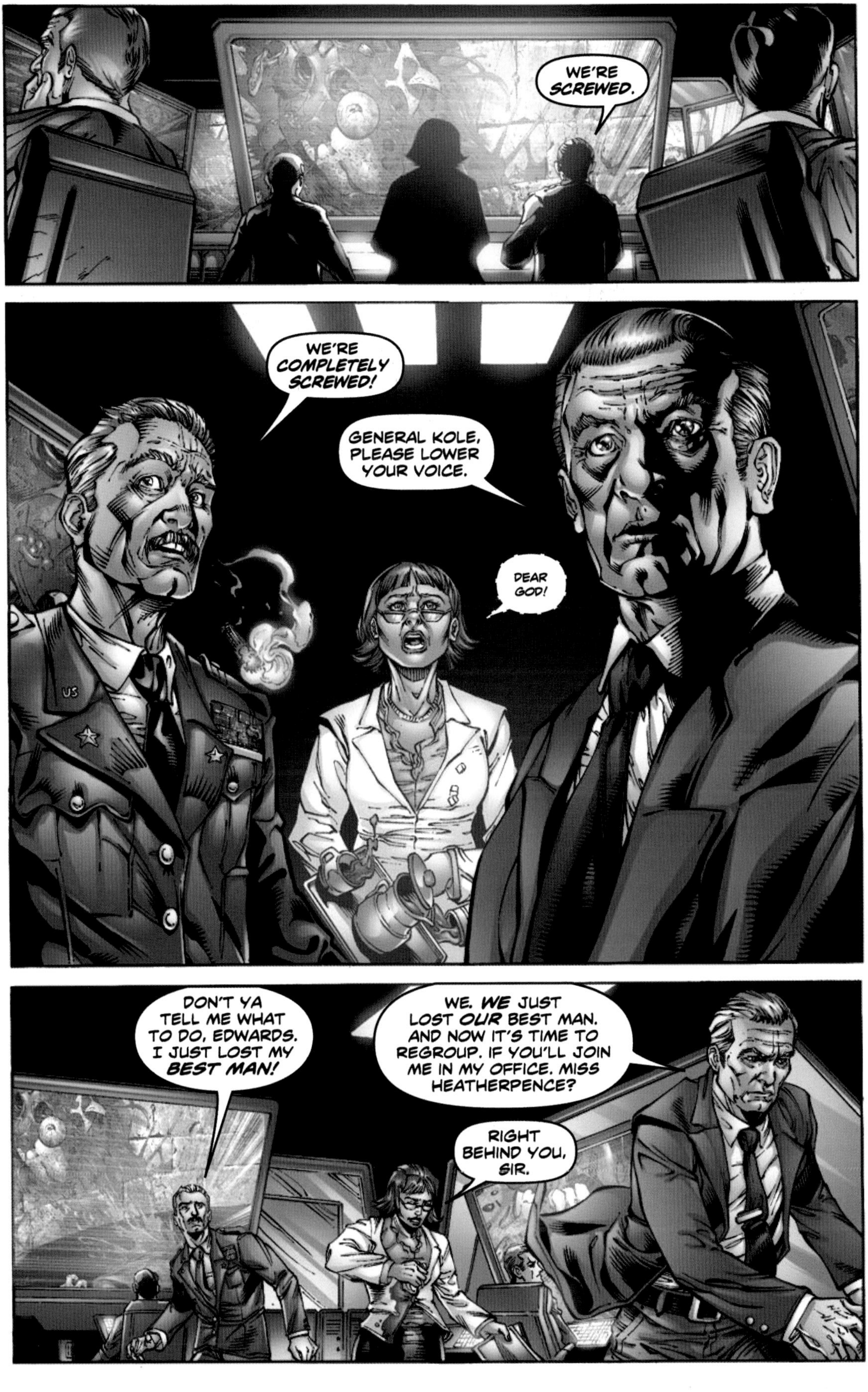
WE'RE SCREWED.
WE'RE COMPLETELY SCREWED!
GENERAL KOLE, PLEASE LOWER YOUR VOICE.
DEAR GOD!
DON'T YA TELL ME WHAT TO DO, EDWARDS. I JUST LOST MY BEST MAN!
WE. WE JUST LOST OUR BEST MAN. AND NOW IT'S TIME TO REGROUP. IF YOU'LL JOIN ME IN MY OFFICE. MISS HEATHERPENCE?
RIGHT BEHIND YOU, SIR.
US

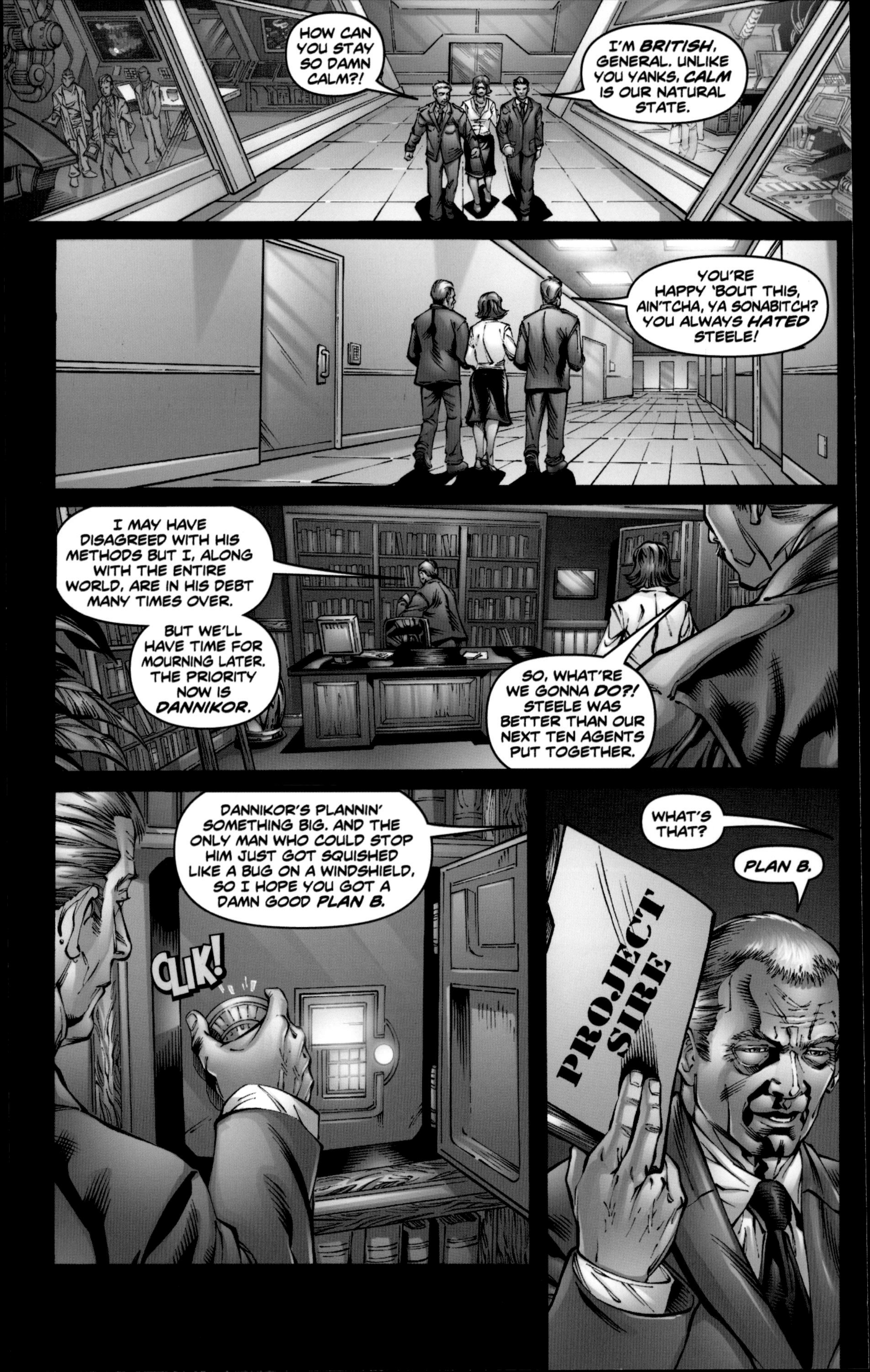
HOW CAN YOU STAY SO DAMN CALM?!
I'M BRITISH, GENERAL. UNLIKE YOU YANKS, CALM IS OUR NATURAL STATE.
YOU'RE HAPPY 'BOUT THIS, AIN'TCHA, YA SONABITCH? YOU ALWAYS HATED STEELE!
I MAY HAVE DISAGREED WITH HIS METHODS BUT I, ALONG WITH THE ENTIRE WORLD, ARE IN HIS DEBT MANY TIMES OVER.
BUT WE'LL HAVE TIME FOR MOURNING LATER. THE PRIORITY NOW IS DANNIKOR.
SO, WHAT'RE WE GONNA DO?! STEELE WAS BETTER THAN OUR NEXT TEN AGENTS PUT TOGETHER.
DANNIKOR'S PLANNIN' SOMETHING BIG. AND THE ONLY MAN WHO COULD STOP HIM JUST GOT SQUISHED LIKE A BUG ON A WINDSHIELD, SO I HOPE YOU GOT A DAMN GOOD PLAN B.
CLIK!
WHAT'S THAT?
PLAN B.
PROJECT SIRE

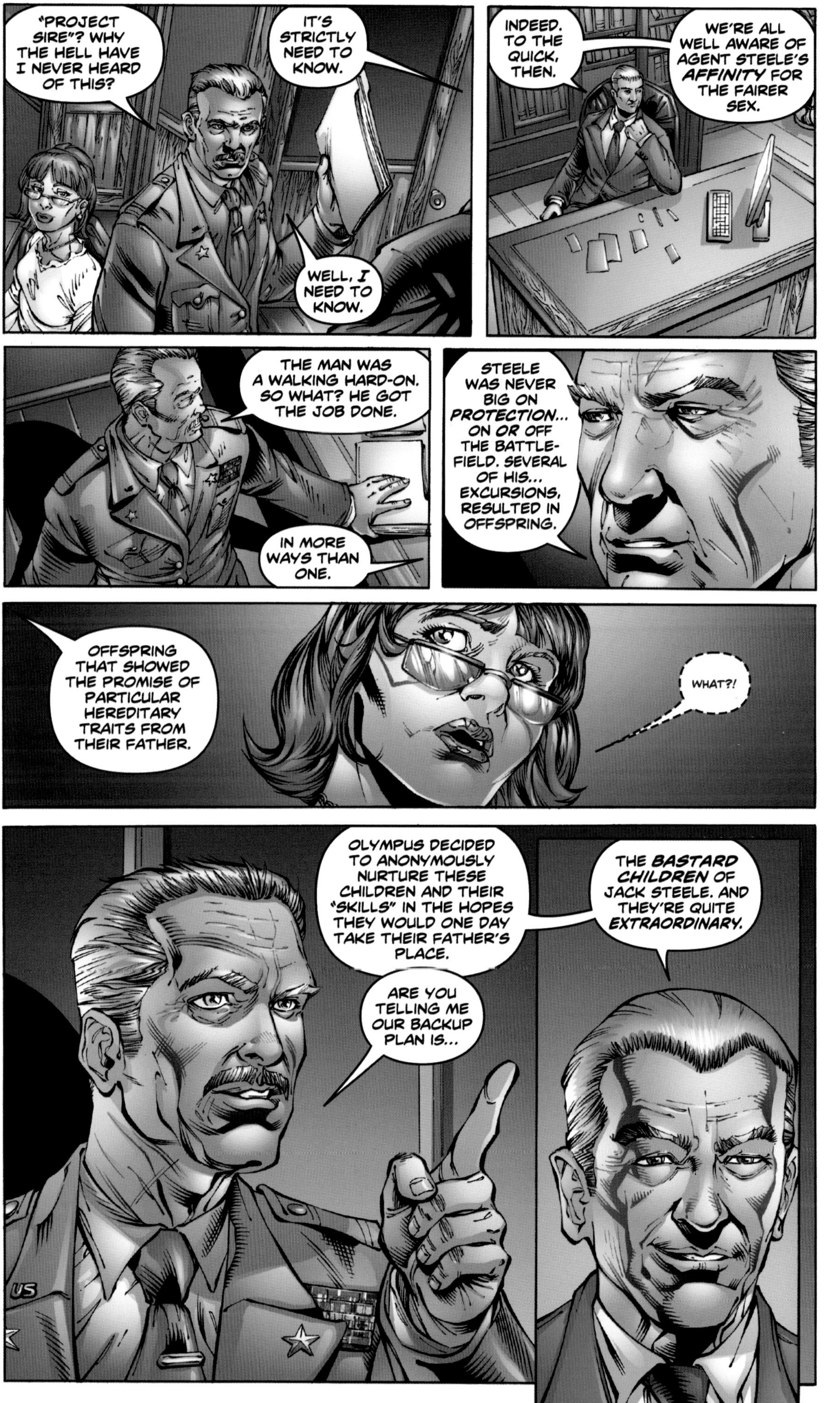
"PROJECT SIRE"? WHY THE HELL HAVE I NEVER HEARD OF THIS?
IT'S STRICTLY NEED TO KNOW.
WELL, I NEED TO KNOW.
INDEED. TO THE QUICK, THEN.
WE'RE ALL WELL AWARE OF AGENT STEELE'S AFFINITY FOR THE FAIRER SEX.
THE MAN WAS A WALKING HARD-ON. SO WHAT? HE GOT THE JOB DONE.
IN MORE WAYS THAN ONE.
STEELE WAS NEVER BIG ON PROTECTION... ON OR OFF THE BATTLE-FIELD. SEVERAL OF HIS... EXCURSIONS, RESULTED IN OFFSPRING.
OFFSPRING THAT SHOWED THE PROMISE OF PARTICULAR HEREDITARY TRAITS FROM THEIR FATHER.
WHAT?!
OLYMPUS DECIDED TO ANONYMOUSLY NURTURE THESE CHILDREN AND THEIR "SKILLS" IN THE HOPES THEY WOULD ONE DAY TAKE THEIR FATHER'S PLACE.
ARE YOU TELLING ME OUR BACKUP PLAN IS...
THE BASTARD CHILDREN OF JACK STEELE. AND THEY'RE QUITE EXTRAORDINARY.
US

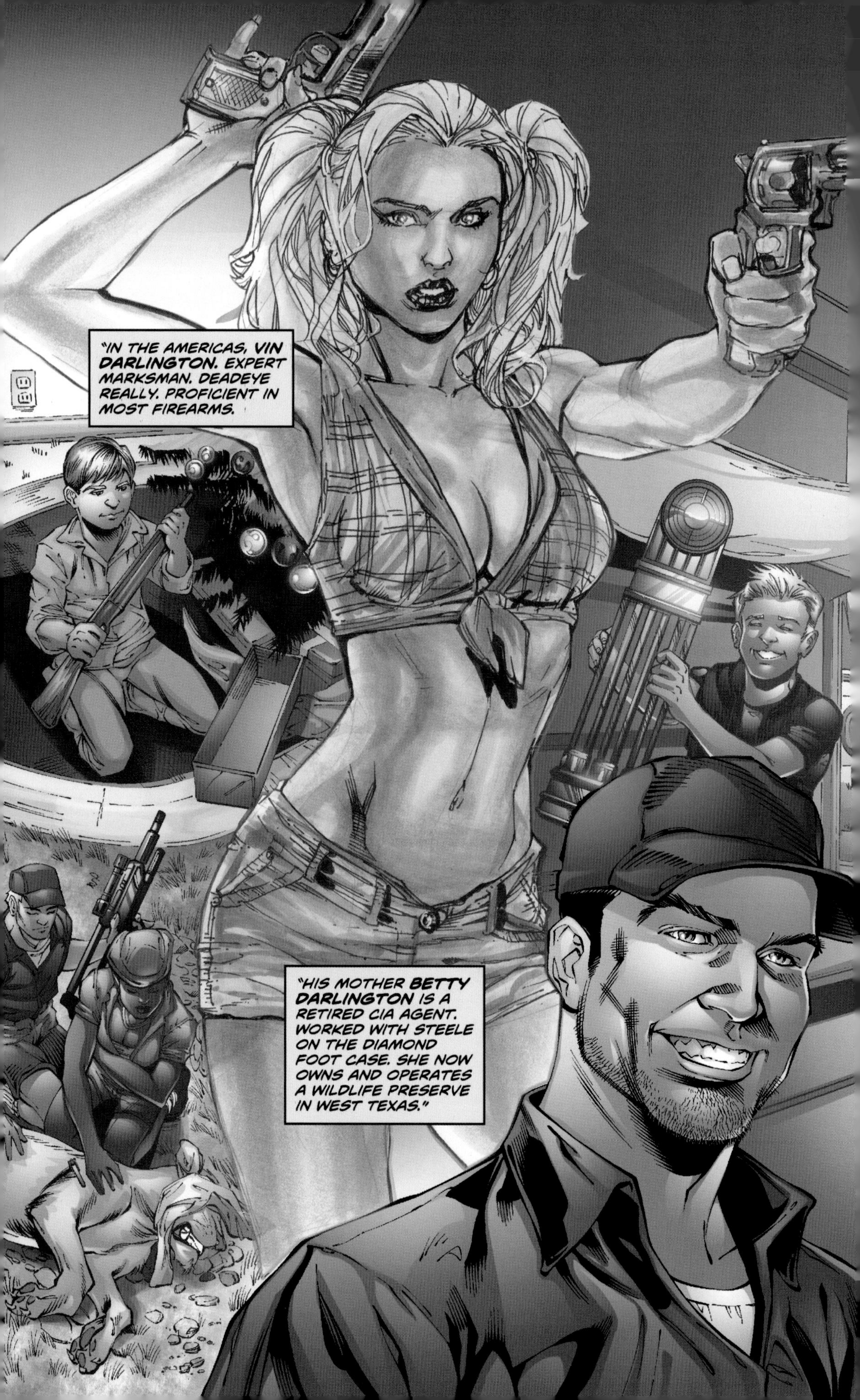
"IN THE AMERICAS, VIN DARLINGTON. EXPERT MARKSMAN. DEADEYE REALLY. PROFICIENT IN MOST FIREARMS.
"HIS MOTHER BETTY DARLINGTON IS A RETIRED CIA AGENT. WORKED WITH STEELE ON THE DIAMOND FOOT CASE. SHE NOW OWNS AND OPERATES A WILDLIFE PRESERVE IN WEST TEXAS."

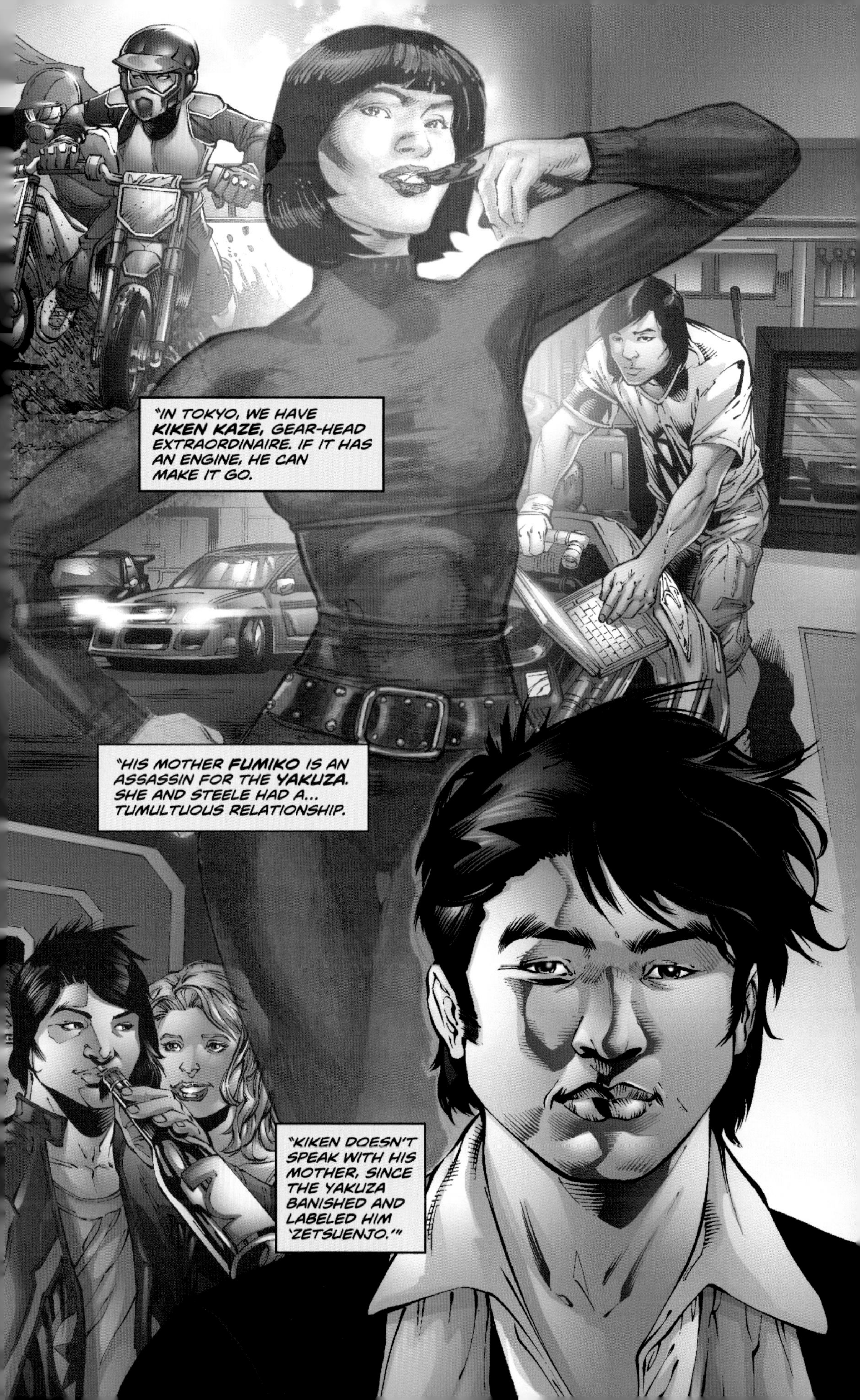
"IN TOKYO, WE HAVE KIKEN KAZE, GEAR-HEAD EXTRAORDINAIRE. IF IT HAS AN ENGINE, HE CAN MAKE IT GO.
"HIS MOTHER FUMIKO IS AN ASSASSIN FOR THE YAKUZA. SHE AND STEELE HAD A... TUMULTUOUS RELATIONSHIP.
"KIKEN DOESN'T SPEAK WITH HIS MOTHER, SINCE THE YAKUZA BANISHED AND LABELED HIM 'ZETSUENJO.'"

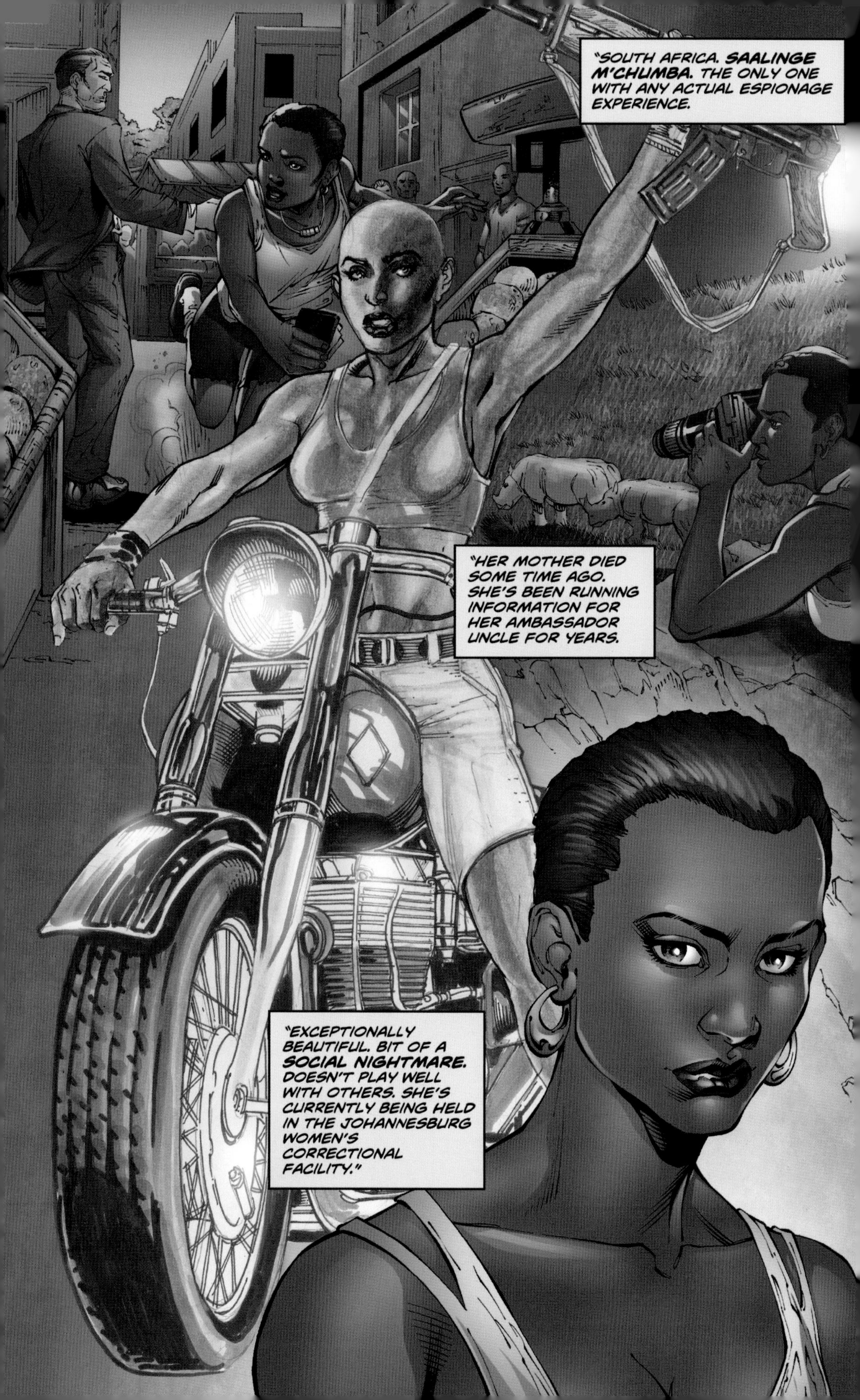
"SOUTH AFRICA. SAALINGE M'CHUMBA. THE ONLY ONE WITH ANY ACTUAL ESPIONAGE EXPERIENCE.
"HER MOTHER DIED SOME TIME AGO. SHE'S BEEN RUNNING INFORMATION FOR HER AMBASSADOR UNCLE FOR YEARS.
"EXCEPTIONALLY BEAUTIFUL. BIT OF A SOCIAL NIGHTMARE. DOESN'T PLAY WELL WITH OTHERS. SHE'S CURRENTLY BEING HELD IN THE JOHANNESBURG WOMEN'S CORRECTIONAL FACILITY."

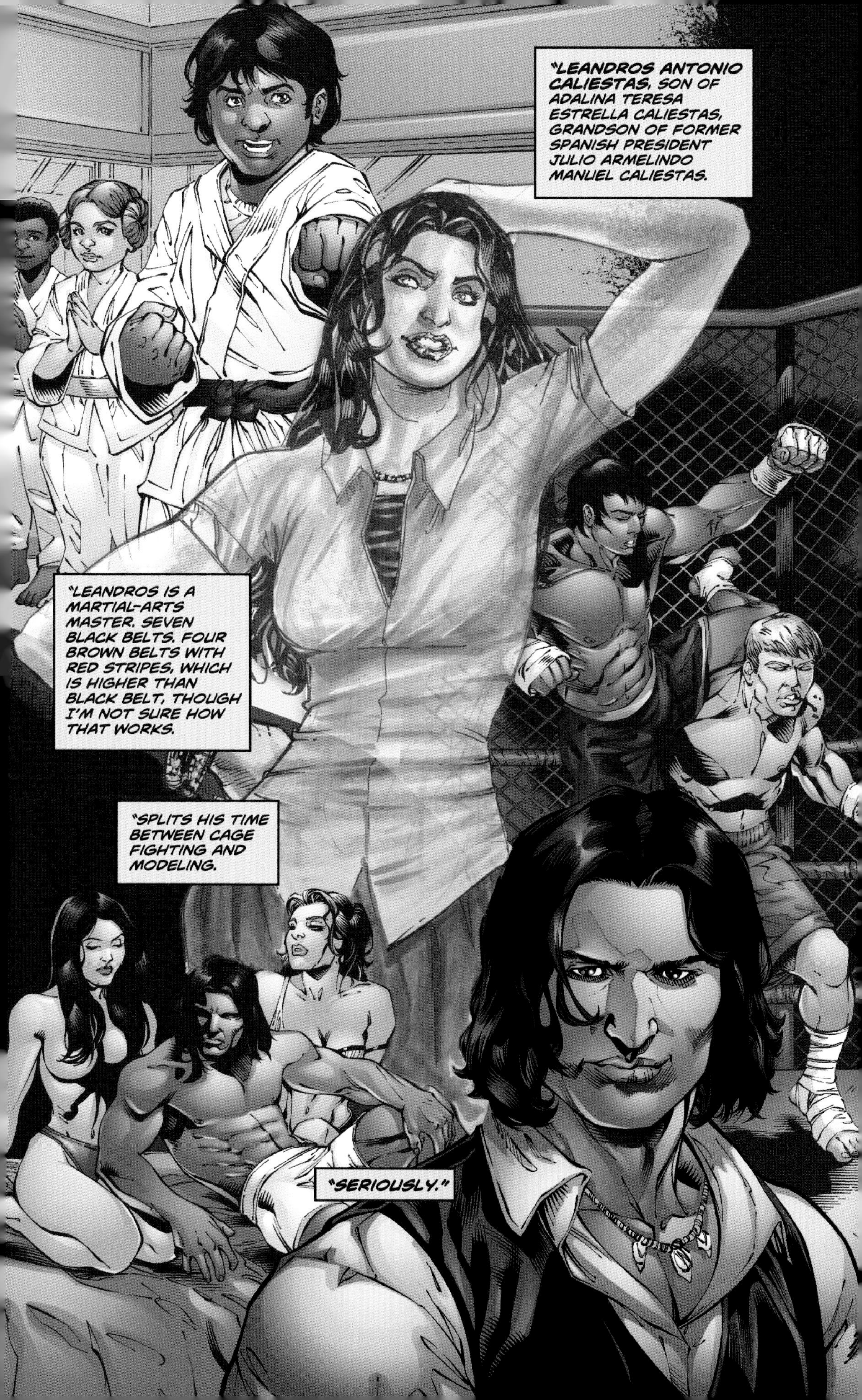
"LEANDROS ANTONIO CALIESTAS, SON OF ADALINA TERESA ESTRELLA CALIESTAS, GRANDSON OF FORMER SPANISH PRESIDENT JULIO ARMELINDO MANUEL CALIESTAS.
"LEANDROS IS A MARTIAL-ARTS MASTER. SEVEN BLACK BELTS. FOUR BROWN BELTS WITH RED STRIPES, WHICH IS HIGHER THAN BLACK BELT, THOUGH I'M NOT SURE HOW THAT WORKS.
"SPLITS HIS TIME BETWEEN CAGE FIGHTING AND MODELING.
"SERIOUSLY."

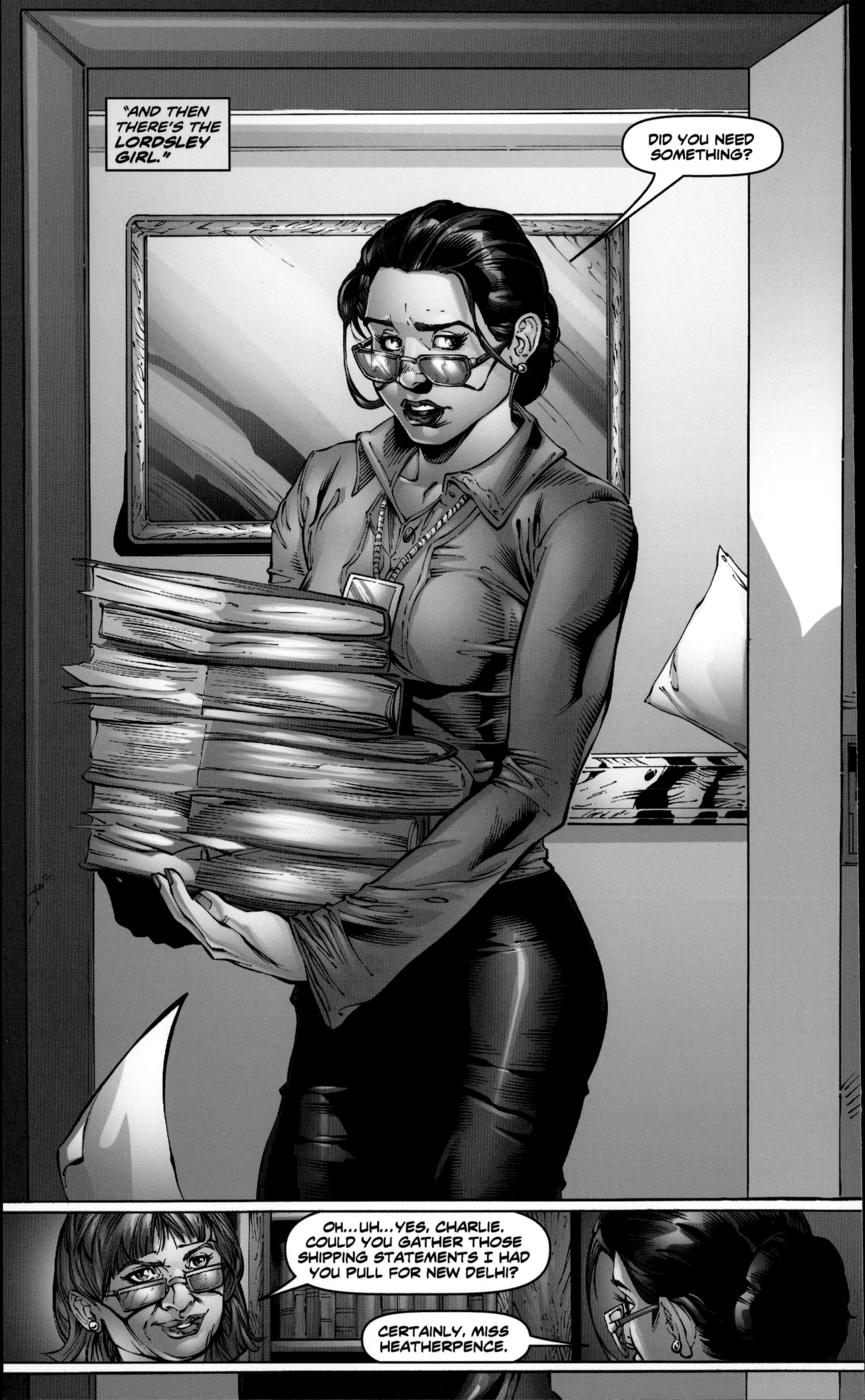
"AND THEN THERE'S THE LORDSLEY GIRL."
DID YOU NEED SOMETHING?
OH...UH...YES, CHARLIE. COULD YOU GATHER THOSE SHIPPING STATEMENTS I HAD YOU PULL FOR NEW DELHI?
CERTAINLY, MISS HEATHERPENCE.

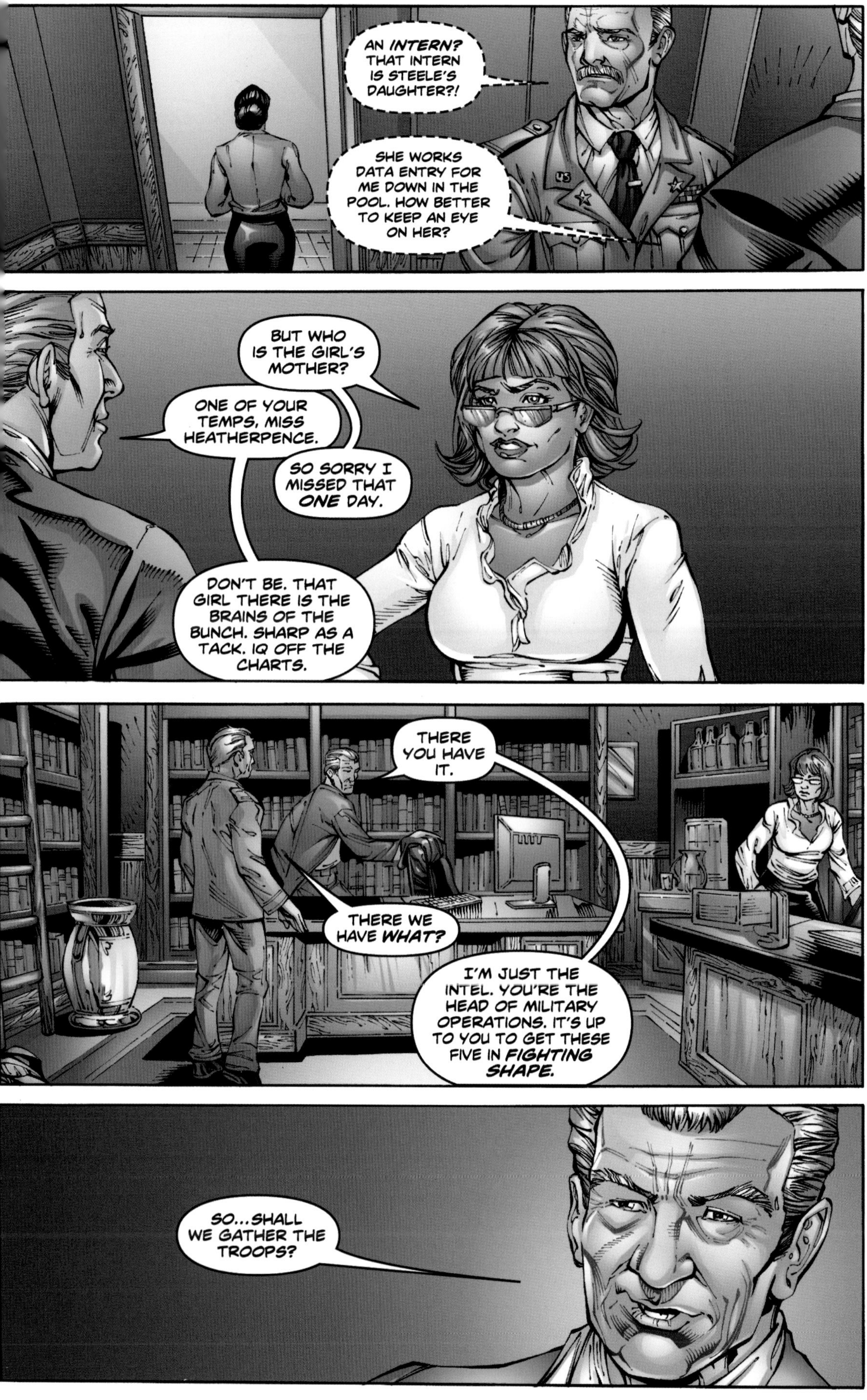
AN *INTERN?* THAT INTERN IS STEELE'S DAUGHTER?!
SHE WORKS DATA ENTRY FOR ME DOWN IN THE POOL. HOW BETTER TO KEEP AN EYE ON HER?
BUT WHO IS THE GIRL'S MOTHER?
ONE OF YOUR TEMPS, MISS HEATHERPENCE.
SO SORRY I MISSED THAT *ONE* DAY.
DON'T BE. THAT GIRL THERE IS THE BRAINS OF THE BUNCH. SHARP AS A TACK. IQ OFF THE CHARTS.
THERE YOU HAVE IT.
THERE WE HAVE *WHAT?*
I'M JUST THE INTEL. YOU'RE THE HEAD OF MILITARY OPERATIONS. IT'S UP TO YOU TO GET THESE FIVE IN *FIGHTING SHAPE.*
SO...SHALL WE GATHER THE TROOPS?

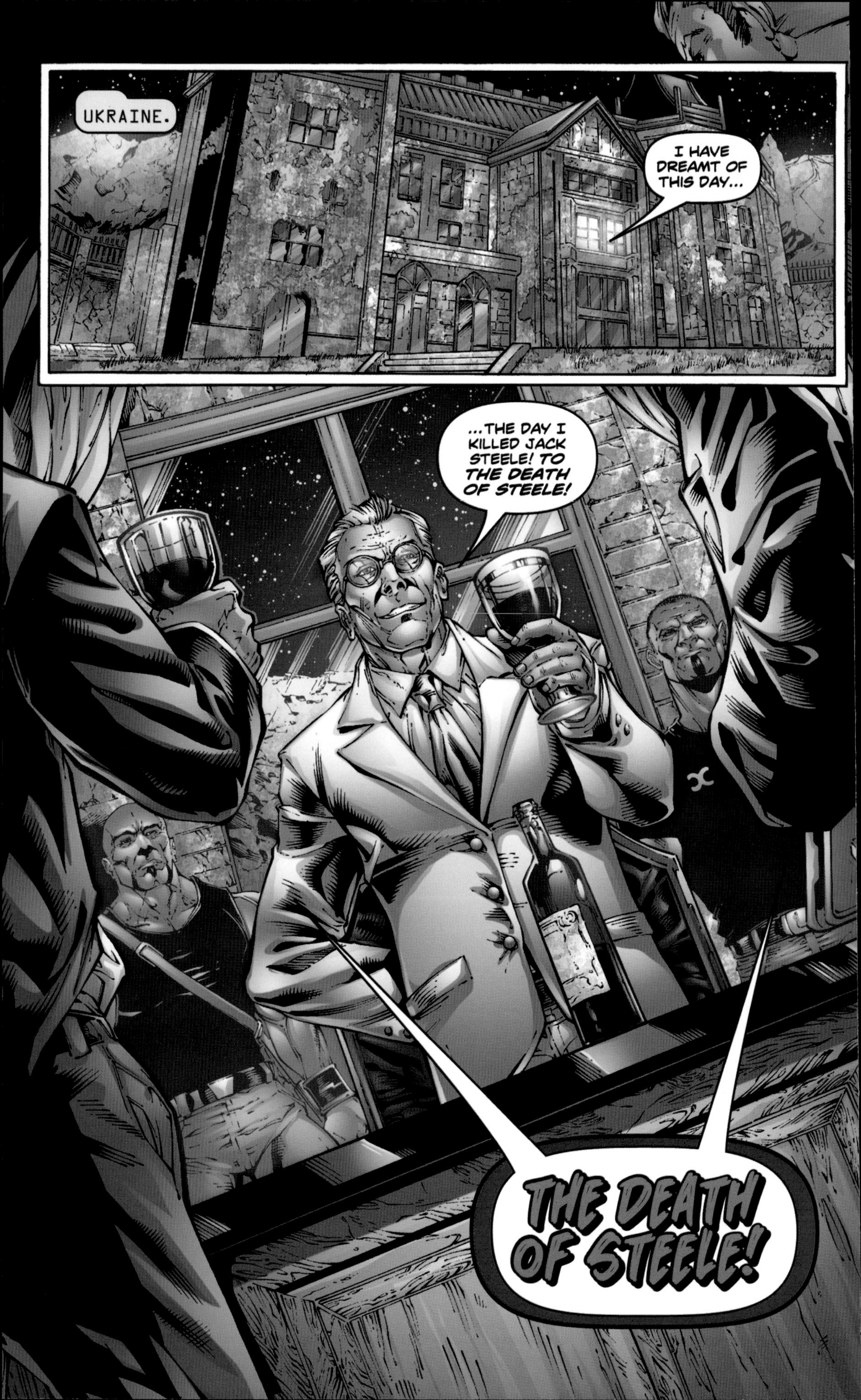
UKRAINE.
I HAVE DREAMT OF THIS DAY...
...THE DAY I KILLED JACK STEELE! TO THE DEATH OF STEELE!
THE DEATH OF STEELE!

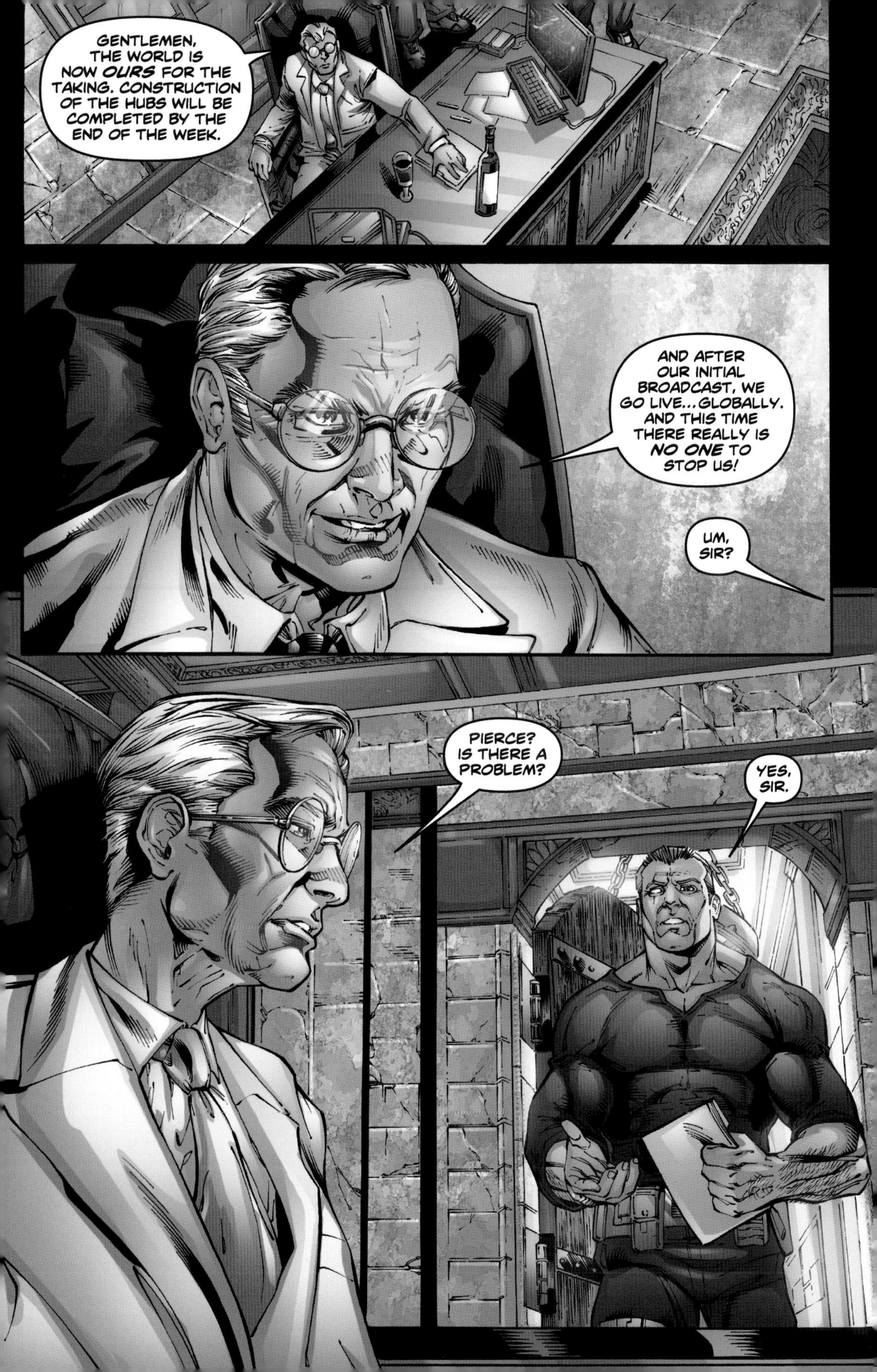
GENTLEMEN, THE WORLD IS NOW OURS FOR THE TAKING. CONSTRUCTION OF THE HUBS WILL BE COMPLETED BY THE END OF THE WEEK.
AND AFTER OUR INITIAL BROADCAST, WE GO LIVE...GLOBALLY. AND THIS TIME THERE REALLY IS NO ONE TO STOP US!
UM, SIR?
PIERCE? IS THERE A PROBLEM?
YES, SIR.

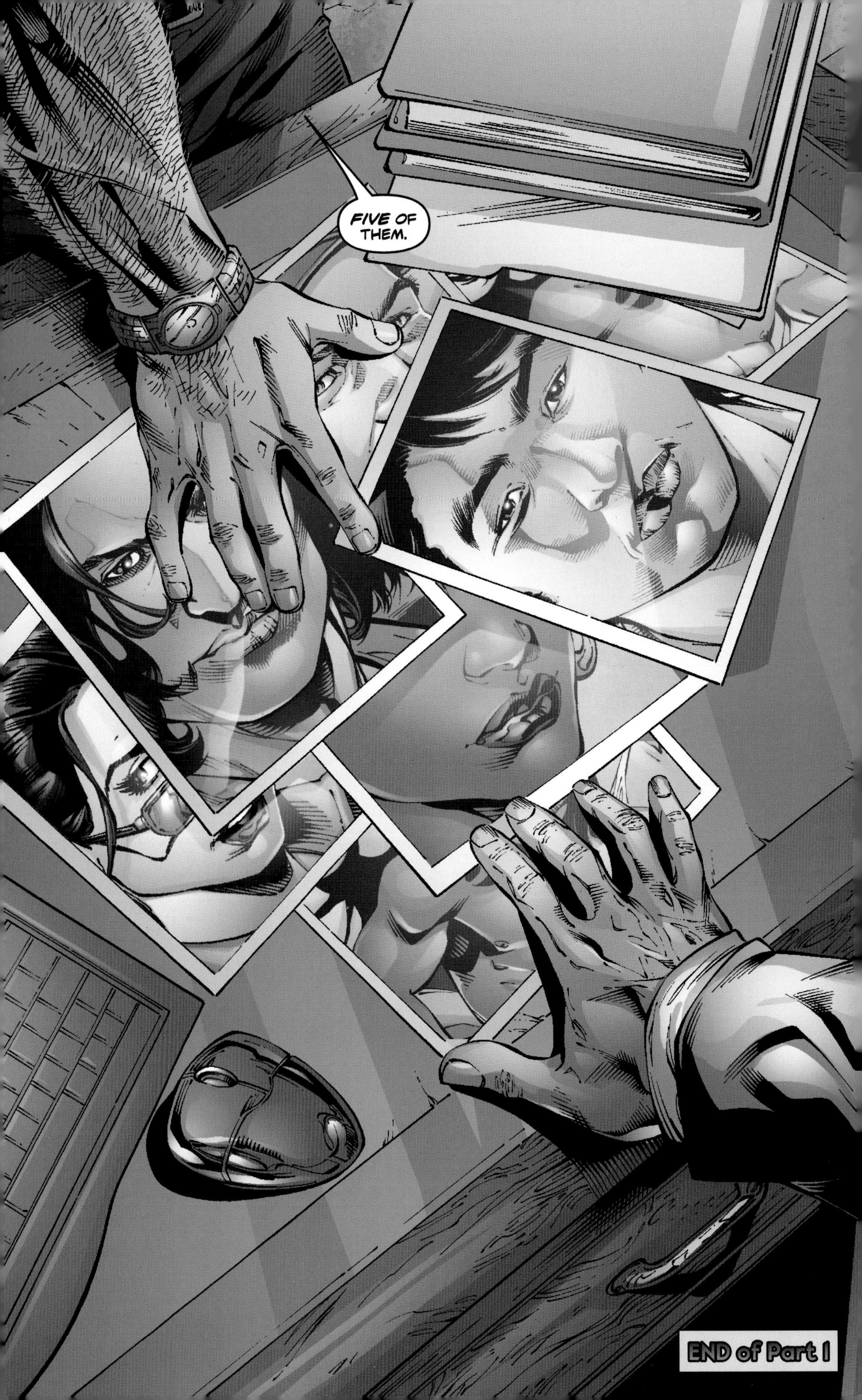
FIVE OF THEM.
END of Part 1

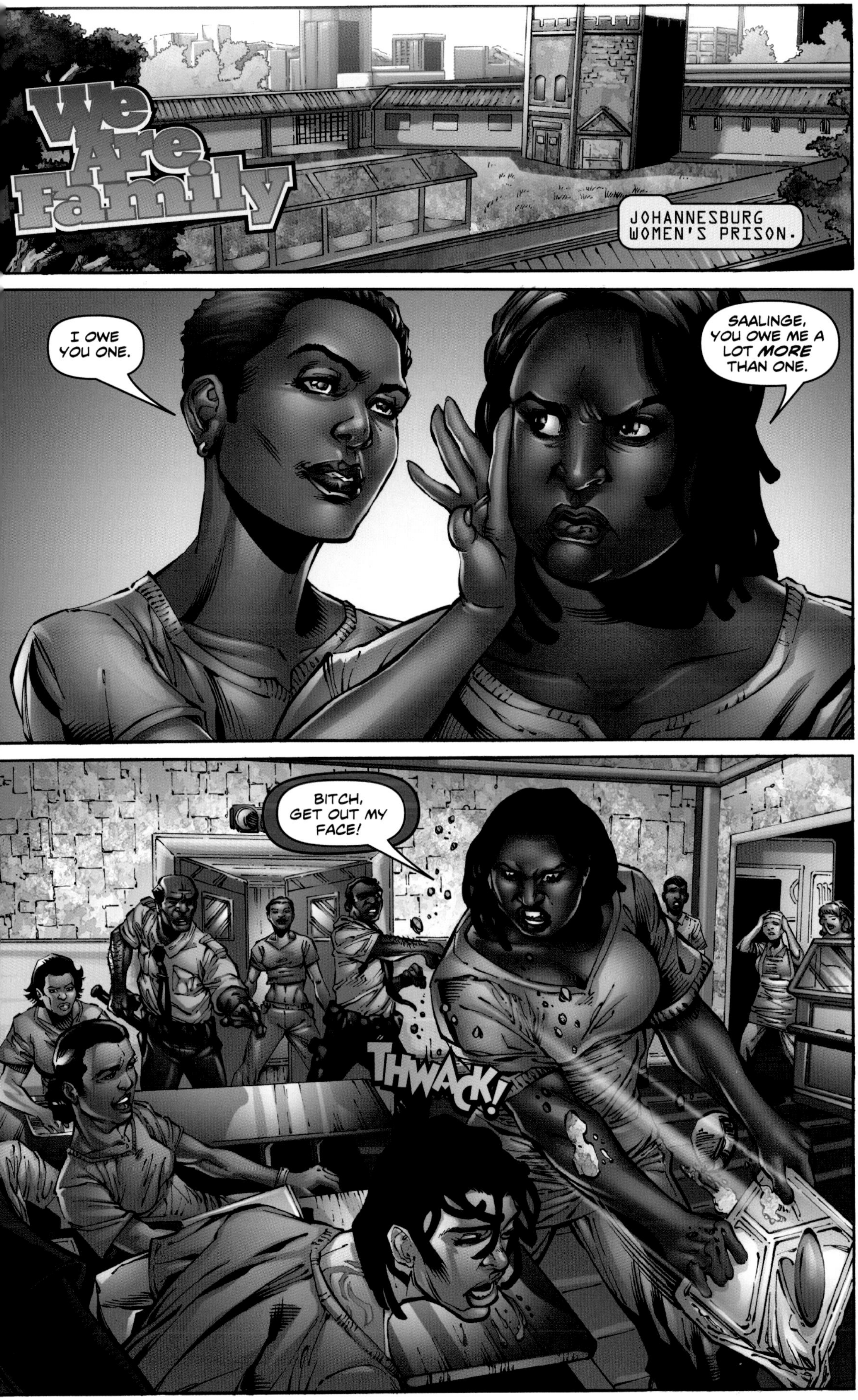
We Are Family
JOHANNESBURG WOMEN'S PRISON.
I OWE YOU ONE.
SAALINGE, YOU OWE ME A LOT MORE THAN ONE.
BITCH, GET OUT MY FACE!
THWACK!

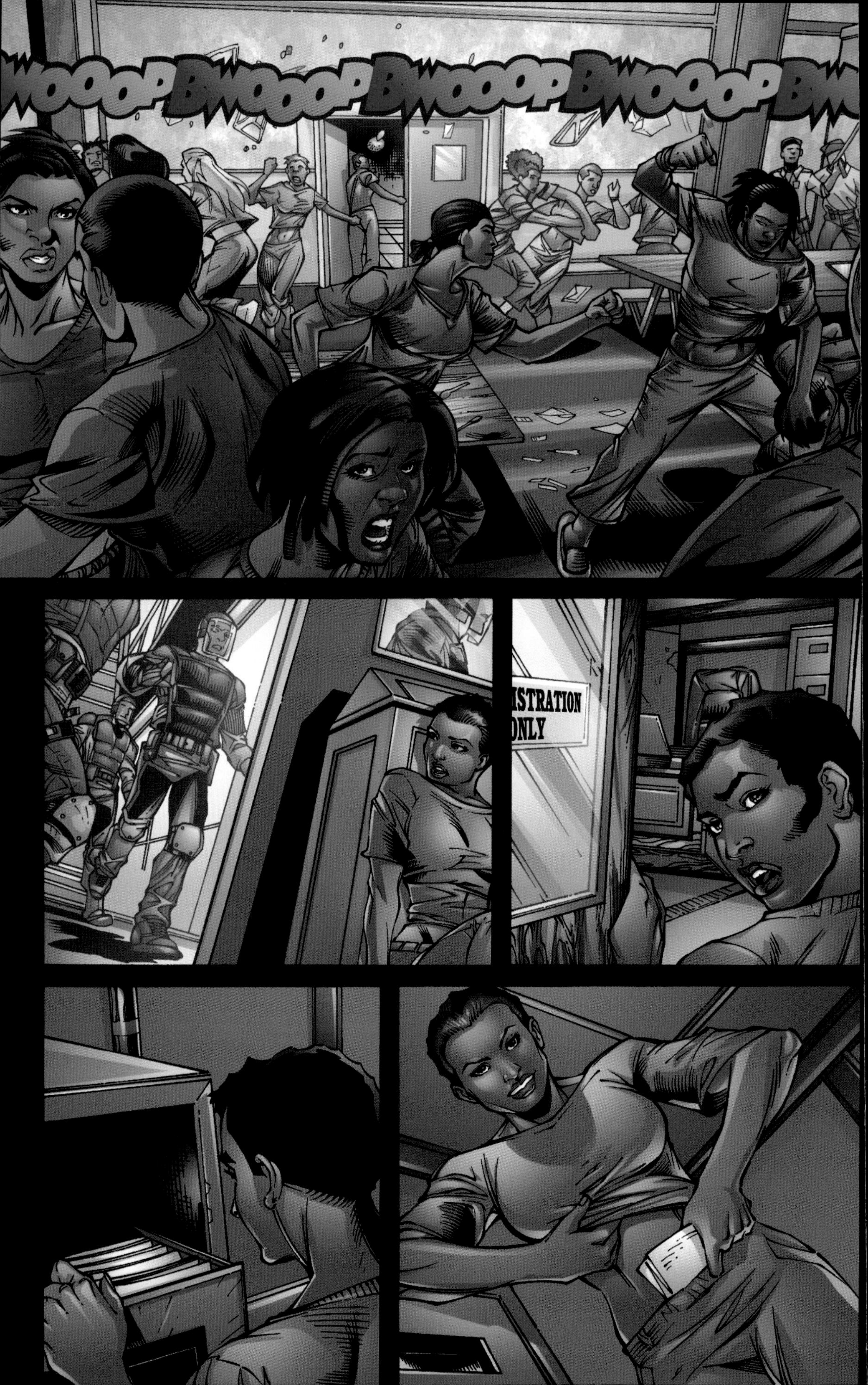
WOOOP BWOOOP BWOOOP BWOOOP BW
ISTRATION
ONLY

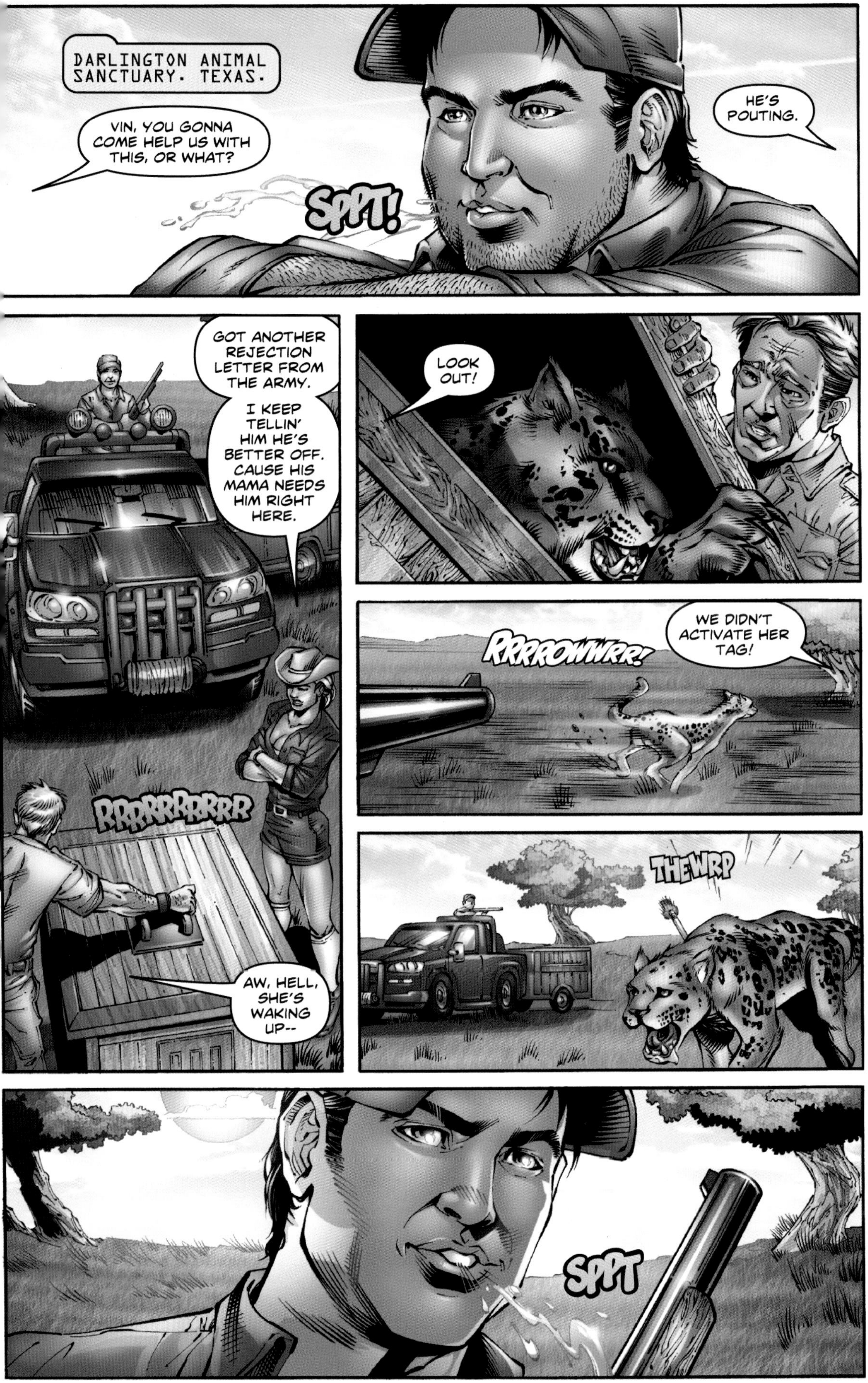
DARLINGTON ANIMAL SANCTUARY. TEXAS.
VIN, YOU GONNA COME HELP US WITH THIS, OR WHAT?
HE'S POUTING.
SPPT!
GOT ANOTHER REJECTION LETTER FROM THE ARMY.
I KEEP TELLIN' HIM HE'S BETTER OFF. CAUSE HIS MAMA NEEDS HIM RIGHT HERE.
RRRRRRRRRR
AW, HELL, SHE'S WAKING UP--
LOOK OUT!
RRRROWWRR!
WE DIDN'T ACTIVATE HER TAG!
THEWRP
SPPT

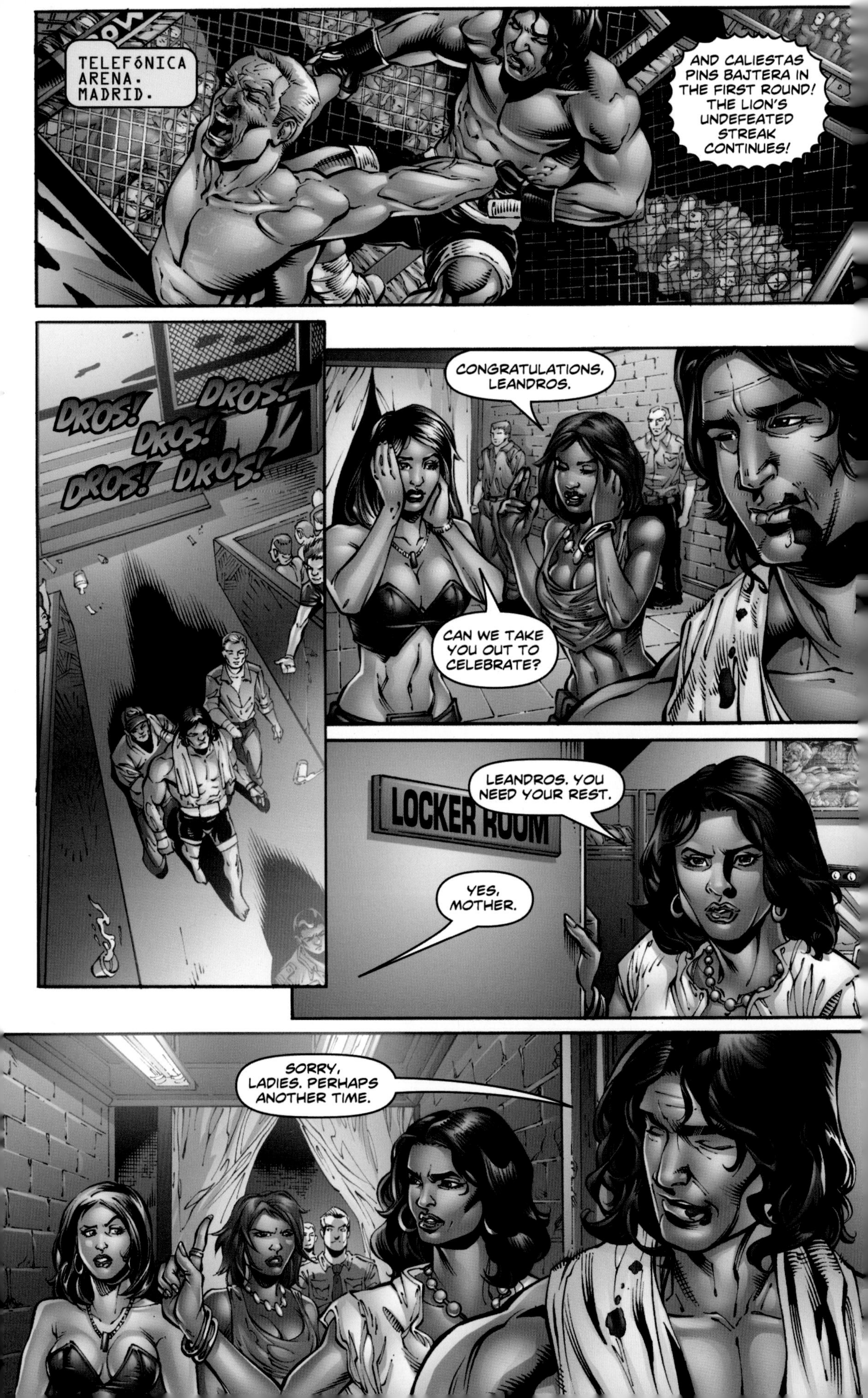
TELEFÓNICA ARENA. MADRID.
AND CALIESTAS PINS BAJTERA IN THE FIRST ROUND! THE LION'S UNDEFEATED STREAK CONTINUES!
DROS! DROS! DROS! DROS! DROS!
CONGRATULATIONS, LEANDROS.
CAN WE TAKE YOU OUT TO CELEBRATE?
LOCKER ROOM
LEANDROS. YOU NEED YOUR REST.
YES, MOTHER.
SORRY, LADIES. PERHAPS ANOTHER TIME.

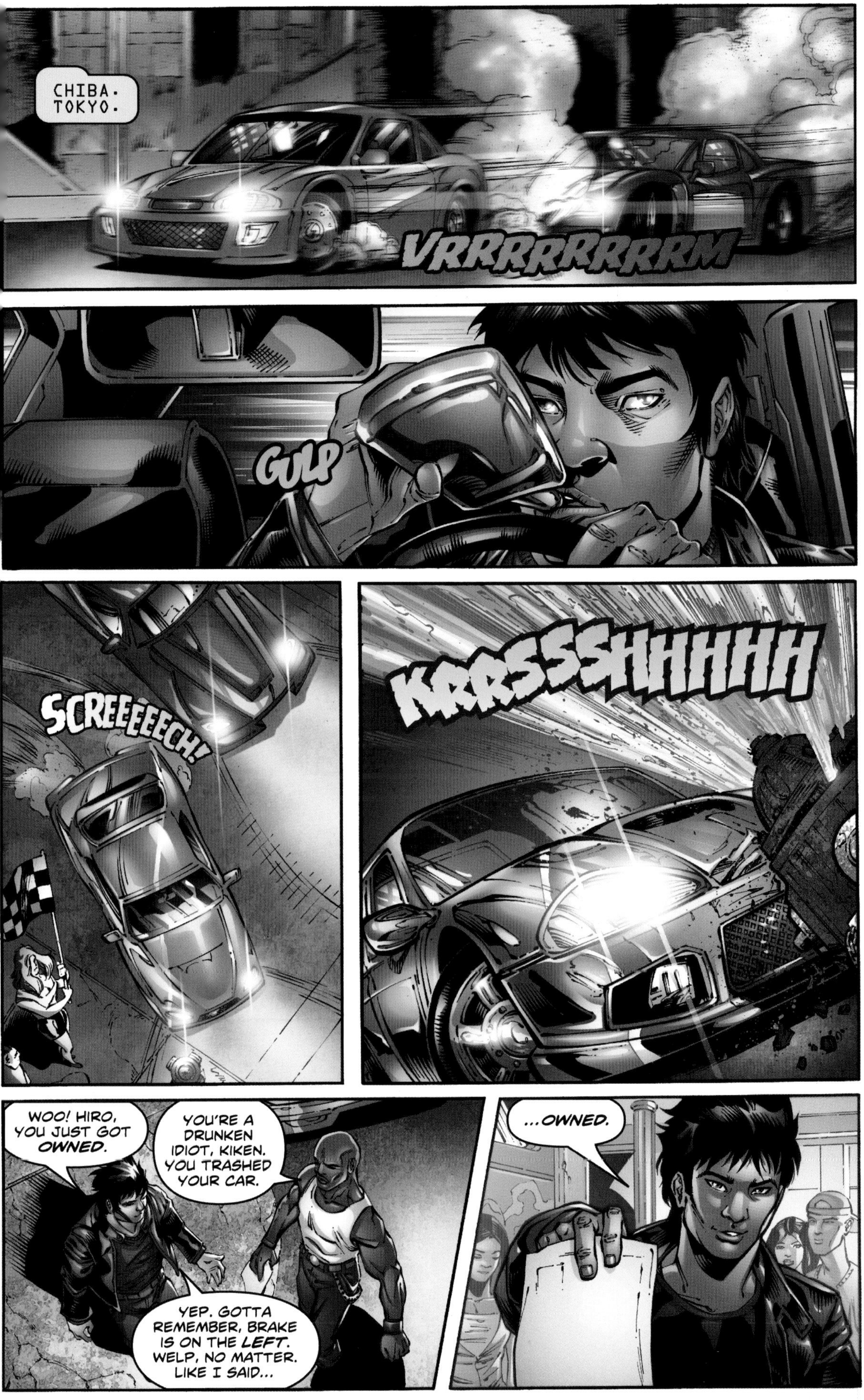
CHIBA. TOKYO.
VRRRRRRRRRM
GULP
SCREEEEECH!
KRRSSSHHHHH
WOO! HIRO, YOU JUST GOT OWNED.
YOU'RE A DRUNKEN IDIOT, KIKEN. YOU TRASHED YOUR CAR.
YEP. GOTTA REMEMBER, BRAKE IS ON THE LEFT. WELP, NO MATTER. LIKE I SAID...
...OWNED.

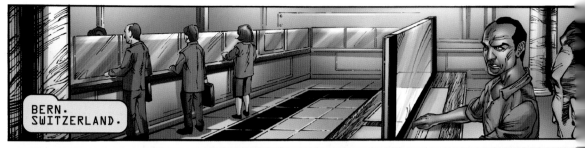

BERN. SWITZERLAND.

SIGN HERE FOR YOUR WITHDRAWAL, MRS. GEHRIG. HOW WOULD YOU LIKE IT?

HUNDREDS IS FINE.

1200 IN 100-EURO NOTES, CORRECT?

YES—

--NO...ALL OF IT...I WANT ALL OF IT...

...YES...ALL OF IT...

ALL OF IT? YOU MEAN YOU WANT TO CLOSE YOUR ACCOUNT?

IS SOMETHING WRONG—

...ALL OF IT.

ALL OF IT.

ALL OF IT.

ALL OF IT.

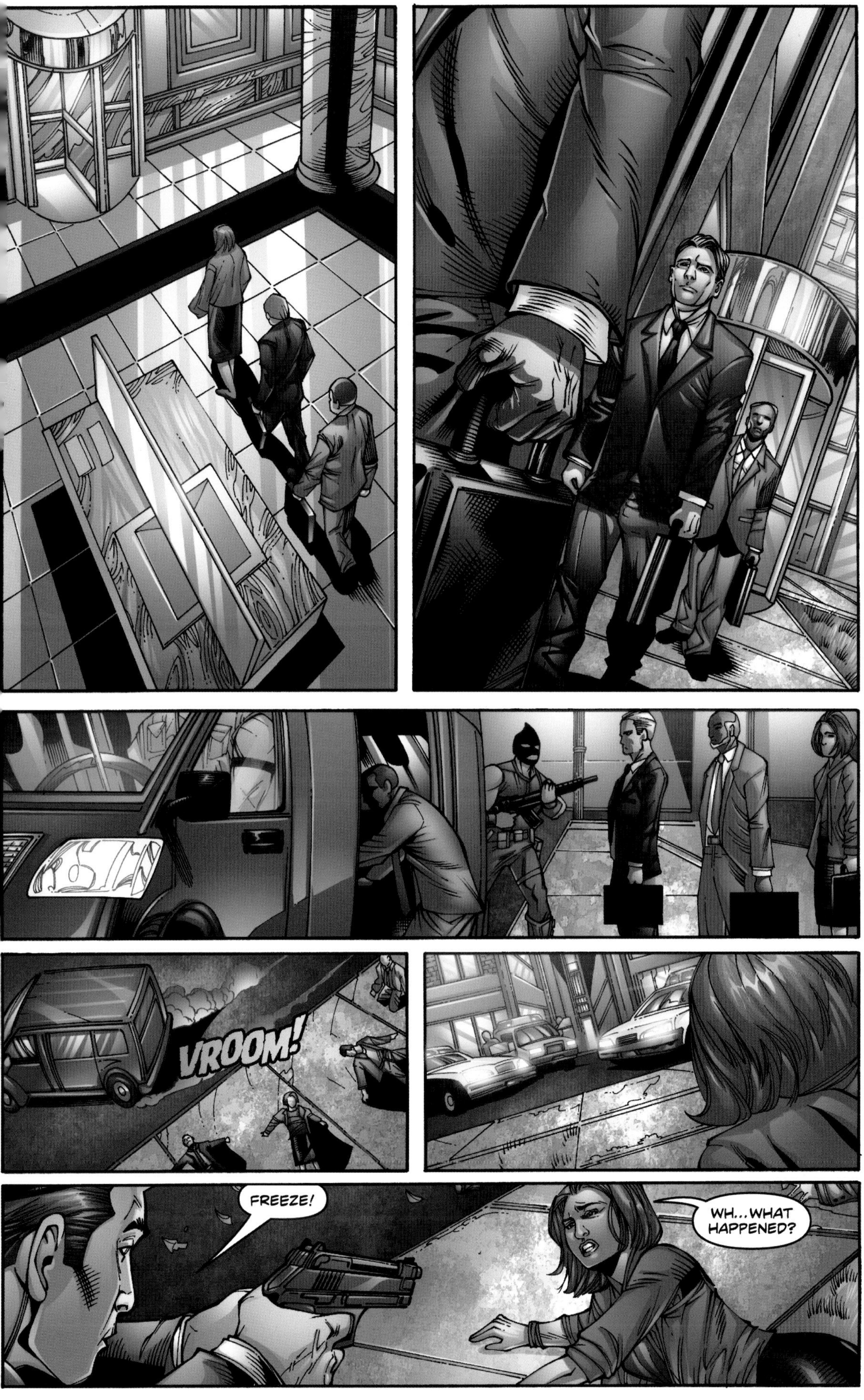
VROOM!
FREEZE!
WH...WHAT HAPPENED?

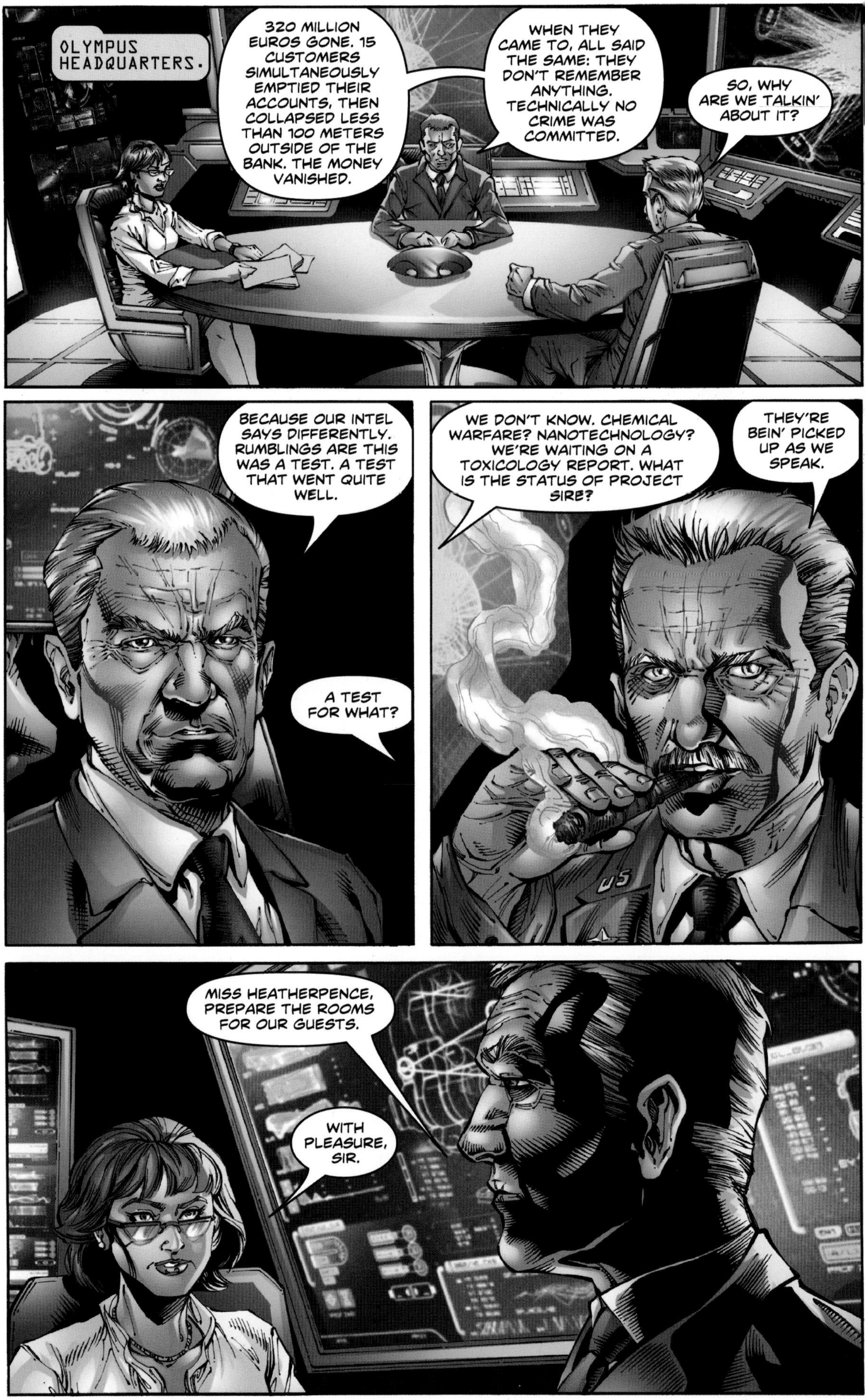
OLYMPUS HEADQUARTERS.
320 MILLION EUROS GONE. 15 CUSTOMERS SIMULTANEOUSLY EMPTIED THEIR ACCOUNTS, THEN COLLAPSED LESS THAN 100 METERS OUTSIDE OF THE BANK. THE MONEY VANISHED.
WHEN THEY CAME TO, ALL SAID THE SAME: THEY DON'T REMEMBER ANYTHING. TECHNICALLY NO CRIME WAS COMMITTED.
SO, WHY ARE WE TALKIN' ABOUT IT?
BECAUSE OUR INTEL SAYS DIFFERENTLY. RUMBLINGS ARE THIS WAS A TEST. A TEST THAT WENT QUITE WELL.
A TEST FOR WHAT?
WE DON'T KNOW. CHEMICAL WARFARE? NANOTECHNOLOGY? WE'RE WAITING ON A TOXICOLOGY REPORT. WHAT IS THE STATUS OF PROJECT SIRE?
THEY'RE BEIN' PICKED UP AS WE SPEAK.
MISS HEATHERPENCE, PREPARE THE ROOMS FOR OUR GUESTS.
WITH PLEASURE, SIR.

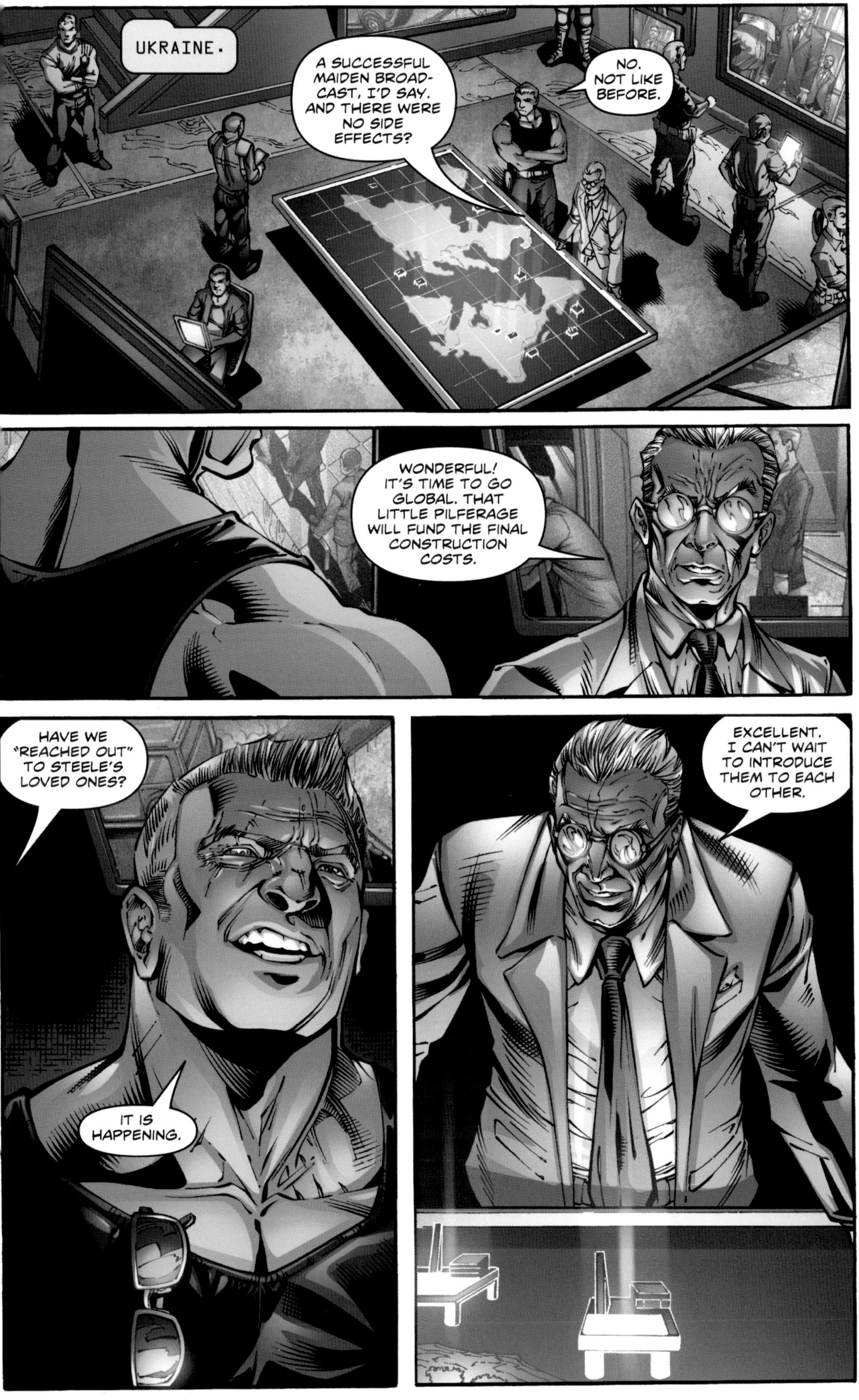
UKRAINE.
A SUCCESSFUL MAIDEN BROAD-CAST, I'D SAY. AND THERE WERE NO SIDE EFFECTS?
NO. NOT LIKE BEFORE.
WONDERFUL! IT'S TIME TO GO GLOBAL. THAT LITTLE PILFERAGE WILL FUND THE FINAL CONSTRUCTION COSTS.
HAVE WE "REACHED OUT" TO STEELE'S LOVED ONES?
IT IS HAPPENING.
EXCELLENT. I CAN'T WAIT TO INTRODUCE THEM TO EACH OTHER.

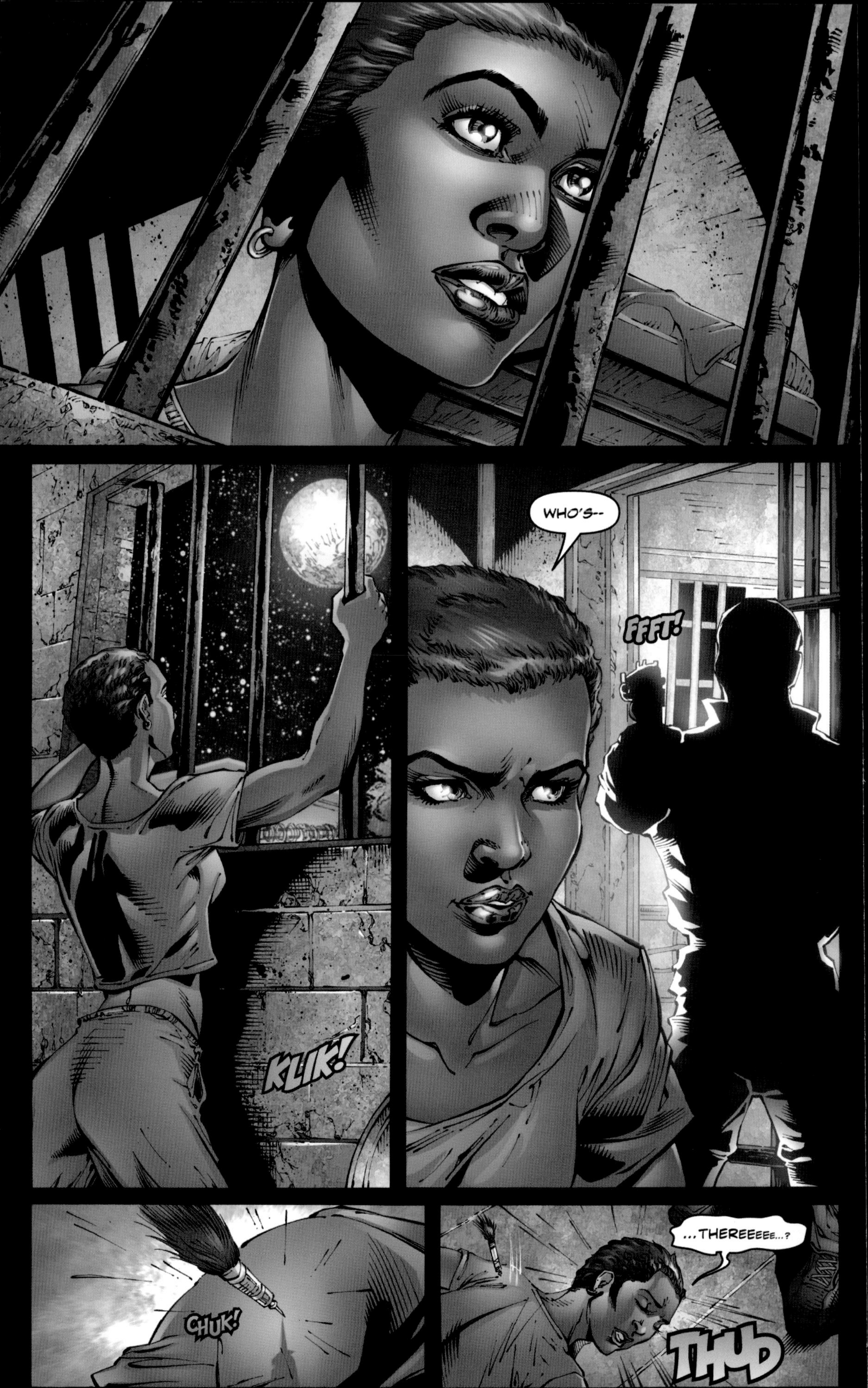
WHO'S--
FFFT!
KLIK!
CHUK!
...THEREEEEE...?
THUD

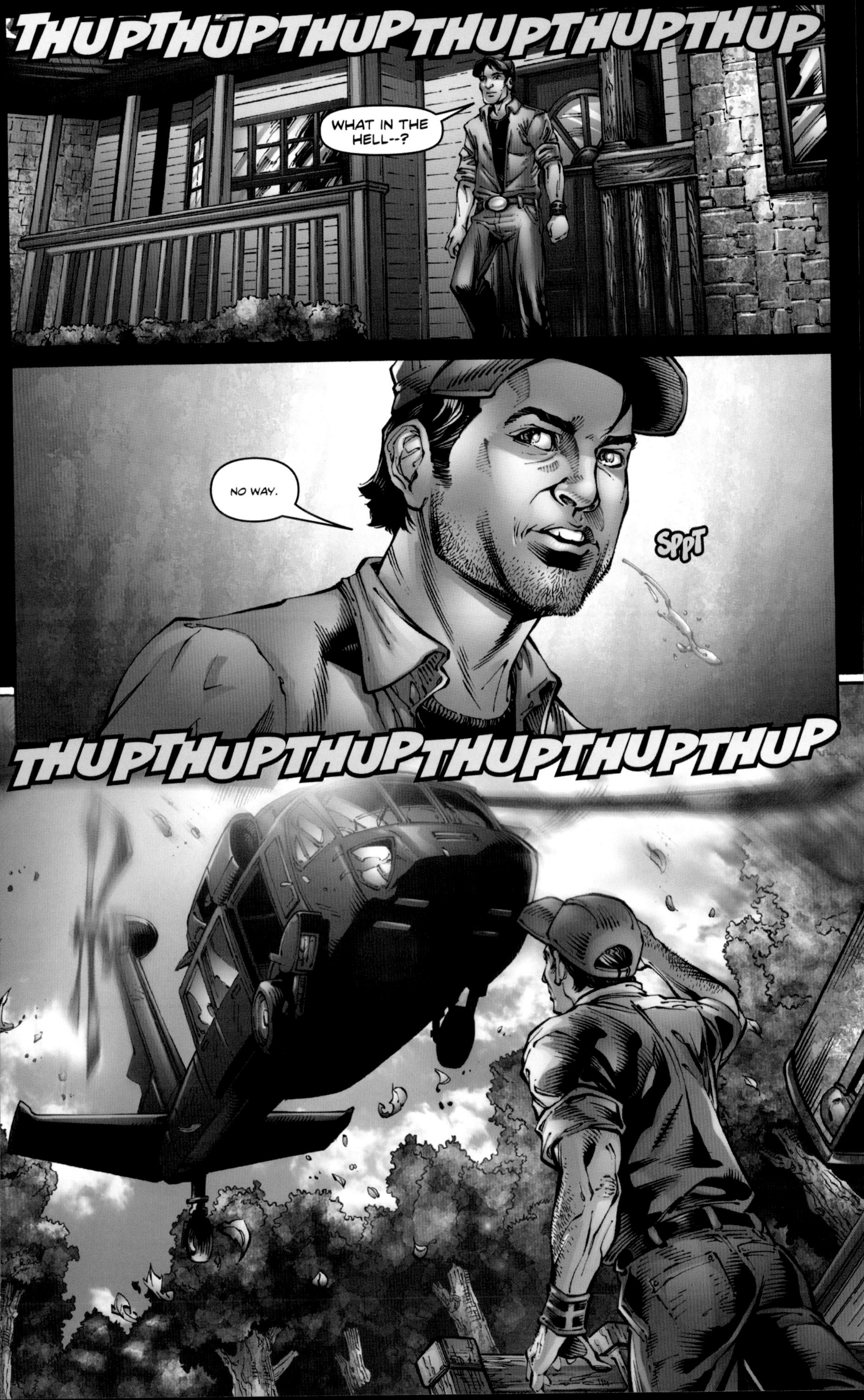
THUPTHUPTHUPTHUPTHUPTHUP
WHAT IN THE HELL--?
NO WAY.
SPPT
THUPTHUPTHUPTHUPTHUPTHUP

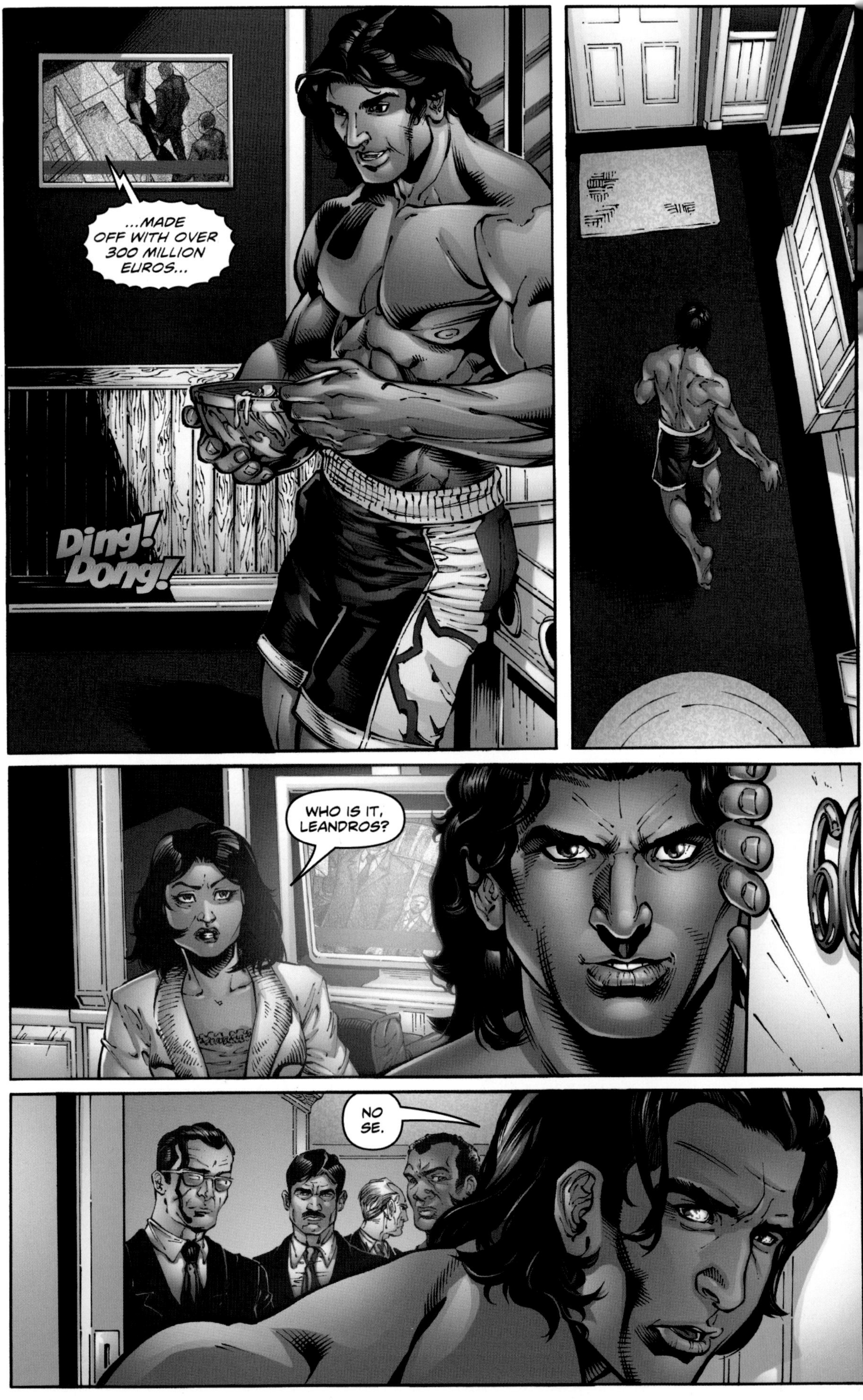
...MADE OFF WITH OVER 300 MILLION EUROS...
Ding! Dong!
WHO IS IT, LEANDROS?
NO SE.

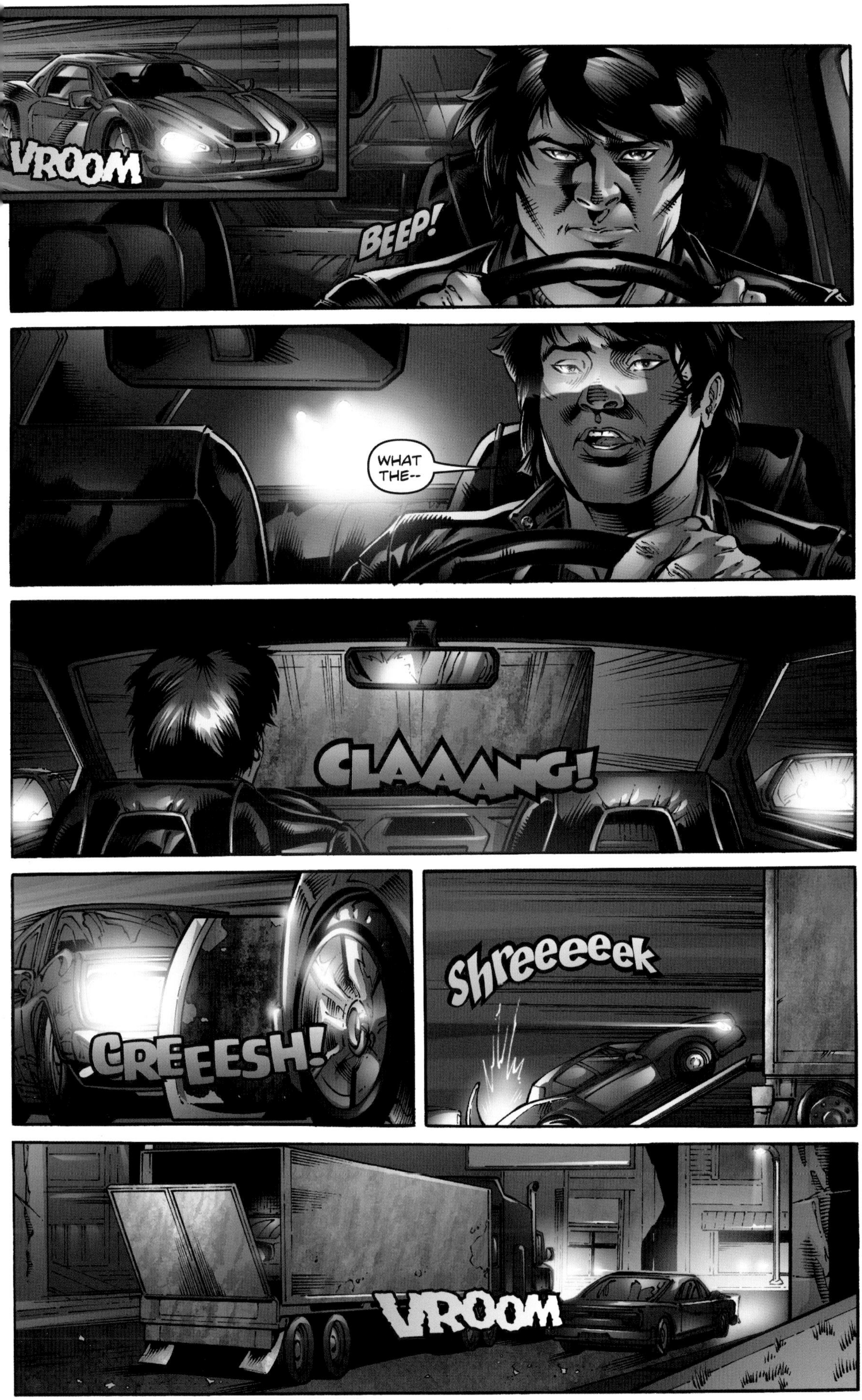
VROOM
BEEP!
WHAT THE--
CLAAANG!
CREEESH!
Shreeeeek
VROOM

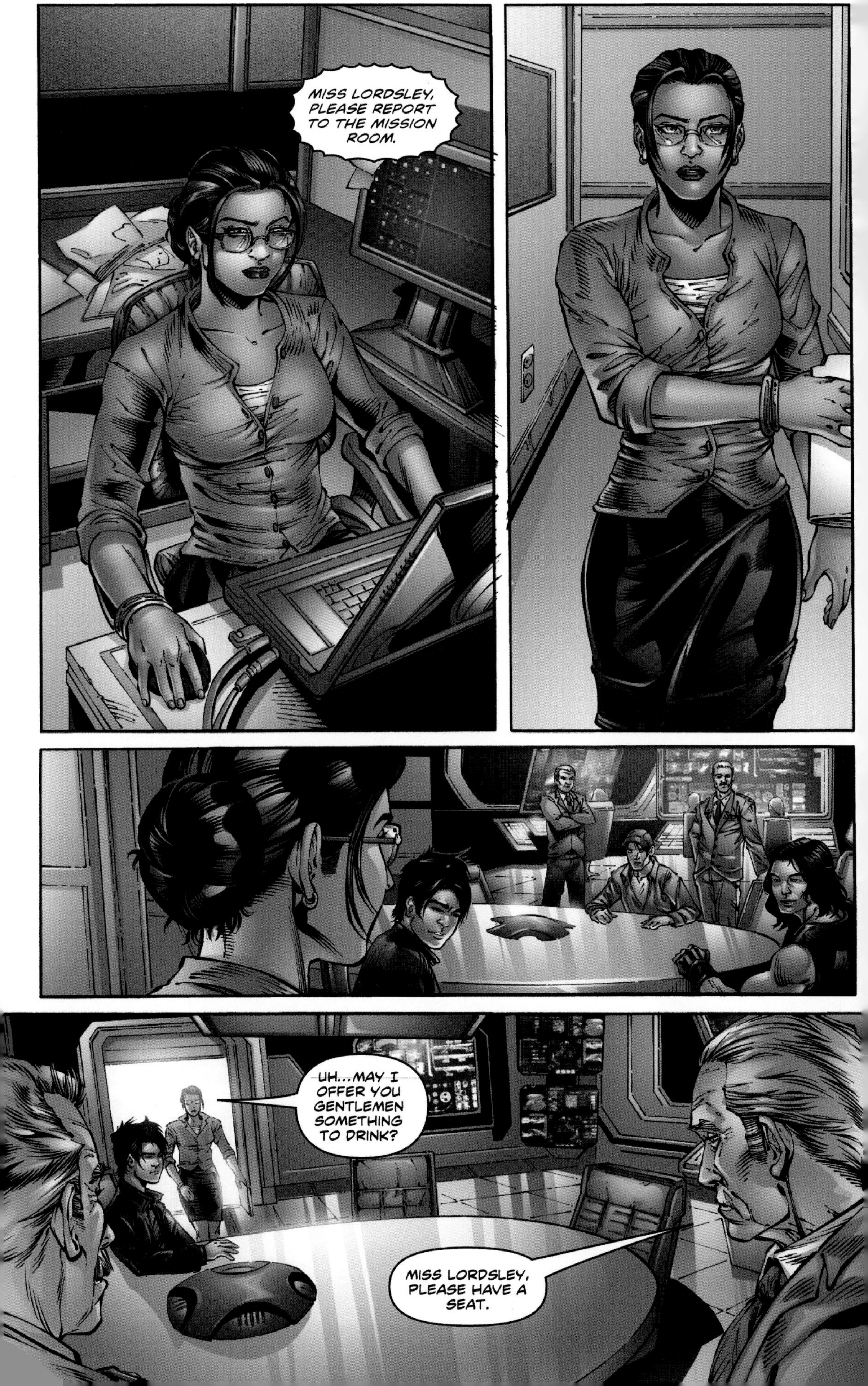
MISS LORDSLEY, PLEASE REPORT TO THE MISSION ROOM.
UH...MAY I OFFER YOU GENTLEMEN SOMETHING TO DRINK?
MISS LORDSLEY, PLEASE HAVE A SEAT.

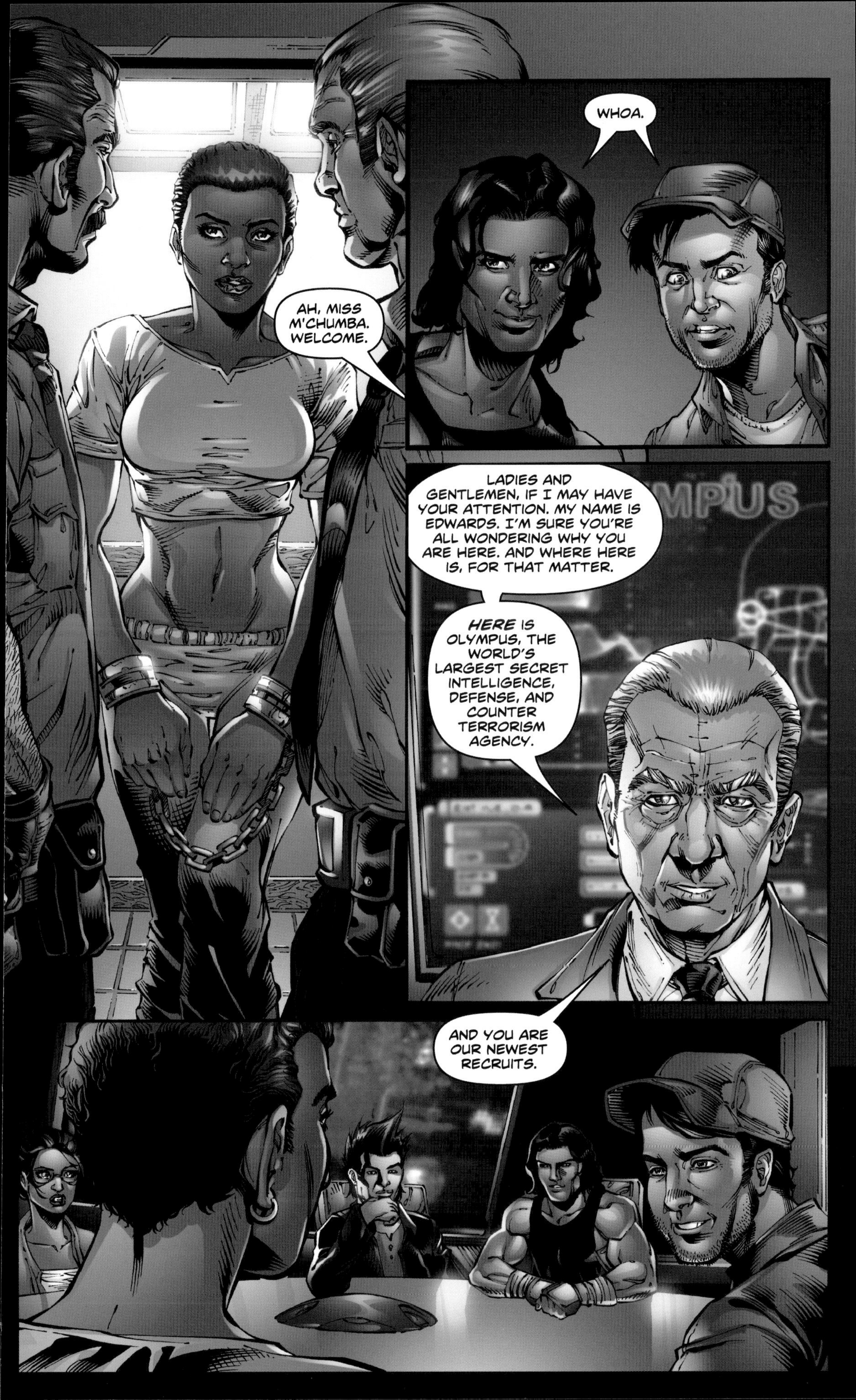
AH, MISS M'CHUMBA. WELCOME.
WHOA.
LADIES AND GENTLEMEN, IF I MAY HAVE YOUR ATTENTION. MY NAME IS EDWARDS. I'M SURE YOU'RE ALL WONDERING WHY YOU ARE HERE. AND WHERE HERE IS, FOR THAT MATTER.
HERE IS OLYMPUS, THE WORLD'S LARGEST SECRET INTELLIGENCE, DEFENSE, AND COUNTER TERRORISM AGENCY.
AND YOU ARE OUR NEWEST RECRUITS.

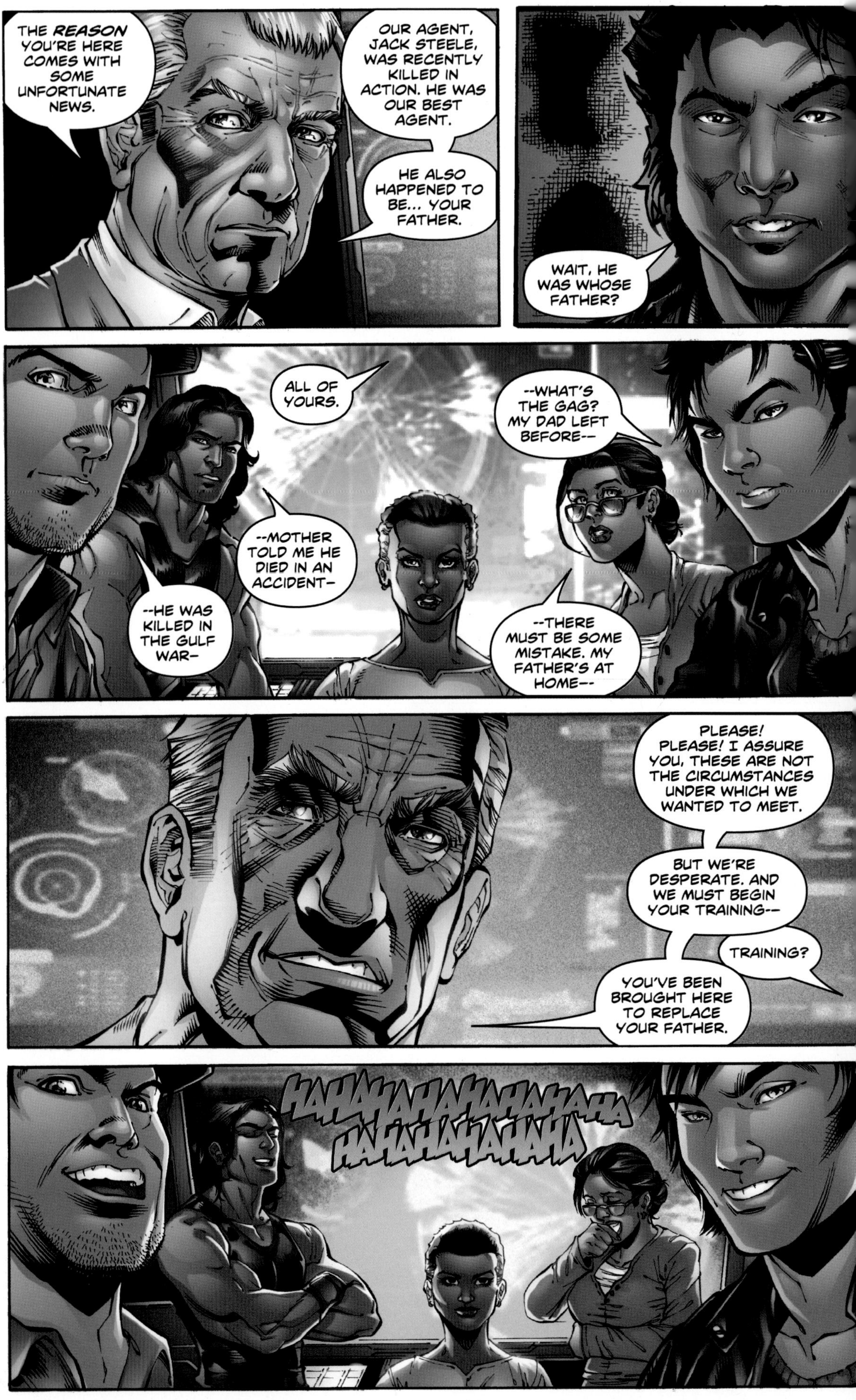
THE *REASON* YOU'RE HERE COMES WITH SOME UNFORTUNATE NEWS.
OUR AGENT, JACK STEELE, WAS RECENTLY KILLED IN ACTION. HE WAS OUR BEST AGENT.
HE ALSO HAPPENED TO BE... YOUR FATHER.
WAIT, HE WAS WHOSE FATHER?
ALL OF YOURS.
--WHAT'S THE GAG? MY DAD LEFT BEFORE--
--MOTHER TOLD ME HE DIED IN AN ACCIDENT-
--HE WAS KILLED IN THE GULF WAR-
--THERE MUST BE SOME MISTAKE. MY FATHER'S AT HOME--
PLEASE! PLEASE! I ASSURE YOU, THESE ARE NOT THE CIRCUMSTANCES UNDER WHICH WE WANTED TO MEET.
BUT WE'RE DESPERATE. AND WE MUST BEGIN YOUR TRAINING--
TRAINING?
YOU'VE BEEN BROUGHT HERE TO REPLACE YOUR FATHER.
HAHAHAHAHAHAHAHAHAHA
HAHAHAHAHAHAHAHA

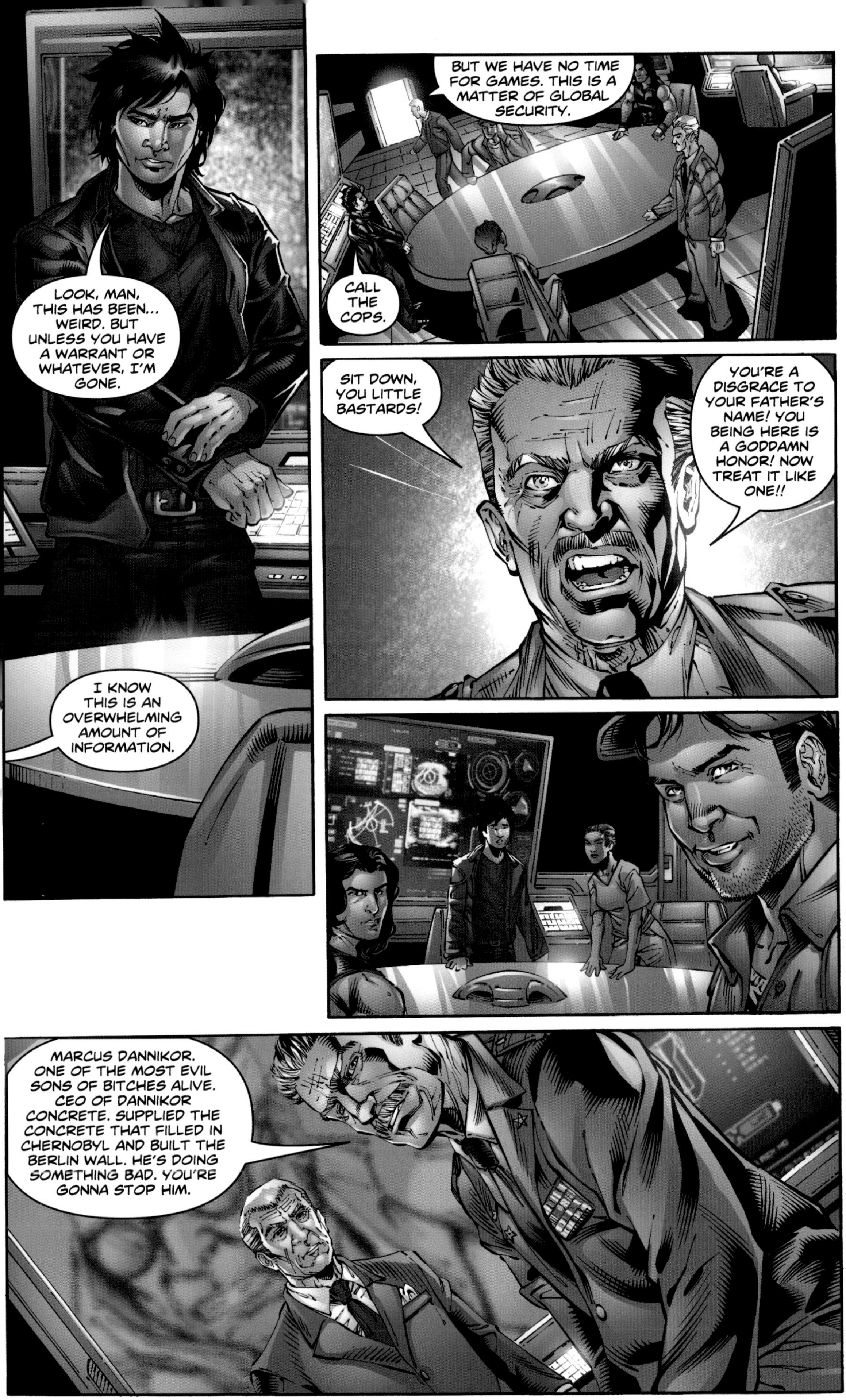
LOOK, MAN, THIS HAS BEEN... WEIRD. BUT UNLESS YOU HAVE A WARRANT OR WHATEVER, I'M GONE.
BUT WE HAVE NO TIME FOR GAMES. THIS IS A MATTER OF GLOBAL SECURITY.
CALL THE COPS.
I KNOW THIS IS AN OVERWHELMING AMOUNT OF INFORMATION.
SIT DOWN, YOU LITTLE BASTARDS!
YOU'RE A DISGRACE TO YOUR FATHER'S NAME! YOU BEING HERE IS A GODDAMN HONOR! NOW TREAT IT LIKE ONE!!
MARCUS DANNIKOR. ONE OF THE MOST EVIL SONS OF BITCHES ALIVE. CEO OF DANNIKOR CONCRETE. SUPPLIED THE CONCRETE THAT FILLED IN CHERNOBYL AND BUILT THE BERLIN WALL. HE'S DOING SOMETHING BAD. YOU'RE GONNA STOP HIM.

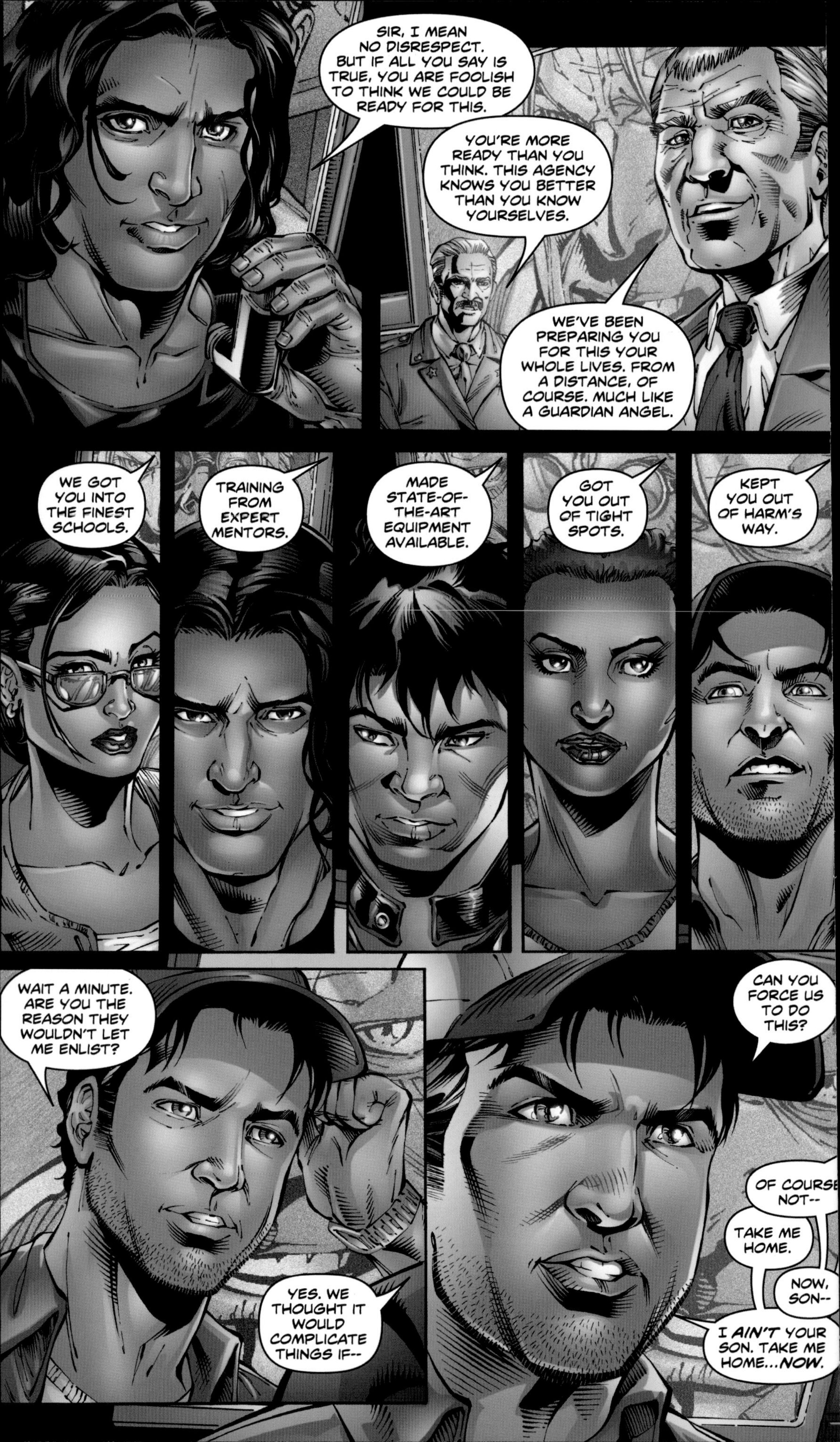
SIR, I MEAN NO DISRESPECT. BUT IF ALL YOU SAY IS TRUE, YOU ARE FOOLISH TO THINK WE COULD BE READY FOR THIS.
YOU'RE MORE READY THAN YOU THINK. THIS AGENCY KNOWS YOU BETTER THAN YOU KNOW YOURSELVES.
WE'VE BEEN PREPARING YOU FOR THIS YOUR WHOLE LIVES. FROM A DISTANCE, OF COURSE. MUCH LIKE A GUARDIAN ANGEL.
WE GOT YOU INTO THE FINEST SCHOOLS.
TRAINING FROM EXPERT MENTORS.
MADE STATE-OF-THE-ART EQUIPMENT AVAILABLE.
GOT YOU OUT OF TIGHT SPOTS.
KEPT YOU OUT OF HARM'S WAY.
WAIT A MINUTE. ARE YOU THE REASON THEY WOULDN'T LET ME ENLIST?
YES. WE THOUGHT IT WOULD COMPLICATE THINGS IF--
CAN YOU FORCE US TO DO THIS?
OF COURSE NOT--
TAKE ME HOME.
NOW, SON--
I *AIN'T* YOUR SON. TAKE ME HOME...*NOW*.

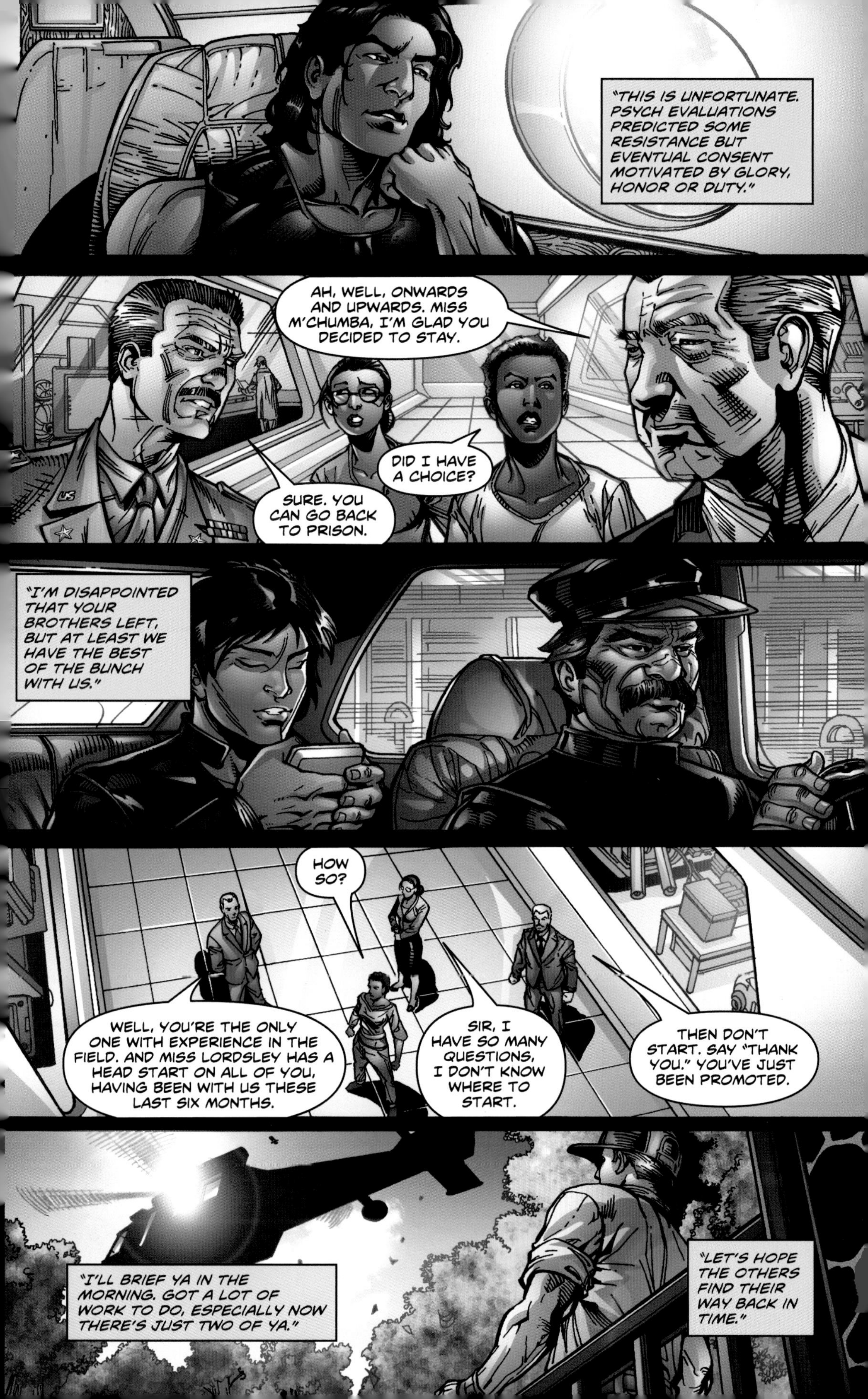
"THIS IS UNFORTUNATE. PSYCH EVALUATIONS PREDICTED SOME RESISTANCE BUT EVENTUAL CONSENT MOTIVATED BY GLORY, HONOR OR DUTY."
AH, WELL, ONWARDS AND UPWARDS. MISS M'CHUMBA, I'M GLAD YOU DECIDED TO STAY.
DID I HAVE A CHOICE?
SURE. YOU CAN GO BACK TO PRISON.
"I'M DISAPPOINTED THAT YOUR BROTHERS LEFT, BUT AT LEAST WE HAVE THE BEST OF THE BUNCH WITH US."
HOW SO?
WELL, YOU'RE THE ONLY ONE WITH EXPERIENCE IN THE FIELD. AND MISS LORDSLEY HAS A HEAD START ON ALL OF YOU, HAVING BEEN WITH US THESE LAST SIX MONTHS.
SIR, I HAVE SO MANY QUESTIONS, I DON'T KNOW WHERE TO START.
THEN DON'T START. SAY "THANK YOU." YOU'VE JUST BEEN PROMOTED.
"I'LL BRIEF YA IN THE MORNING. GOT A LOT OF WORK TO DO, ESPECIALLY NOW THERE'S JUST TWO OF YA."
"LET'S HOPE THE OTHERS FIND THEIR WAY BACK IN TIME."

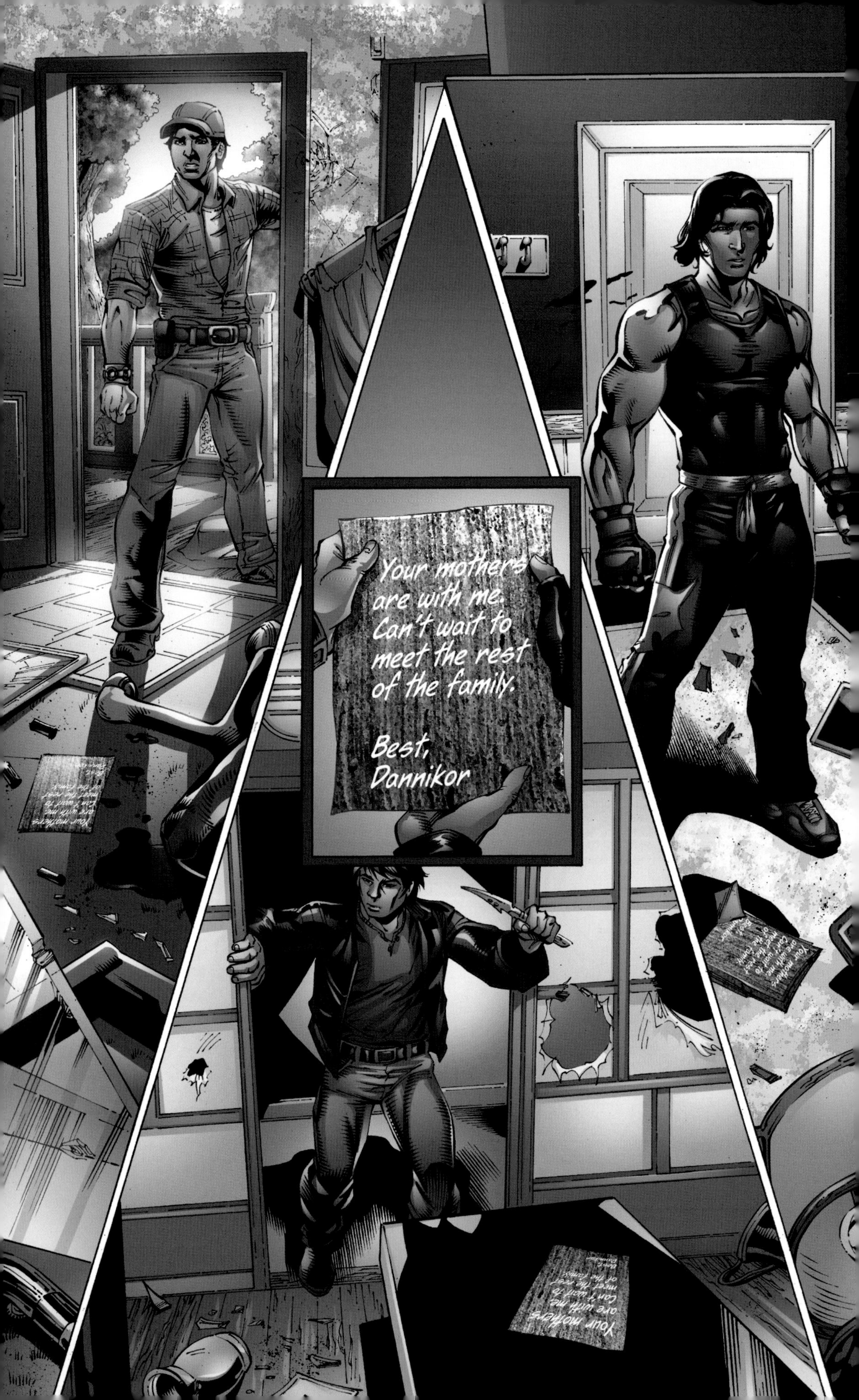
Your mothers are with me. Can't wait to meet the rest of the family.
Best,
Dannikor

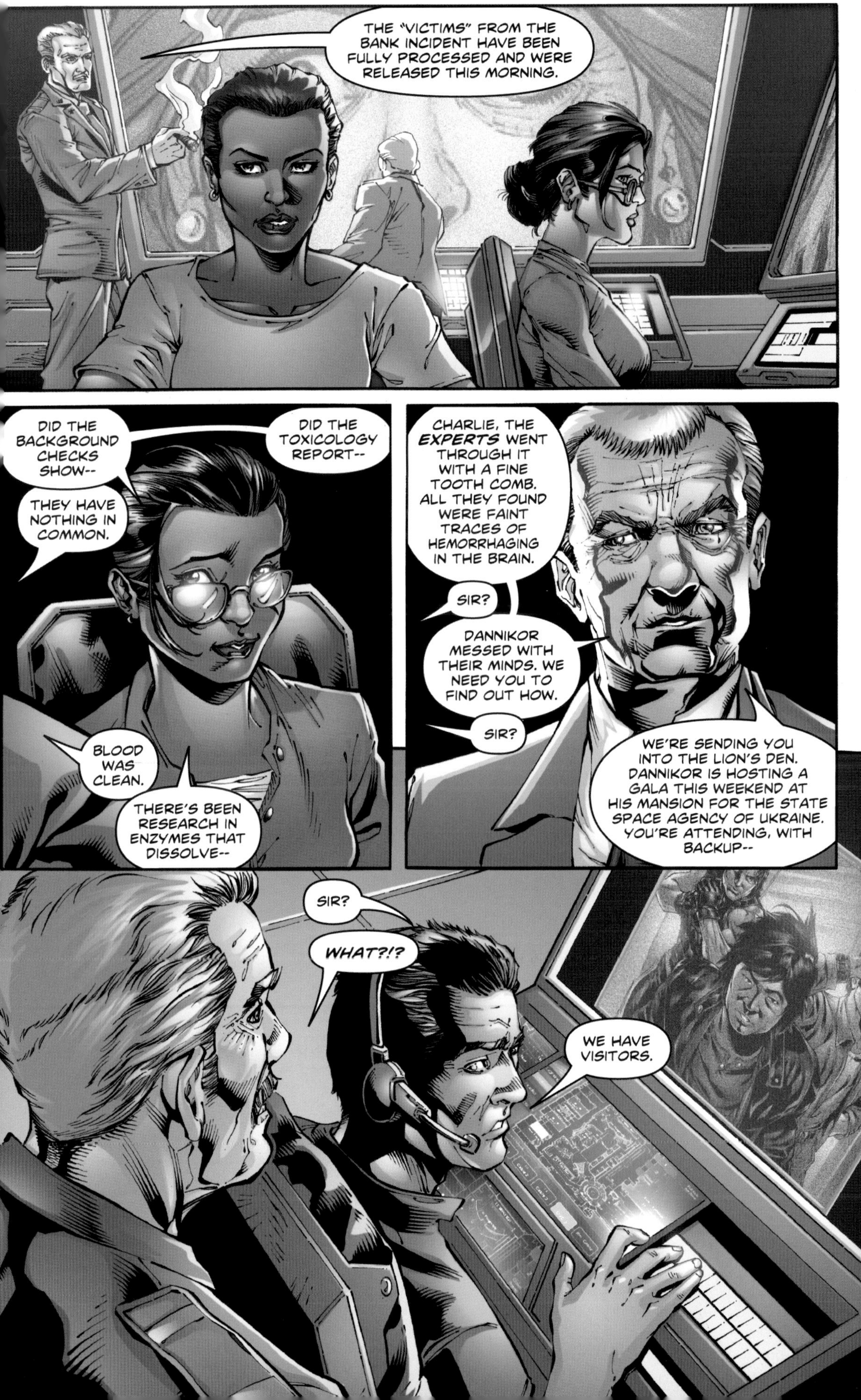
THE "VICTIMS" FROM THE BANK INCIDENT HAVE BEEN FULLY PROCESSED AND WERE RELEASED THIS MORNING.
DID THE BACKGROUND CHECKS SHOW--
DID THE TOXICOLOGY REPORT--
THEY HAVE NOTHING IN COMMON.
BLOOD WAS CLEAN.
THERE'S BEEN RESEARCH IN ENZYMES THAT DISSOLVE--
CHARLIE, THE *EXPERTS* WENT THROUGH IT WITH A FINE TOOTH COMB. ALL THEY FOUND WERE FAINT TRACES OF HEMORRHAGING IN THE BRAIN.
SIR?
DANNIKOR MESSED WITH THEIR MINDS. WE NEED YOU TO FIND OUT HOW.
SIR?
WE'RE SENDING YOU INTO THE LION'S DEN. DANNIKOR IS HOSTING A GALA THIS WEEKEND AT HIS MANSION FOR THE STATE SPACE AGENCY OF UKRAINE. YOU'RE ATTENDING, WITH BACKUP--
SIR?
WHAT?!?
WE HAVE VISITORS.

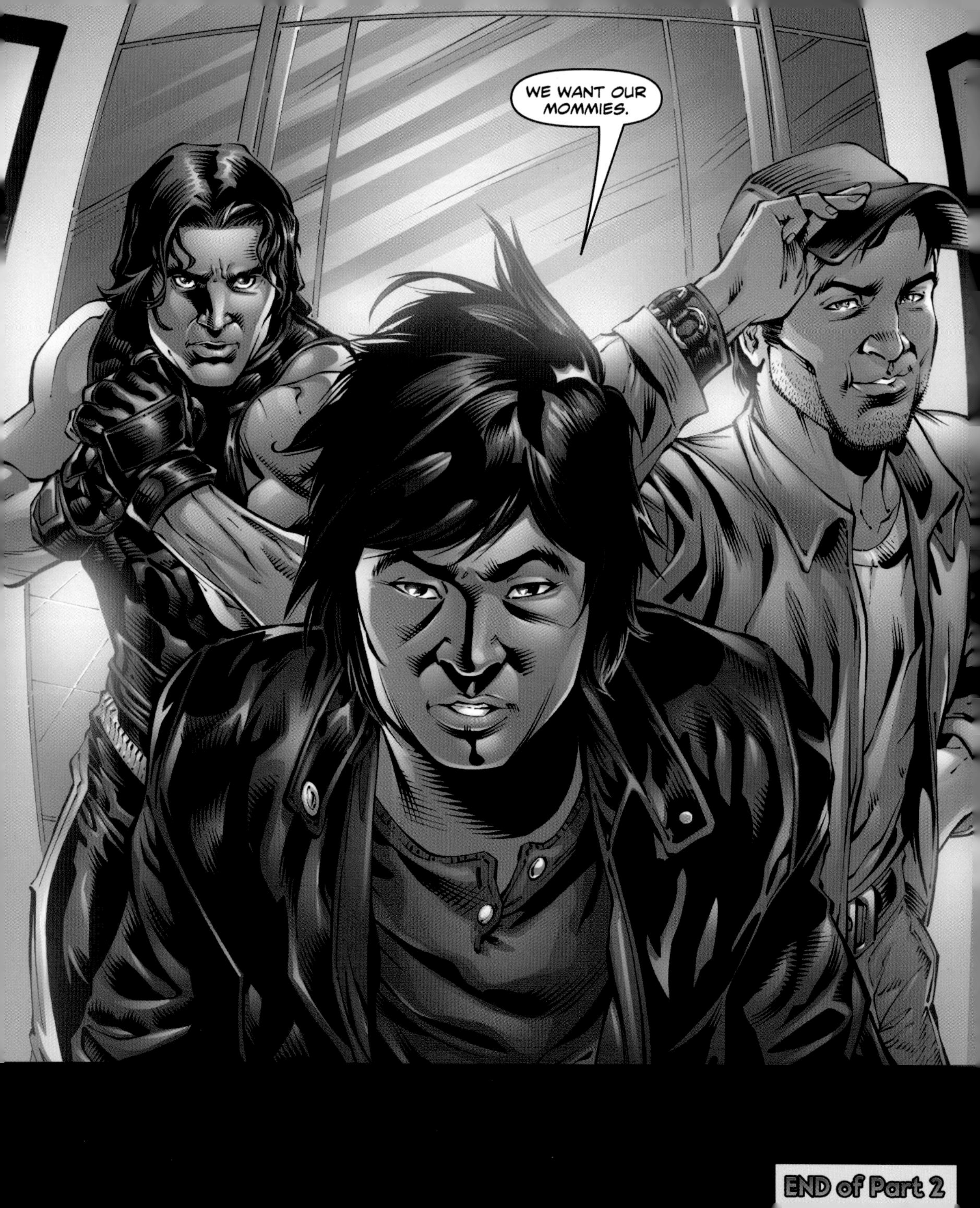
WE WANT OUR MOMMIES.

END of Part 2

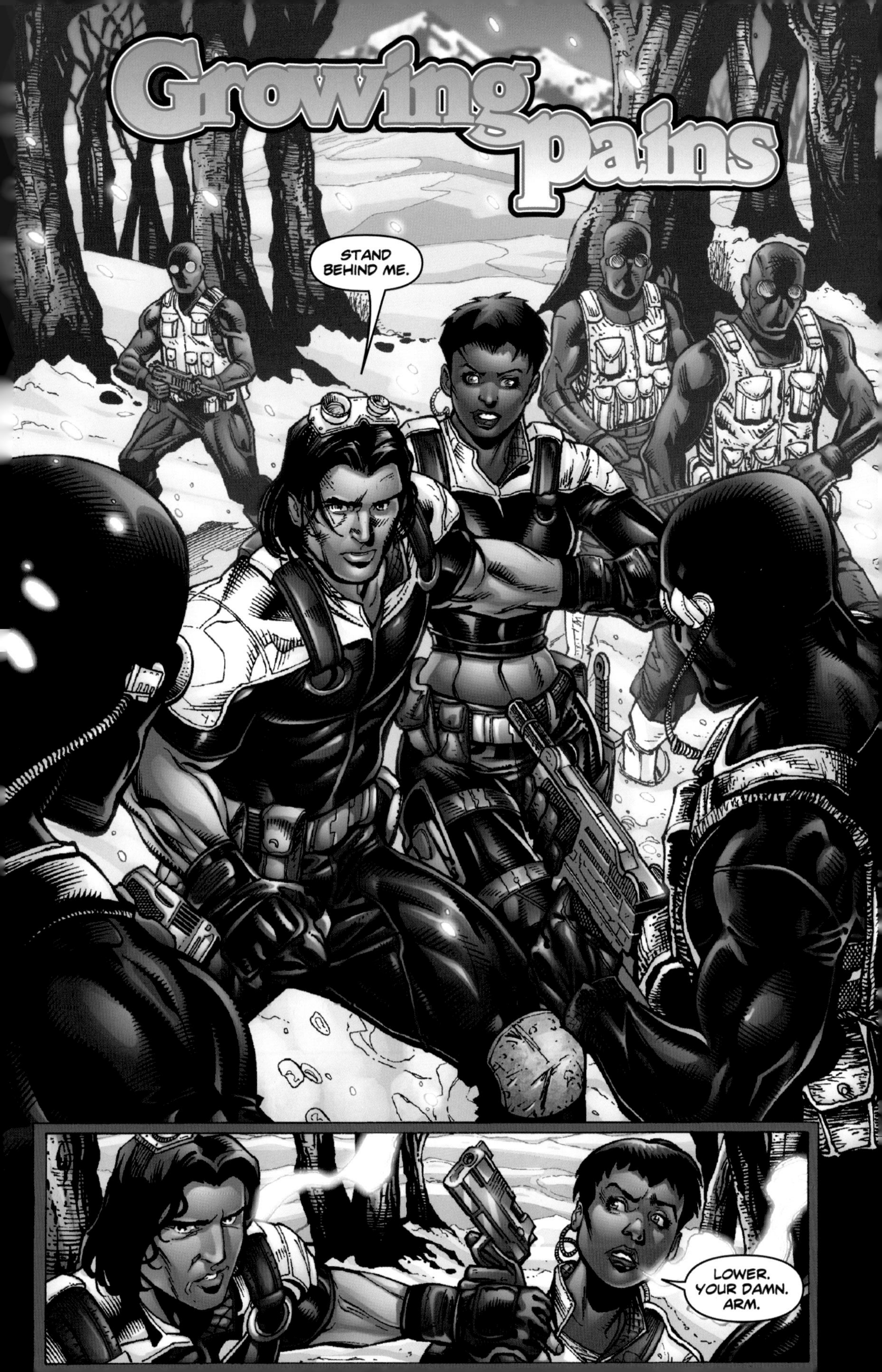
Growing pains
STAND BEHIND ME.
LOWER. YOUR DAMN. ARM.

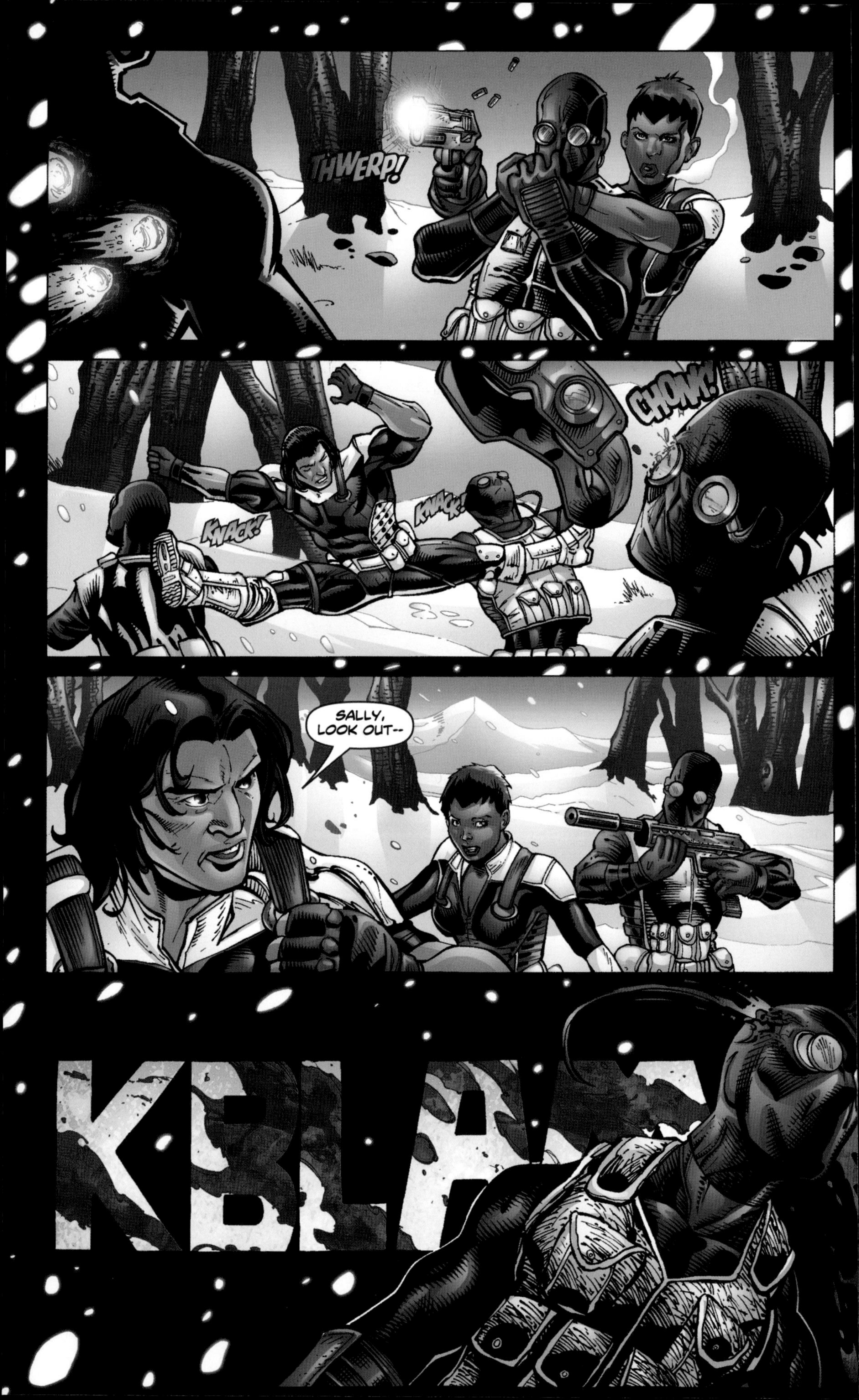
THWERP!
CHONK!
KNACK!
KNACK!
SALLY, LOOK OUT--

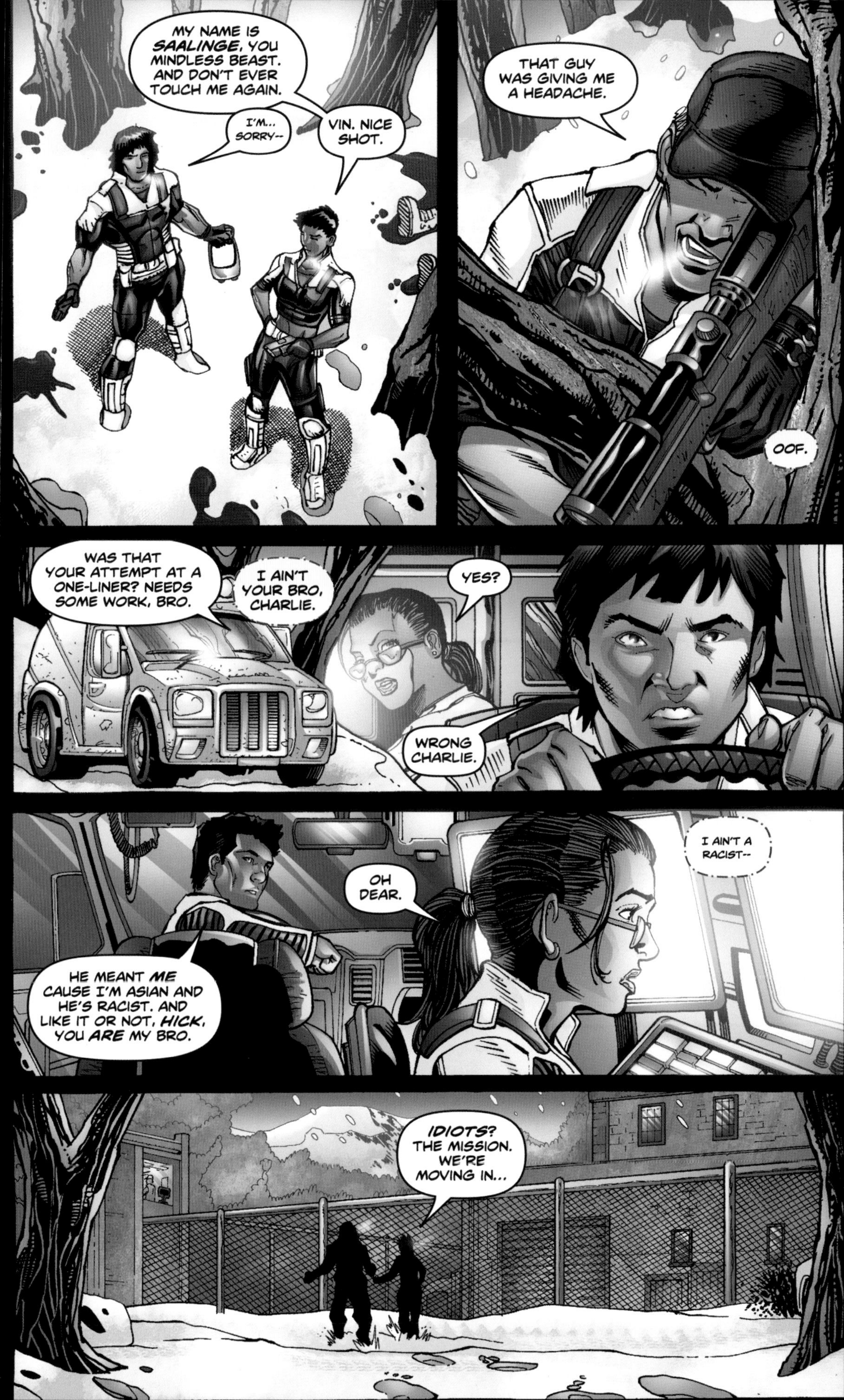

MY NAME IS SAALINGE, YOU MINDLESS BEAST. AND DON'T EVER TOUCH ME AGAIN.
I'M... SORRY--
VIN. NICE SHOT.
THAT GUY WAS GIVING ME A HEADACHE.
OOF.
WAS THAT YOUR ATTEMPT AT A ONE-LINER? NEEDS SOME WORK, BRO.
I AIN'T YOUR BRO, CHARLIE.
YES?
WRONG CHARLIE.
I AIN'T A RACIST--
OH DEAR.
HE MEANT ME CAUSE I'M ASIAN AND HE'S RACIST. AND LIKE IT OR NOT, HICK, YOU ARE MY BRO.
IDIOTS? THE MISSION. WE'RE MOVING IN...

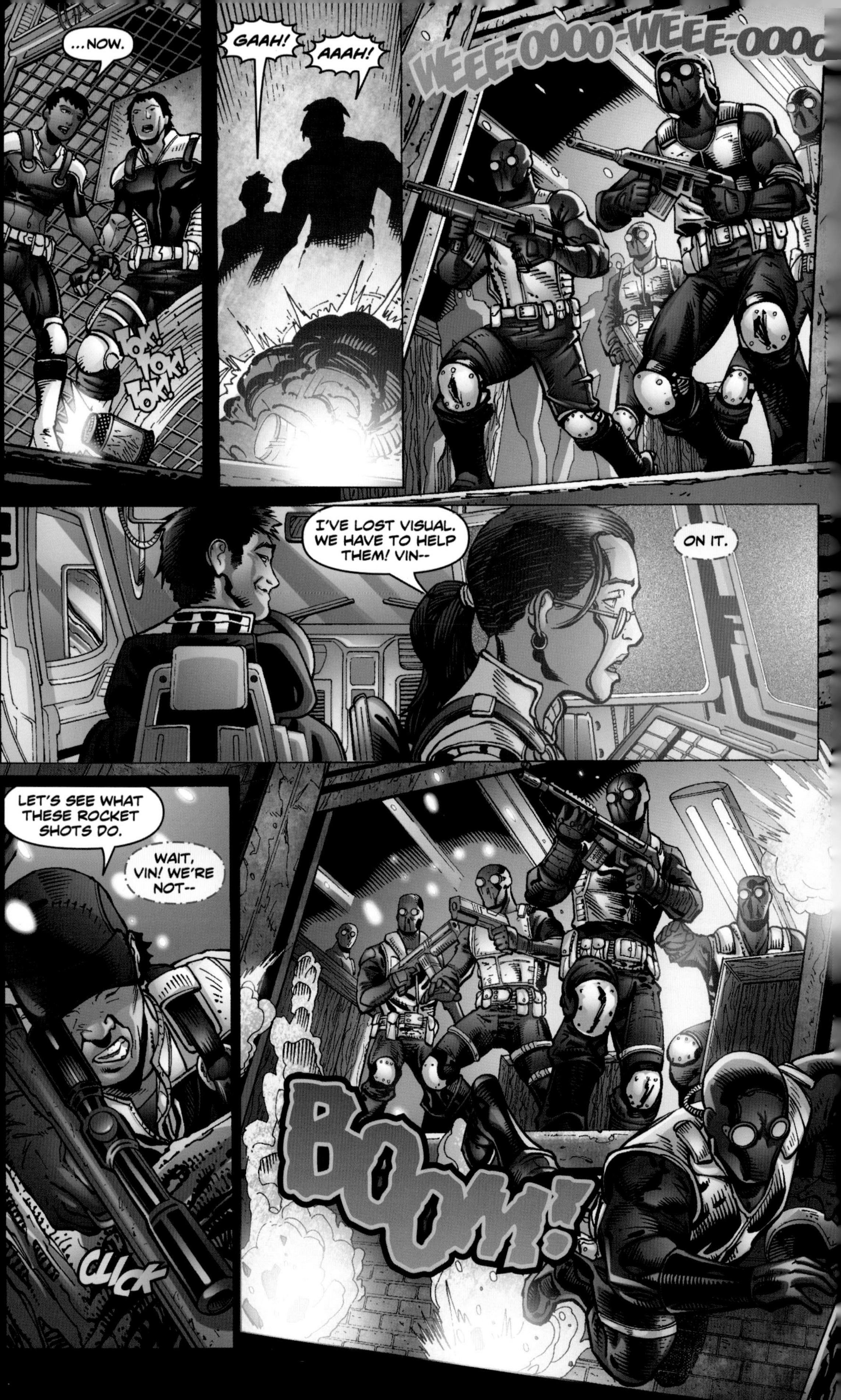
...NOW.
TOK! TOK! TOK!
GAAH!
AAAH!
WEEE-OOOO-WEEE-OOOO
I'VE LOST VISUAL. WE HAVE TO HELP THEM! VIN--
ON IT.
LET'S SEE WHAT THESE ROCKET SHOTS DO.
WAIT, VIN! WE'RE NOT--
CLICK
BOOM!

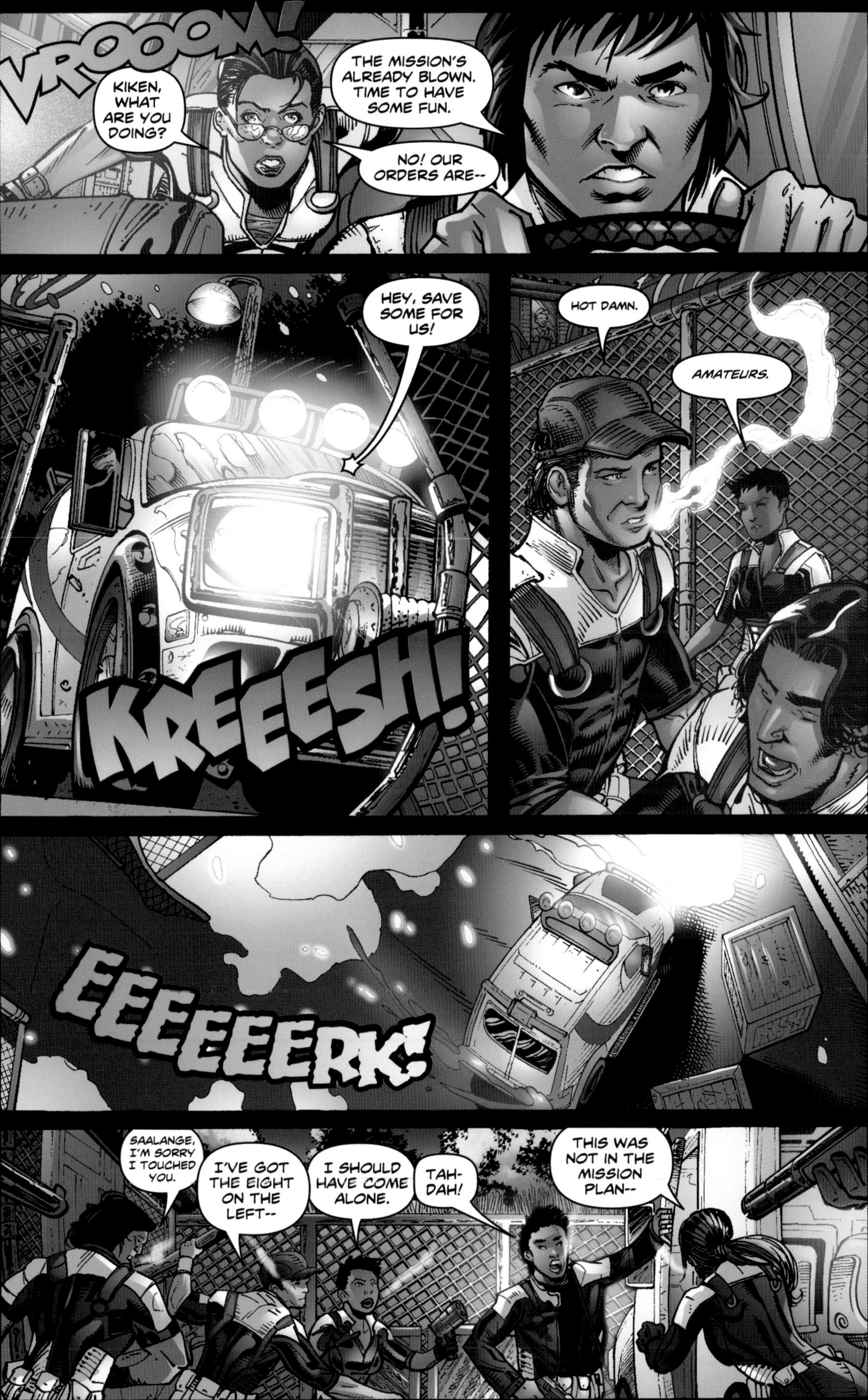
VROOOM!
KIKEN, WHAT ARE YOU DOING?
THE MISSION'S ALREADY BLOWN. TIME TO HAVE SOME FUN.
NO! OUR ORDERS ARE--
HEY, SAVE SOME FOR US!
KREEESH!
HOT DAMN.
AMATEURS.
EEEEEERK!
SAALANGE, I'M SORRY I TOUCHED YOU.
I'VE GOT THE EIGHT ON THE LEFT--
I SHOULD HAVE COME ALONE.
TAH-DAH!
THIS WAS NOT IN THE MISSION PLAN--

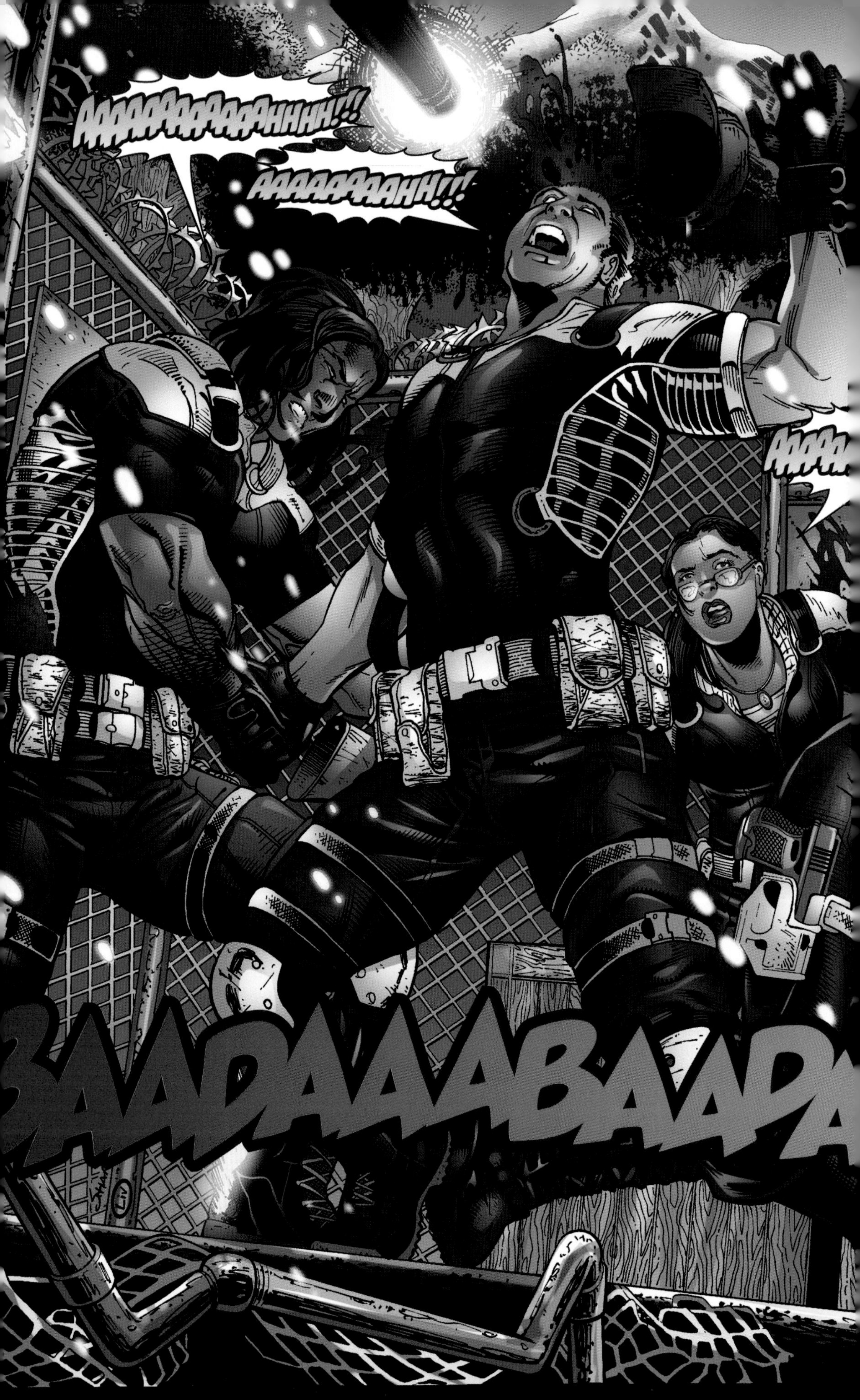
AAAAAAAAAAAHHHH!!!
AAAAAAAAHH!!!

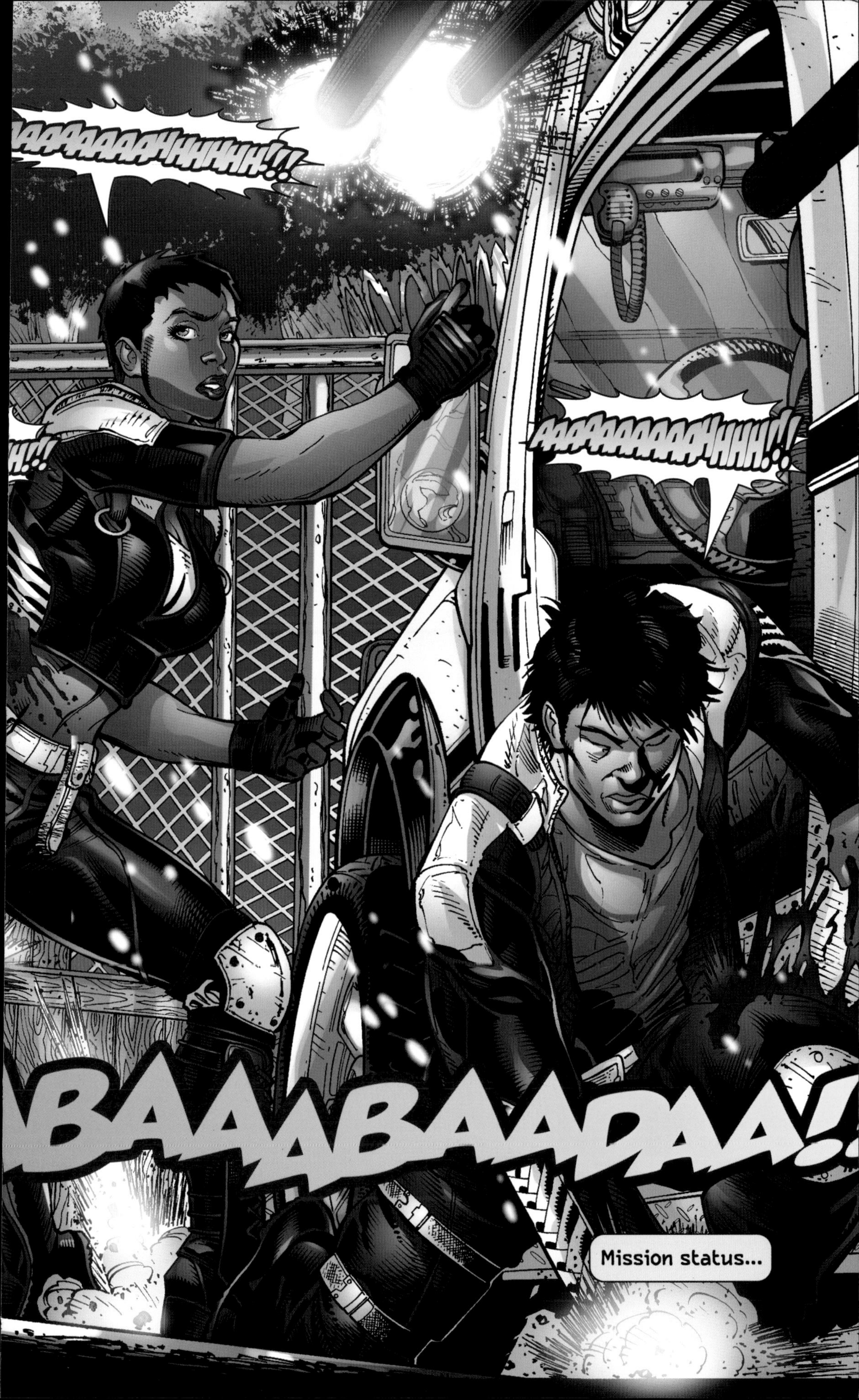
AAAAAAAAHHHHHH!!!
H!!
AAAAAAAAAAHHHH!!
BAAABAAADAA!!
Mission status...

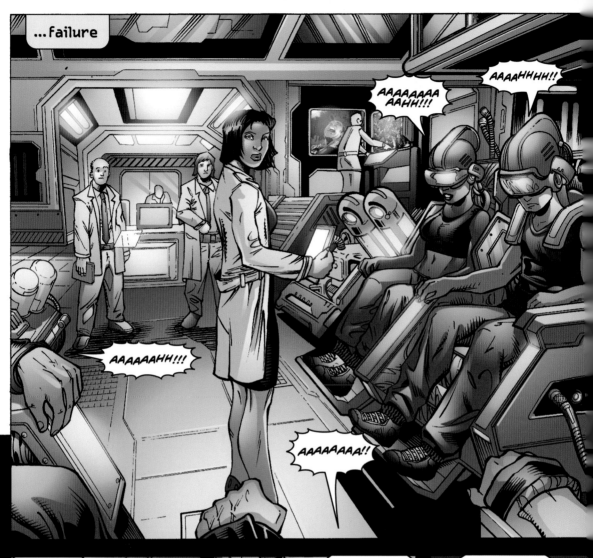

AAAAAAAAAAHH!!!

AAAAHHH!!!

AAAAAAHH!!!

AAAAAAAA!!

GODDAMMIT.

THESE TURDS WOULDN'T KNOW HOW TO WORK TOGETHER IF THEY WERE ATTACHED BRAIN TO BUTT!

GIVE IT TIME.

THERE IS NO TIME. DANNIKOR'S GOT A HEAD START--

WE'VE BEEN AT THIS FOR HOURS. WE NEED A BREAK.

YOU THINK THIS IS A GAME? THERE AIN'T NO "VIRTUAL DEATHS" IN THE REAL WORLD!

WE'RE GOING AGAIN NOW! ANTARCTIC SEQUENCE!

HOW'S THIS VIDEO GAME HELPING US SAVE OUR MOMS?

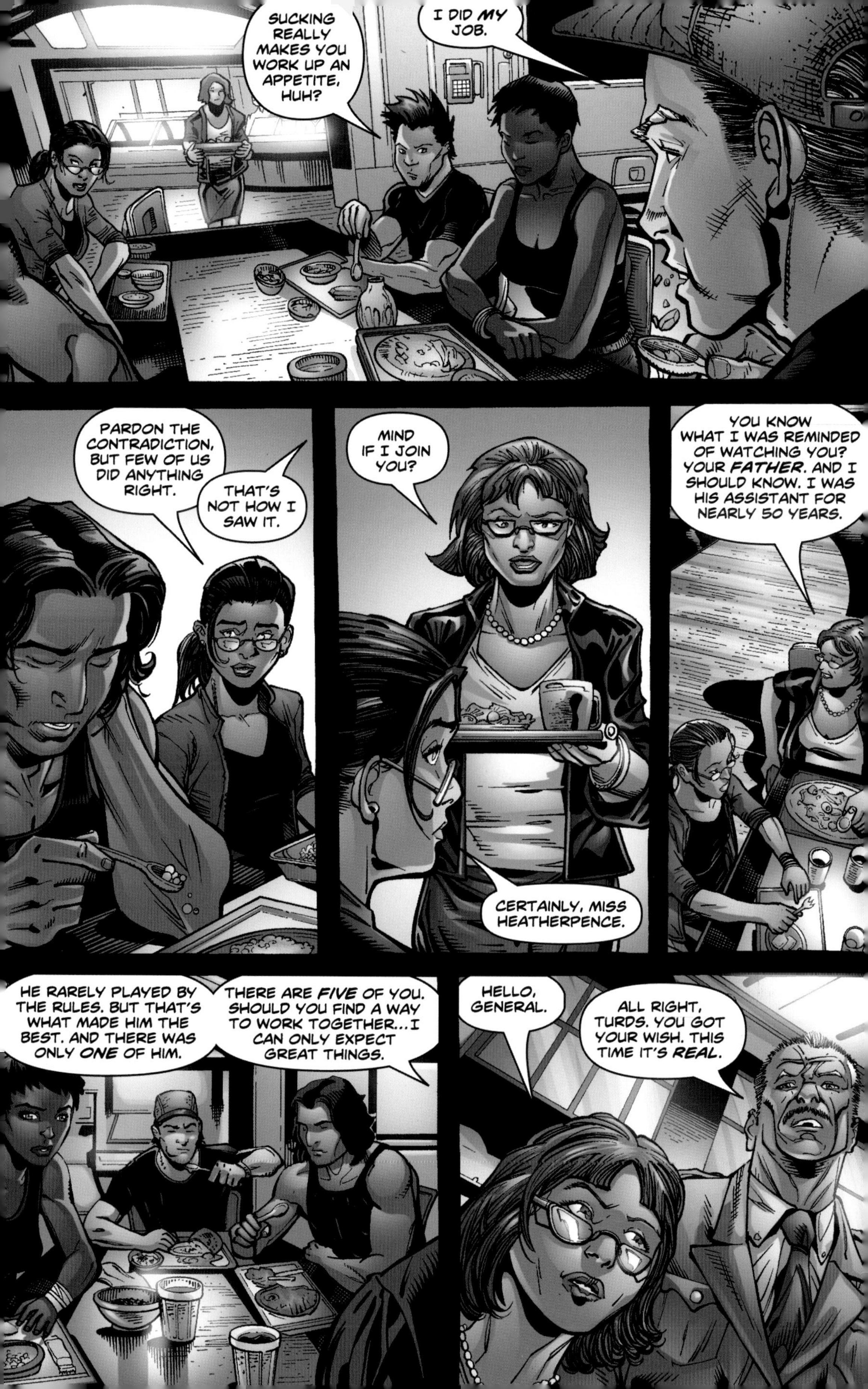
SUCKING REALLY MAKES YOU WORK UP AN APPETITE, HUH?
I DID MY JOB.
PARDON THE CONTRADICTION, BUT FEW OF US DID ANYTHING RIGHT.
THAT'S NOT HOW I SAW IT.
MIND IF I JOIN YOU?
CERTAINLY, MISS HEATHERPENCE.
YOU KNOW WHAT I WAS REMINDED OF WATCHING YOU? YOUR FATHER. AND I SHOULD KNOW. I WAS HIS ASSISTANT FOR NEARLY 50 YEARS.
HE RARELY PLAYED BY THE RULES. BUT THAT'S WHAT MADE HIM THE BEST. AND THERE WAS ONLY ONE OF HIM.
THERE ARE FIVE OF YOU. SHOULD YOU FIND A WAY TO WORK TOGETHER... I CAN ONLY EXPECT GREAT THINGS.
HELLO, GENERAL.
ALL RIGHT, TURDS. YOU GOT YOUR WISH. THIS TIME IT'S REAL.

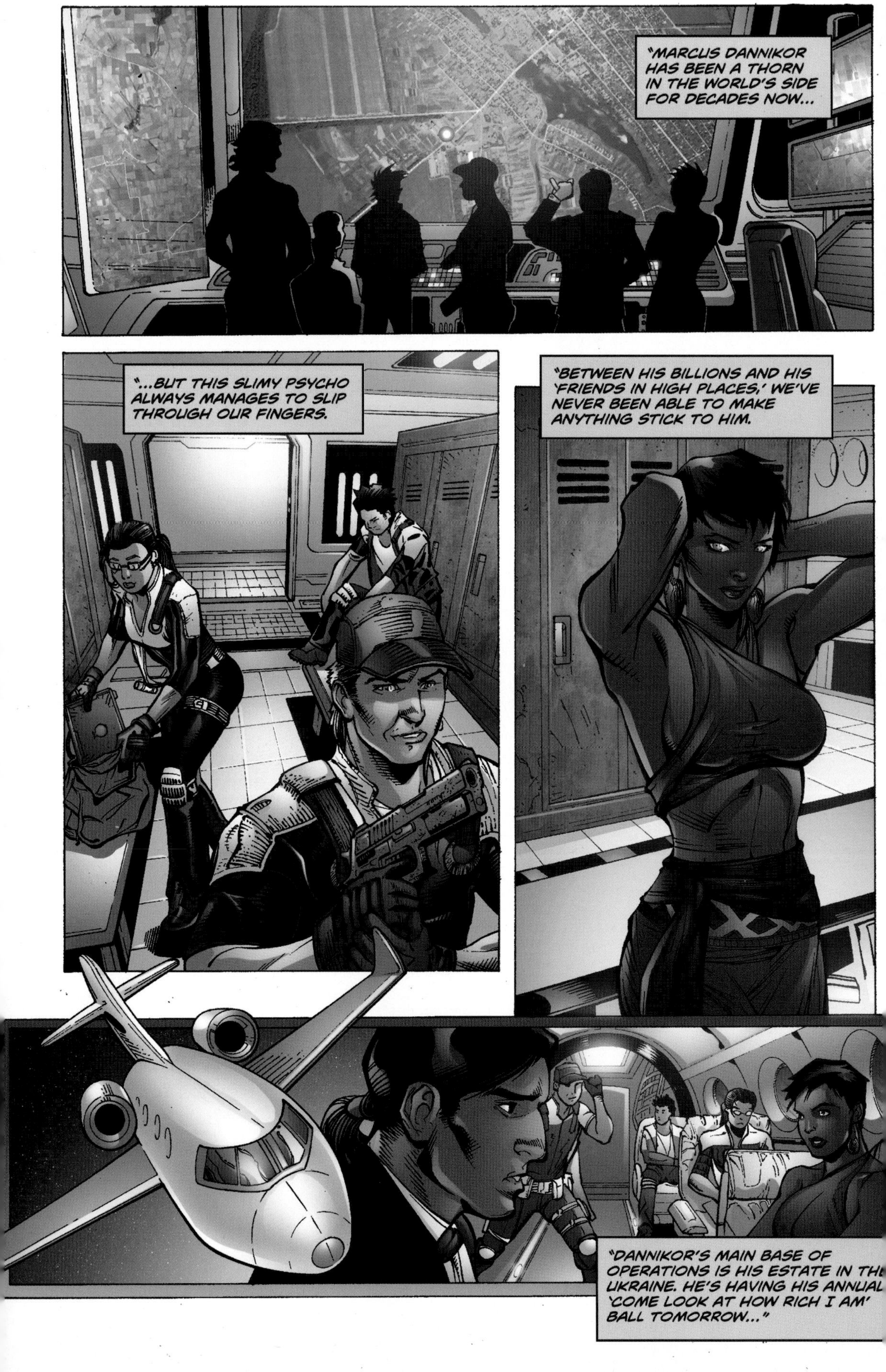
"MARCUS DANNIKOR HAS BEEN A THORN IN THE WORLD'S SIDE FOR DECADES NOW...
"...BUT THIS SLIMY PSYCHO ALWAYS MANAGES TO SLIP THROUGH OUR FINGERS.
"BETWEEN HIS BILLIONS AND HIS 'FRIENDS IN HIGH PLACES,' WE'VE NEVER BEEN ABLE TO MAKE ANYTHING STICK TO HIM.
"DANNIKOR'S MAIN BASE OF OPERATIONS IS HIS ESTATE IN TH UKRAINE. HE'S HAVING HIS ANNUAL 'COME LOOK AT HOW RICH I AM' BALL TOMORROW..."

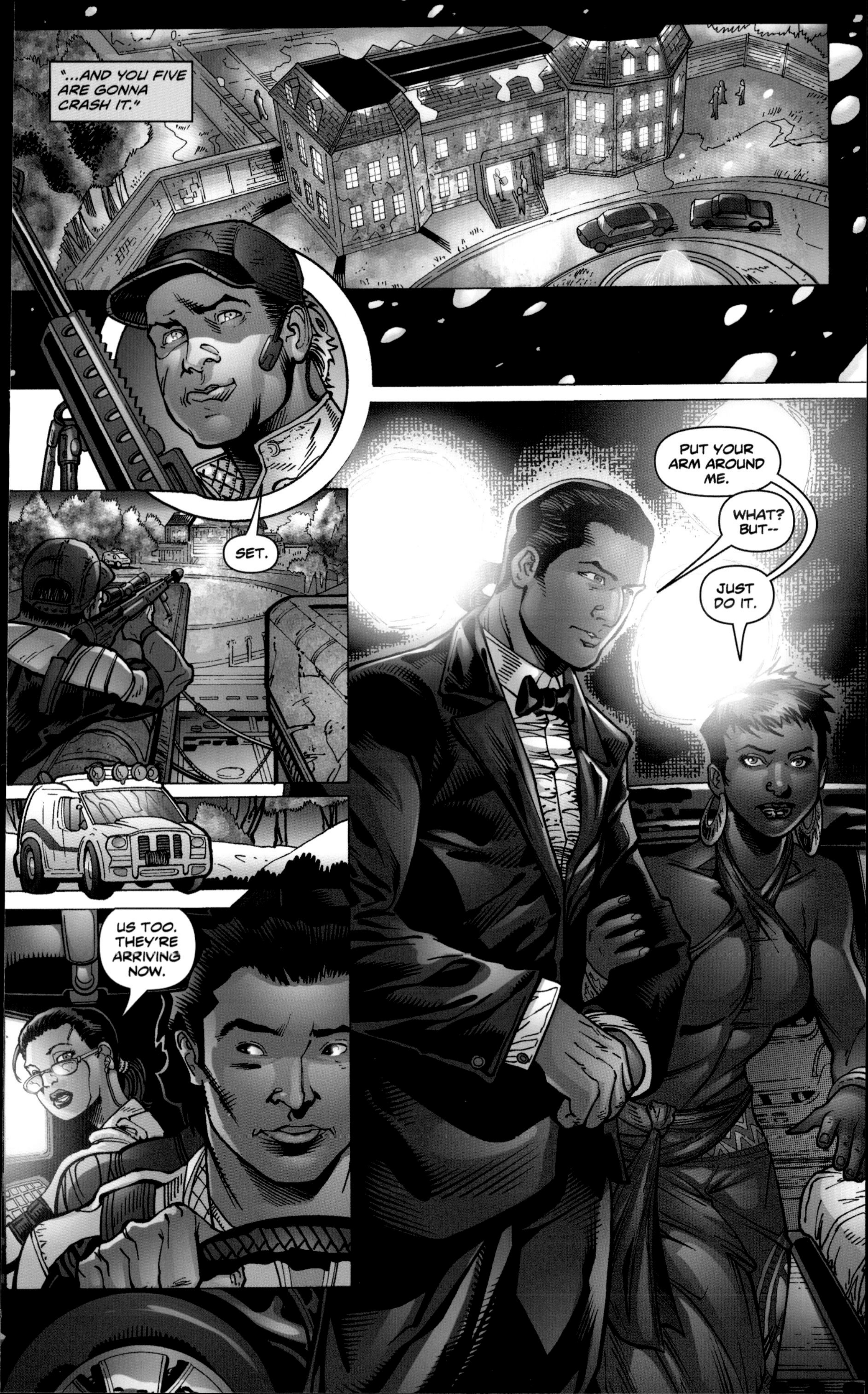
"...AND YOU FIVE ARE GONNA CRASH IT."
SET.
US TOO. THEY'RE ARRIVING NOW.
PUT YOUR ARM AROUND ME.
WHAT? BUT--
JUST DO IT.

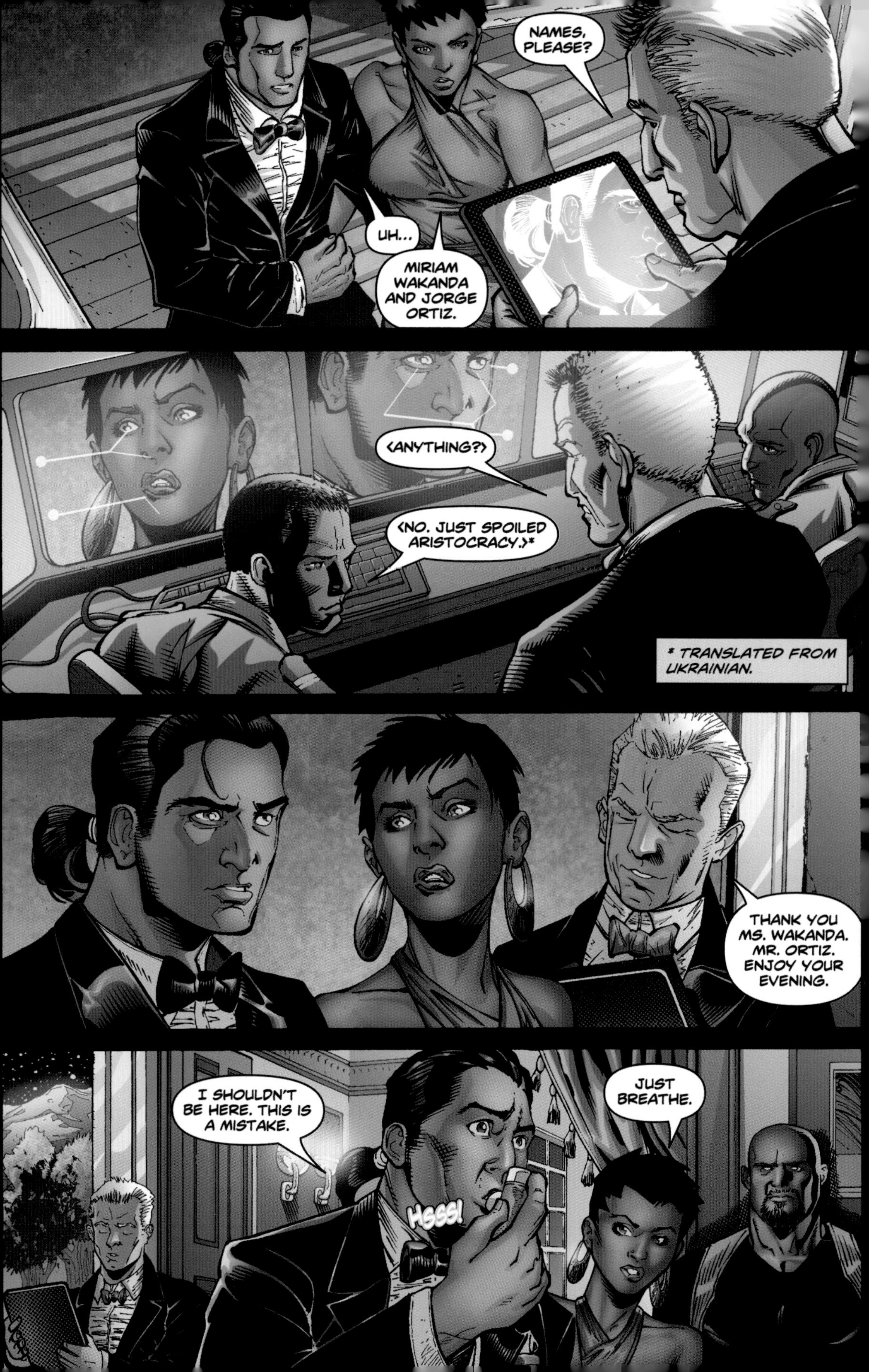
NAMES, PLEASE?
UH...
MIRIAM WAKANDA AND JORGE ORTIZ.
<ANYTHING?>
<NO. JUST SPOILED ARISTOCRACY.>*
* TRANSLATED FROM UKRAINIAN.
THANK YOU MS. WAKANDA. MR. ORTIZ. ENJOY YOUR EVENING.
I SHOULDN'T BE HERE. THIS IS A MISTAKE.
HSSS!
JUST BREATHE.

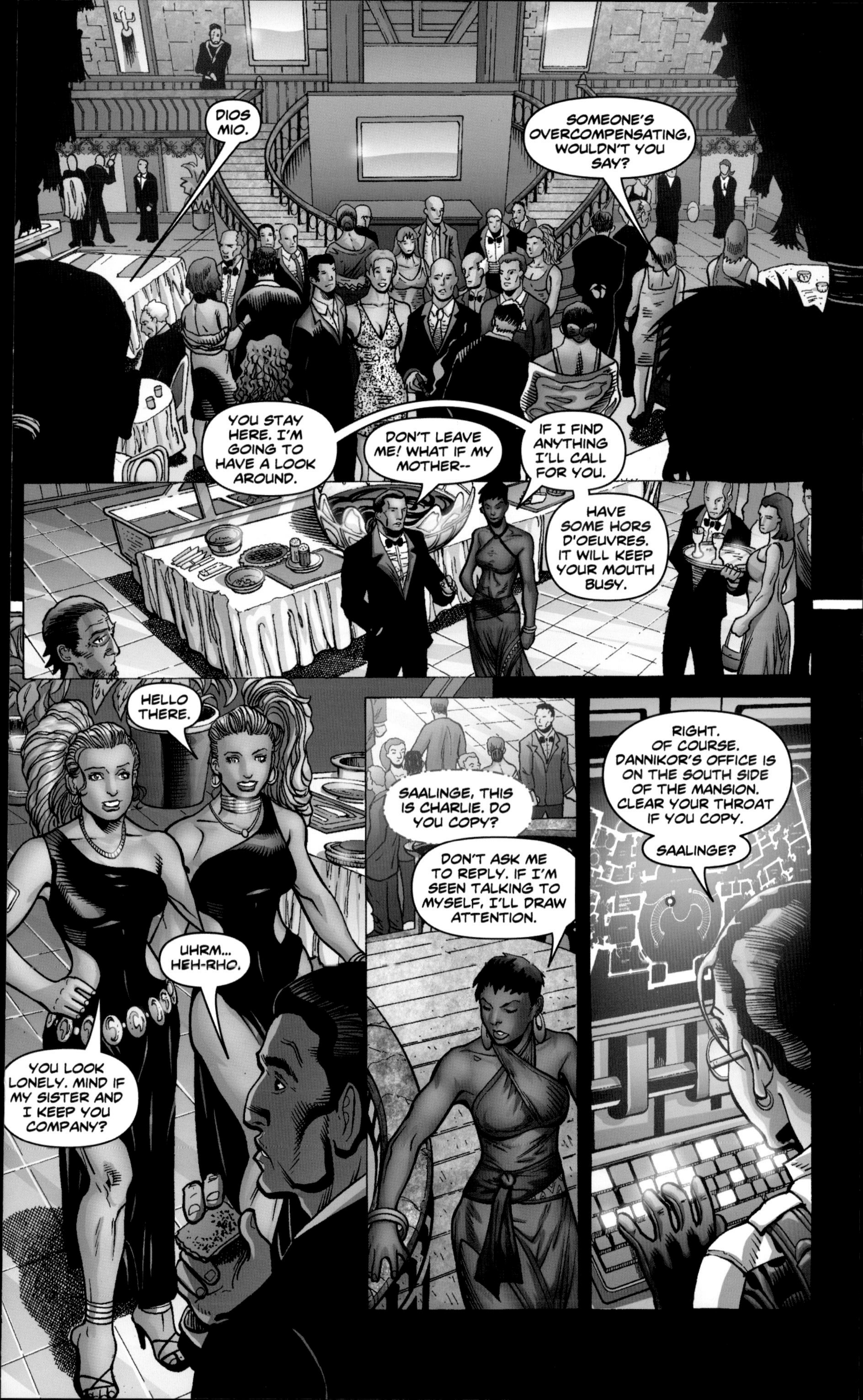
DIOS MIO.
SOMEONE'S OVERCOMPENSATING, WOULDN'T YOU SAY?
YOU STAY HERE. I'M GOING TO HAVE A LOOK AROUND.
DON'T LEAVE ME! WHAT IF MY MOTHER--
IF I FIND ANYTHING I'LL CALL FOR YOU.
HAVE SOME HORS D'OEUVRES. IT WILL KEEP YOUR MOUTH BUSY.
HELLO THERE.
YOU LOOK LONELY. MIND IF MY SISTER AND I KEEP YOU COMPANY?
UHRM... HEH-RHO.
SAALINGE, THIS IS CHARLIE. DO YOU COPY?
DON'T ASK ME TO REPLY. IF I'M SEEN TALKING TO MYSELF, I'LL DRAW ATTENTION.
RIGHT. OF COURSE. DANNIKOR'S OFFICE IS ON THE SOUTH SIDE OF THE MANSION. CLEAR YOUR THROAT IF YOU COPY.
SAALINGE?

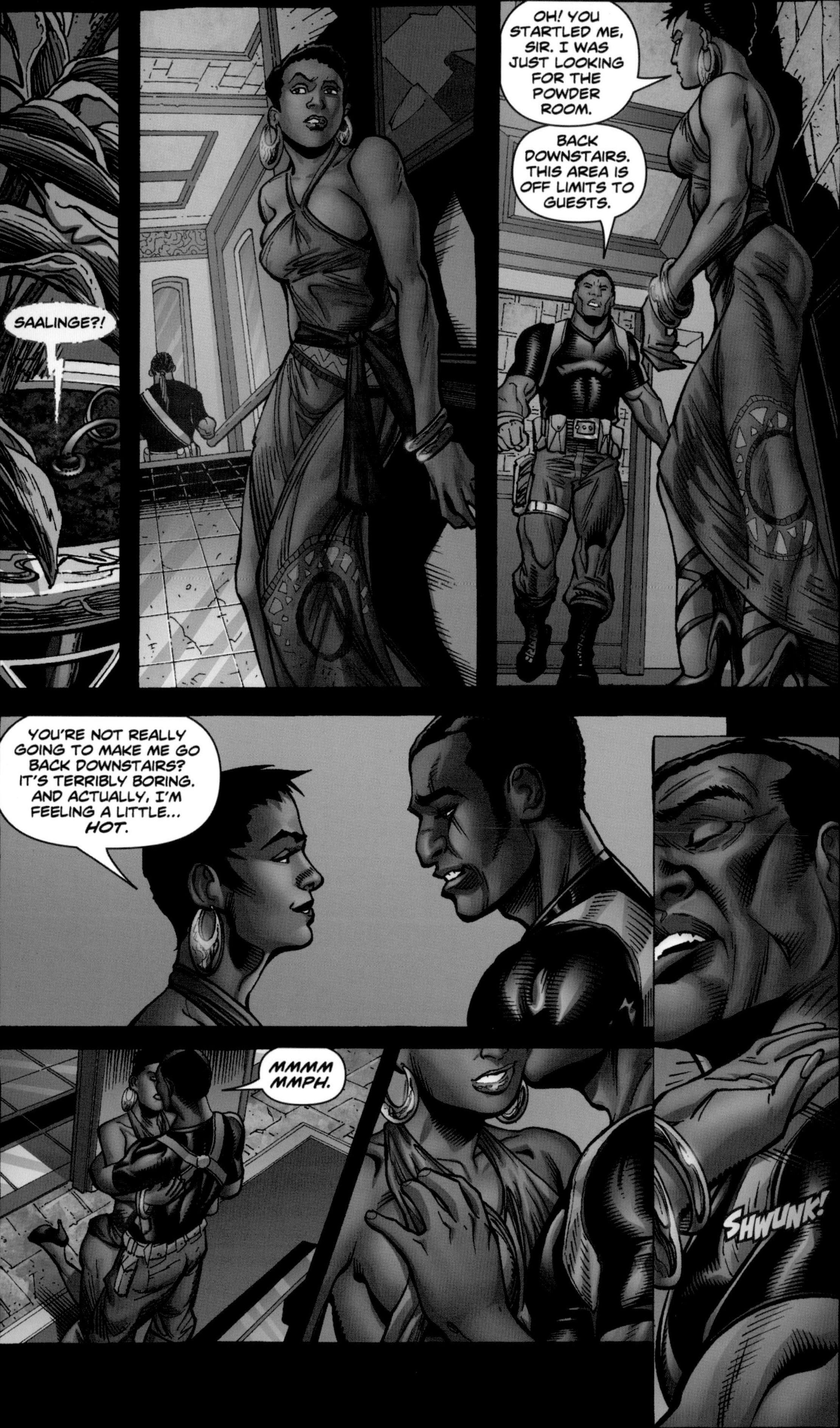
SAALINGE?!
OH! YOU STARTLED ME, SIR. I WAS JUST LOOKING FOR THE POWDER ROOM.
BACK DOWNSTAIRS. THIS AREA IS OFF LIMITS TO GUESTS.
YOU'RE NOT REALLY GOING TO MAKE ME GO BACK DOWNSTAIRS? IT'S TERRIBLY BORING. AND ACTUALLY, I'M FEELING A LITTLE... HOT.
MMMM MMPH.
SHWUNK!

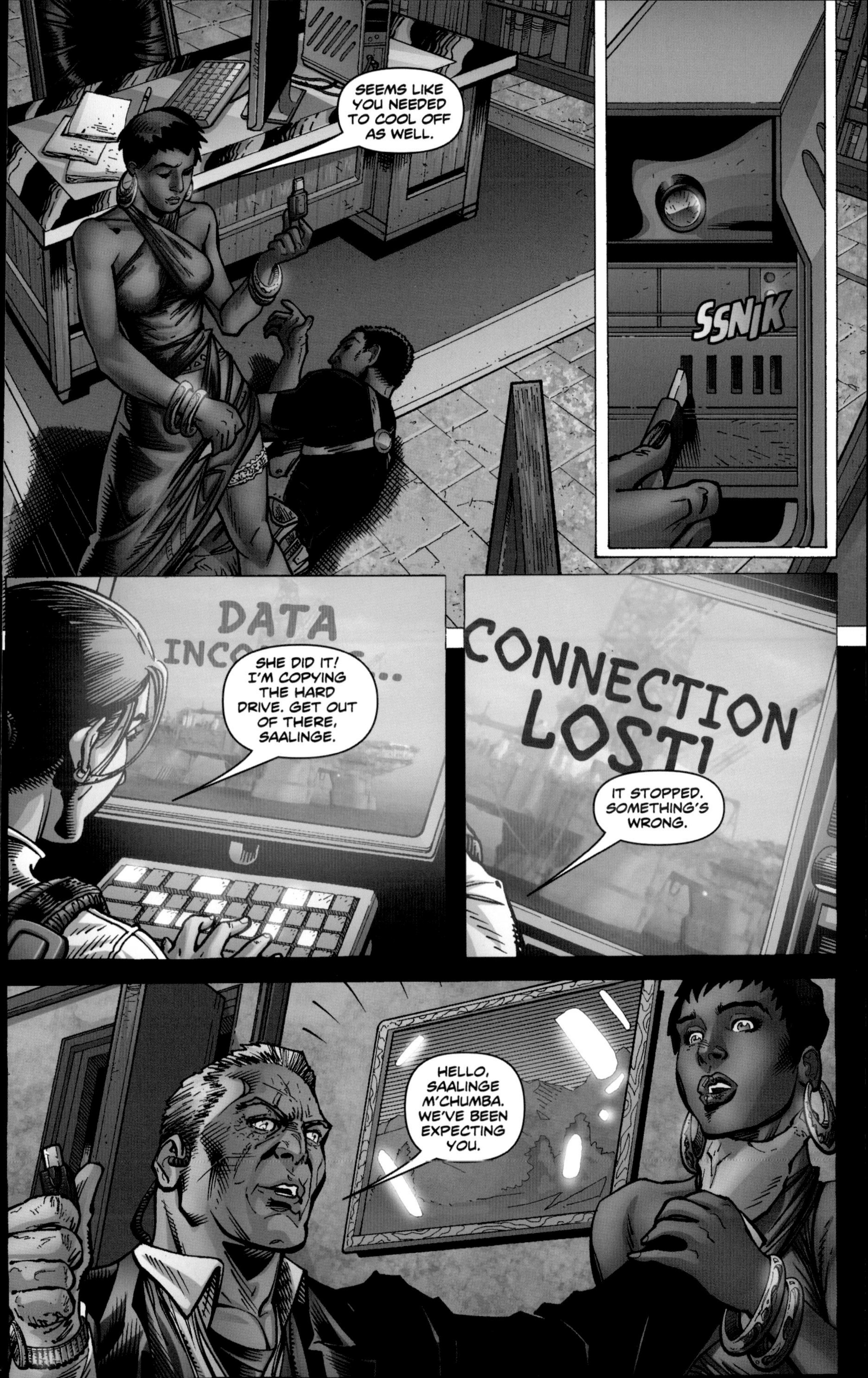
SEEMS LIKE YOU NEEDED TO COOL OFF AS WELL.
SSNIK
DATA
SHE DID IT! I'M COPYING THE HARD DRIVE. GET OUT OF THERE, SAALINGE.
CONNECTION LOST!
IT STOPPED. SOMETHING'S WRONG.
HELLO, SAALINGE M'CHUMBA. WE'VE BEEN EXPECTING YOU.

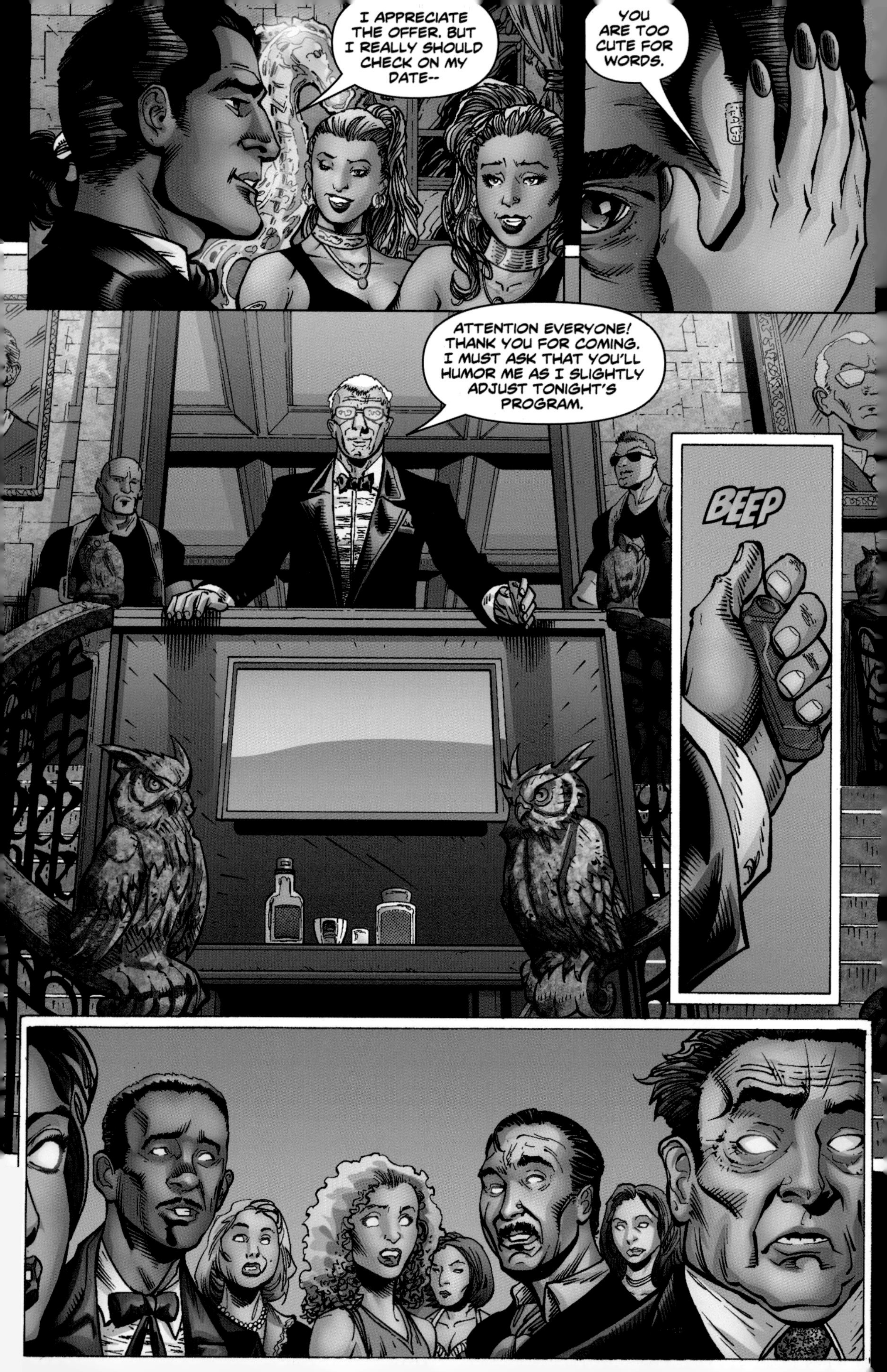
I APPRECIATE THE OFFER. BUT I REALLY SHOULD CHECK ON MY DATE--
YOU ARE TOO CUTE FOR WORDS.
ATTENTION EVERYONE! THANK YOU FOR COMING. I MUST ASK THAT YOU'LL HUMOR ME AS I SLIGHTLY ADJUST TONIGHT'S PROGRAM.
BEEP

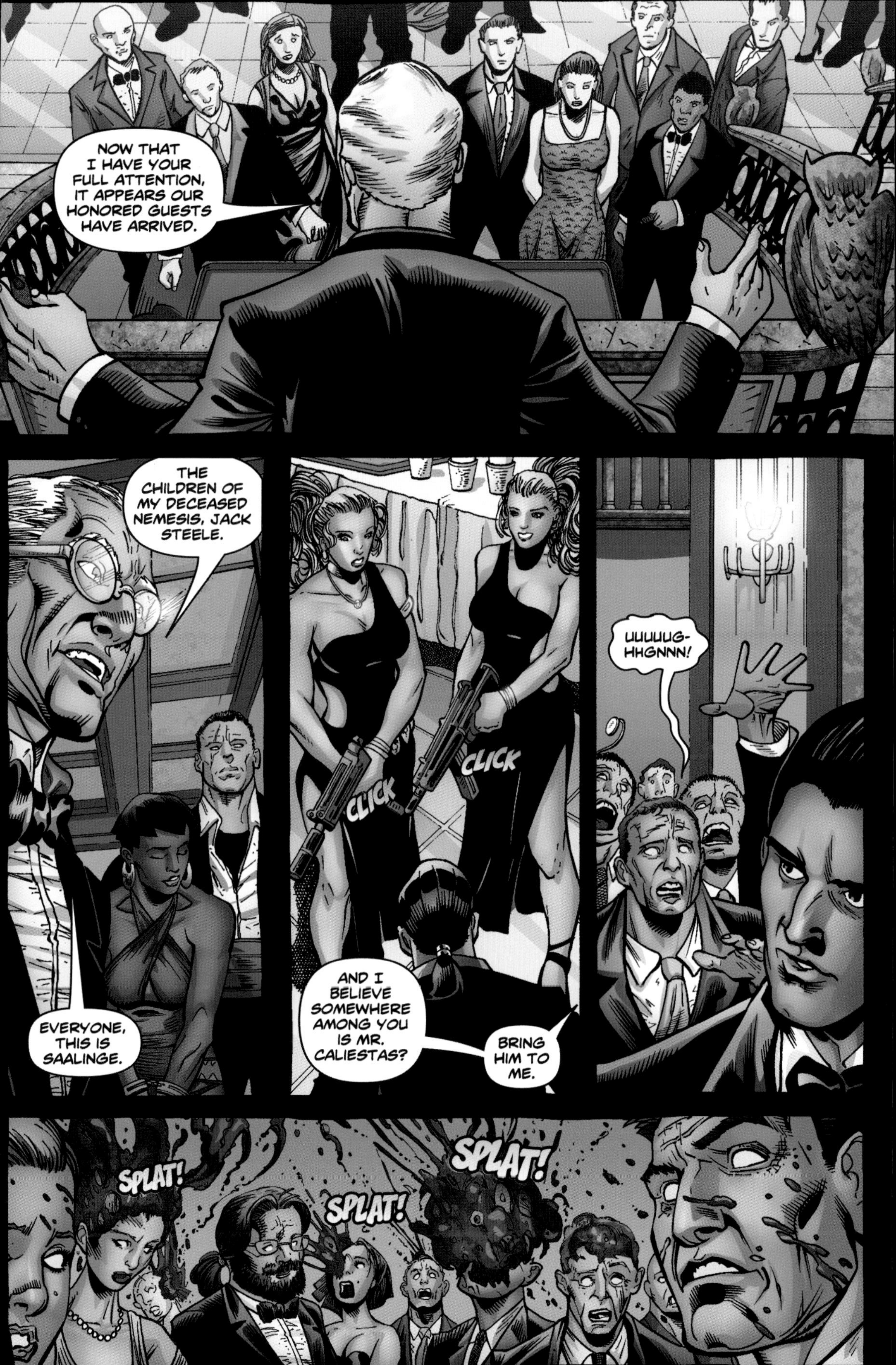
NOW THAT I HAVE YOUR FULL ATTENTION, IT APPEARS OUR HONORED GUESTS HAVE ARRIVED.
THE CHILDREN OF MY DECEASED NEMESIS, JACK STEELE.
EVERYONE, THIS IS SAALINGE.
CLICK
CLICK
AND I BELIEVE SOMEWHERE AMONG YOU IS MR. CALIESTAS?
BRING HIM TO ME.
UUUUUG-HHGNNN!
SPLAT!
SPLAT!
SPLAT!

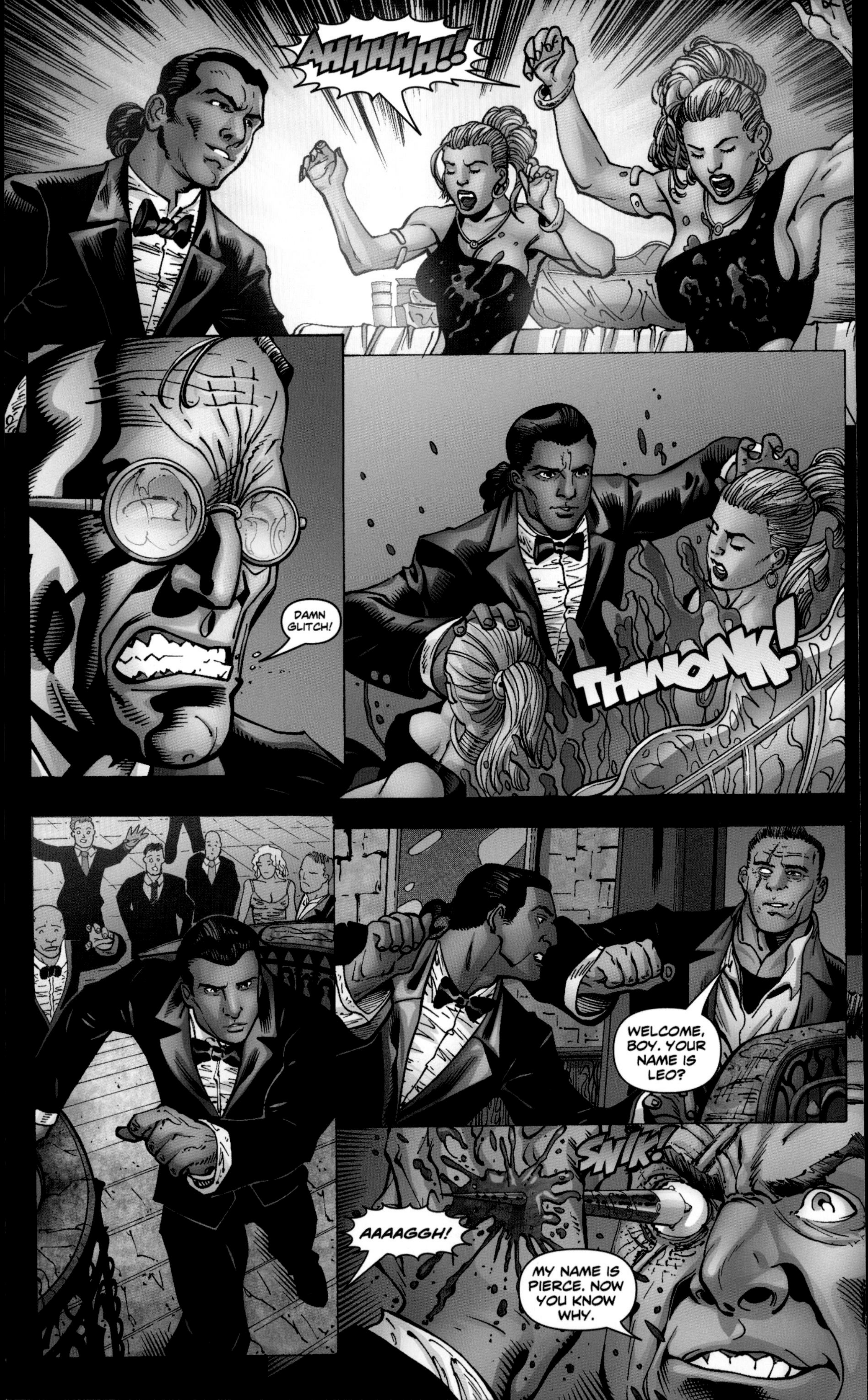
AHHHHH!!
DAMN GLITCH!
THWONK!
WELCOME, BOY. YOUR NAME IS LEO?
SNIK!
AAAAGGH!
MY NAME IS PIERCE. NOW YOU KNOW WHY.

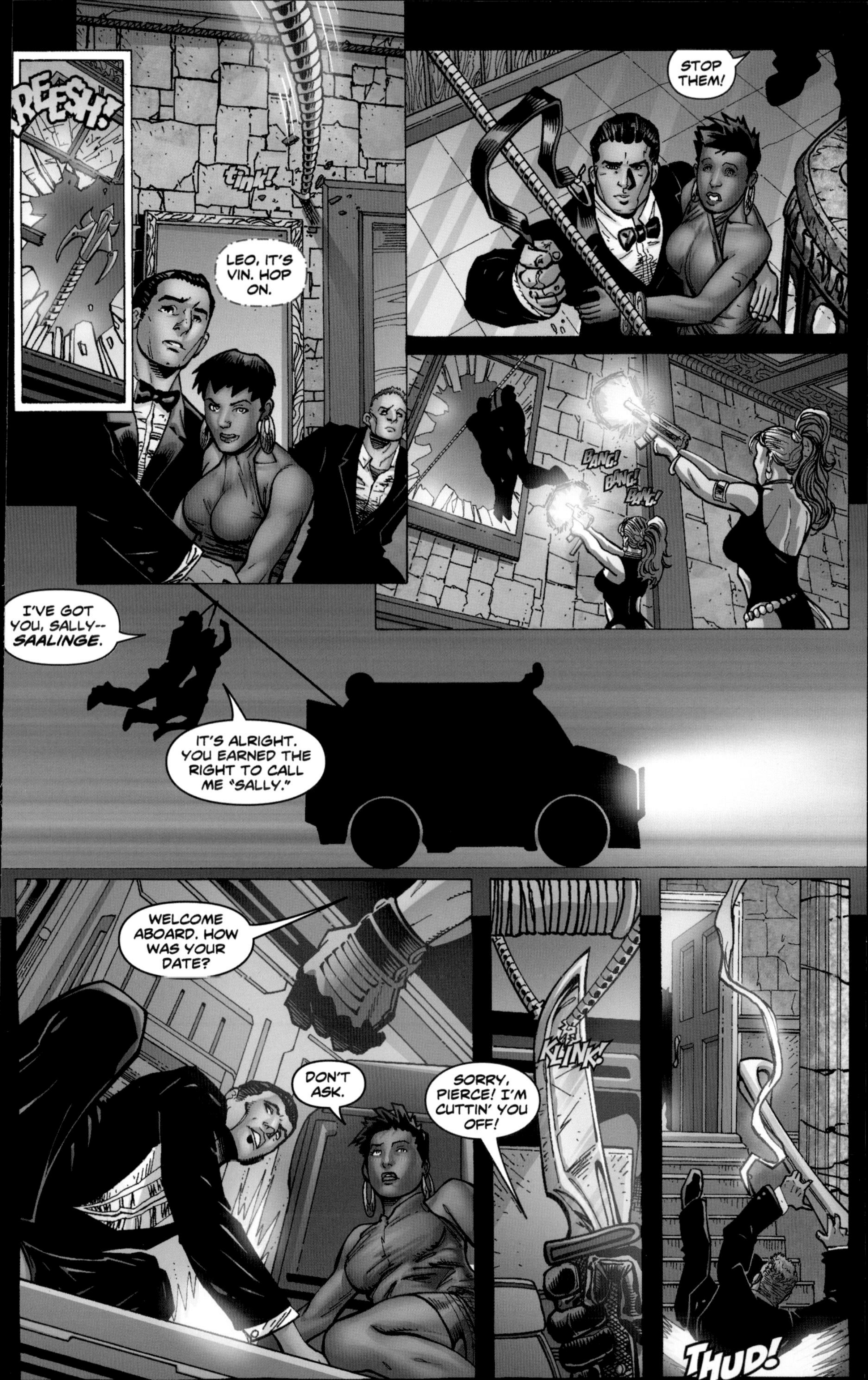

REESH!
tink!
LEO, IT'S VIN. HOP ON.
STOP THEM!
BANG!
BANG!
BANG!
I'VE GOT YOU, SALLY-- SAALINGE.
IT'S ALRIGHT. YOU EARNED THE RIGHT TO CALL ME "SALLY."
WELCOME ABOARD. HOW WAS YOUR DATE?
DON'T ASK.
SORRY, PIERCE! I'M CUTTIN' YOU OFF!
KLINK!
THUD!

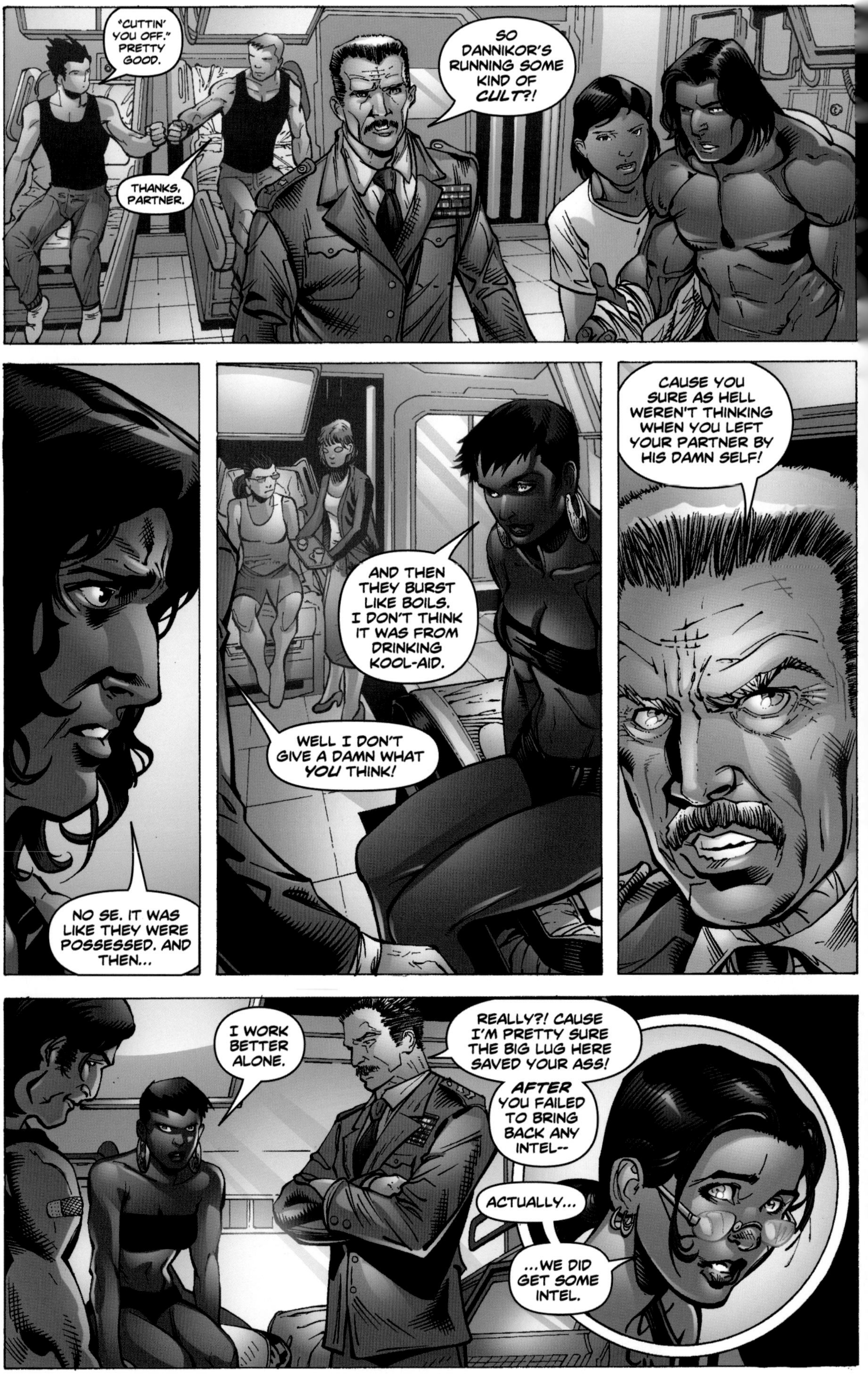
"CUTTIN' YOU OFF." PRETTY GOOD.
THANKS, PARTNER.
SO DANNIKOR'S RUNNING SOME KIND OF CULT?!
NO SE. IT WAS LIKE THEY WERE POSSESSED. AND THEN...
AND THEN THEY BURST LIKE BOILS. I DON'T THINK IT WAS FROM DRINKING KOOL-AID.
WELL I DON'T GIVE A DAMN WHAT YOU THINK!
CAUSE YOU SURE AS HELL WEREN'T THINKING WHEN YOU LEFT YOUR PARTNER BY HIS DAMN SELF!
I WORK BETTER ALONE.
REALLY?! CAUSE I'M PRETTY SURE THE BIG LUG HERE SAVED YOUR ASS!
AFTER YOU FAILED TO BRING BACK ANY INTEL--
ACTUALLY...
...WE DID GET SOME INTEL.

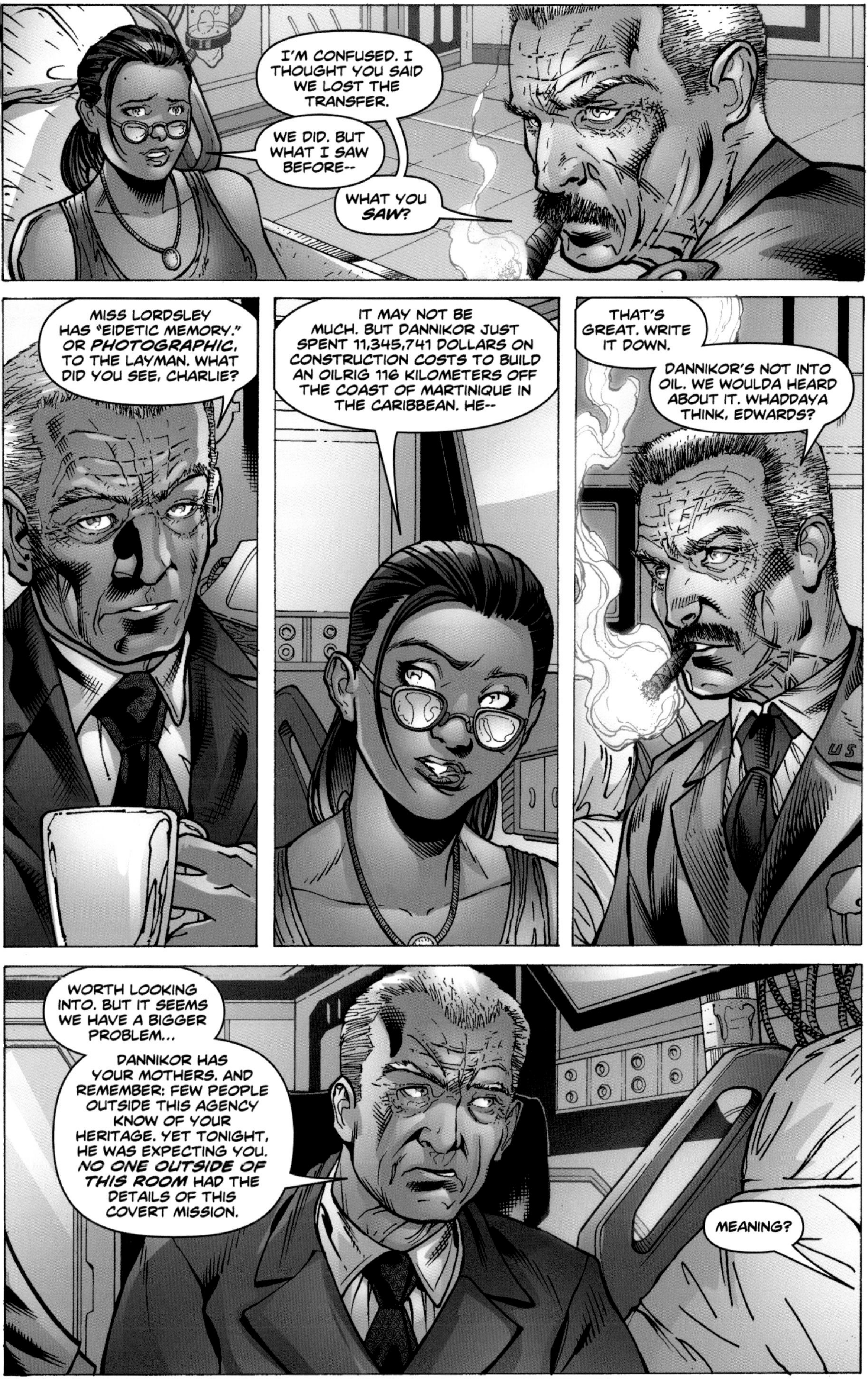
I'M CONFUSED. I THOUGHT YOU SAID WE LOST THE TRANSFER.
WE DID. BUT WHAT I SAW BEFORE--
WHAT YOU *SAW*?
MISS LORDSLEY HAS "EIDETIC MEMORY." OR *PHOTOGRAPHIC*, TO THE LAYMAN. WHAT DID YOU SEE, CHARLIE?
IT MAY NOT BE MUCH. BUT DANNIKOR JUST SPENT 11,345,741 DOLLARS ON CONSTRUCTION COSTS TO BUILD AN OILRIG 116 KILOMETERS OFF THE COAST OF MARTINIQUE IN THE CARIBBEAN. HE--
THAT'S GREAT. WRITE IT DOWN.
DANNIKOR'S NOT INTO OIL. WE WOULDA HEARD ABOUT IT. WHADDAYA THINK, EDWARDS?
US
WORTH LOOKING INTO. BUT IT SEEMS WE HAVE A BIGGER PROBLEM...
DANNIKOR HAS YOUR MOTHERS. AND REMEMBER: FEW PEOPLE OUTSIDE THIS AGENCY KNOW OF YOUR HERITAGE. YET TONIGHT, HE WAS EXPECTING YOU. *NO ONE OUTSIDE OF THIS ROOM* HAD THE DETAILS OF THIS COVERT MISSION.
MEANING?

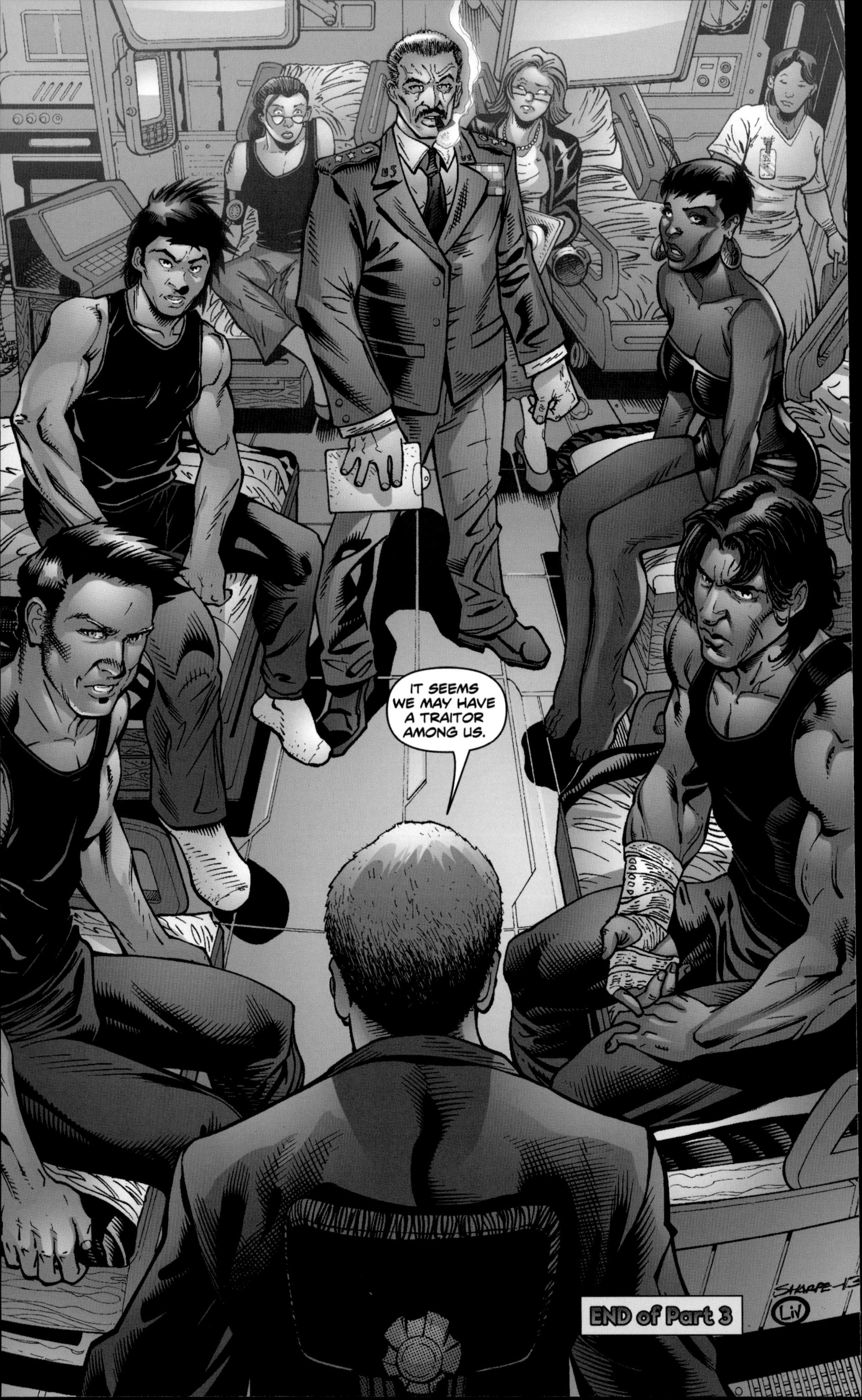
IT SEEMS WE MAY HAVE A TRAITOR AMONG US.
END of Part 3

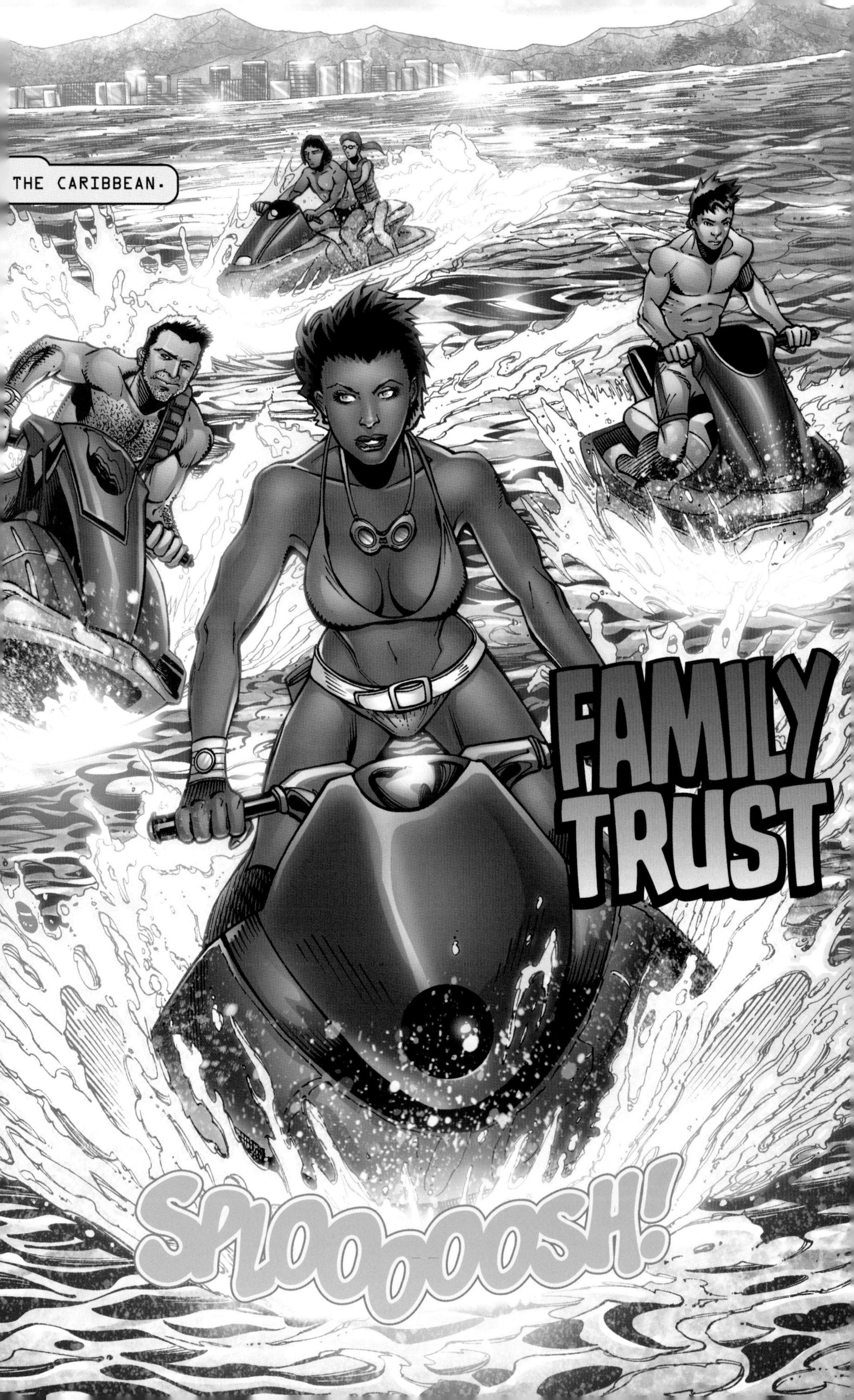
THE CARIBBEAN.
FAMILY TRUST
SPLOOOOOOSH!

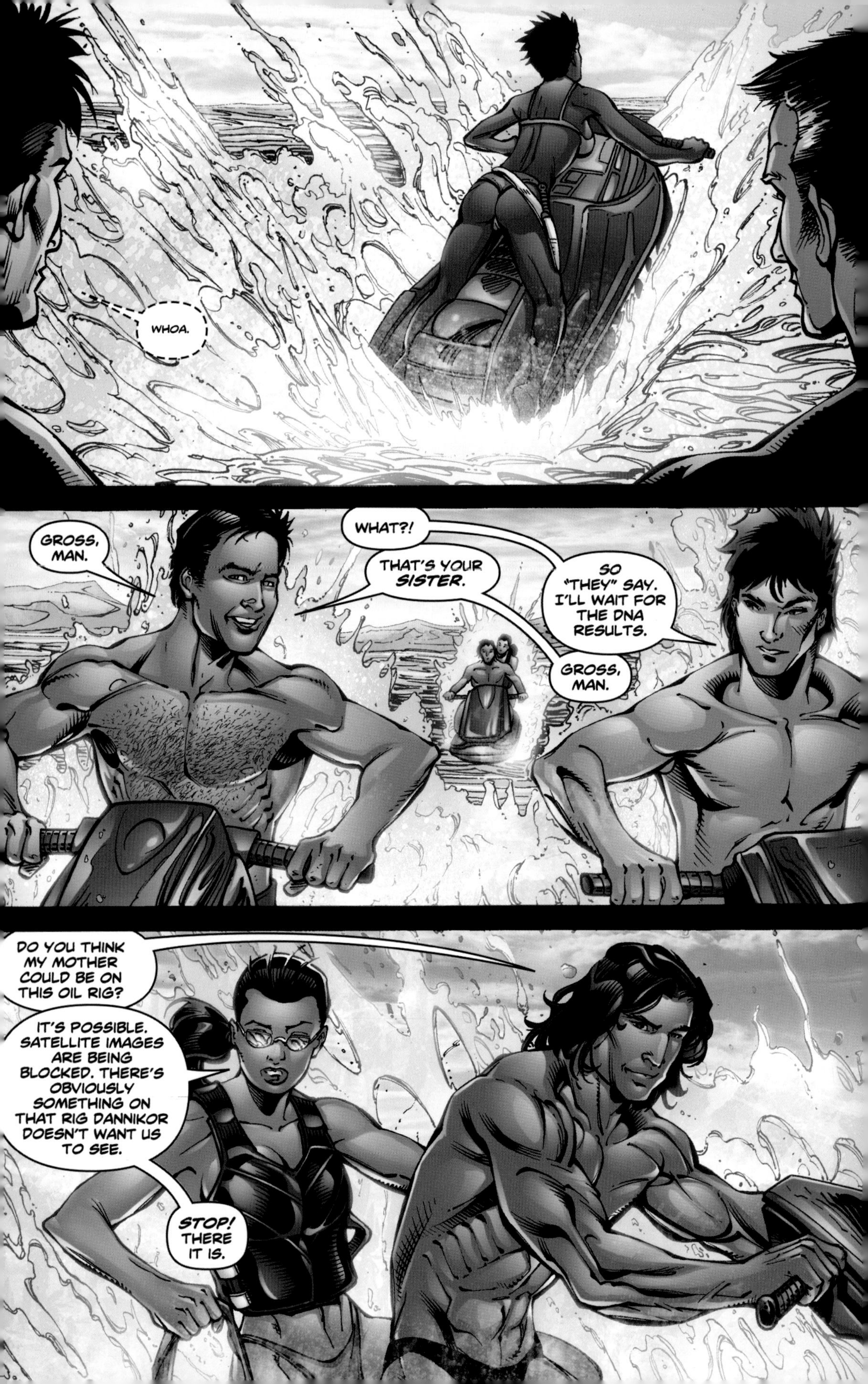
WHOA.
GROSS, MAN.
WHAT?!
THAT'S YOUR SISTER.
SO "THEY" SAY. I'LL WAIT FOR THE DNA RESULTS.
GROSS, MAN.
DO YOU THINK MY MOTHER COULD BE ON THIS OIL RIG?
IT'S POSSIBLE. SATELLITE IMAGES ARE BEING BLOCKED. THERE'S OBVIOUSLY SOMETHING ON THAT RIG DANNIKOR DOESN'T WANT US TO SEE.
STOP! THERE IT IS.

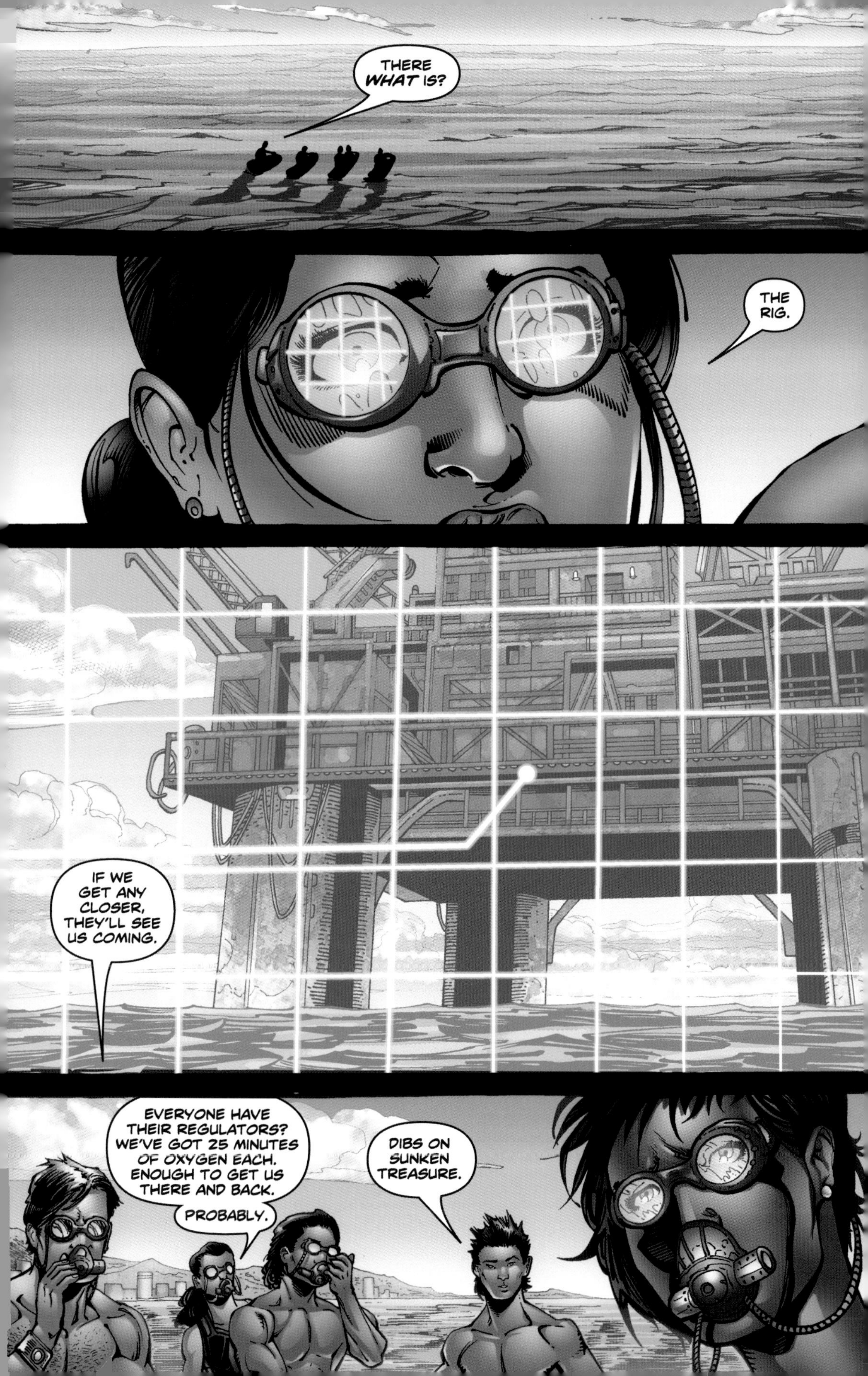
THERE *WHAT* IS?
THE RIG.
IF WE GET ANY CLOSER, THEY'LL SEE US COMING.
EVERYONE HAVE THEIR REGULATORS? WE'VE GOT 25 MINUTES OF OXYGEN EACH. ENOUGH TO GET US THERE AND BACK.
PROBABLY.
DIBS ON SUNKEN TREASURE.

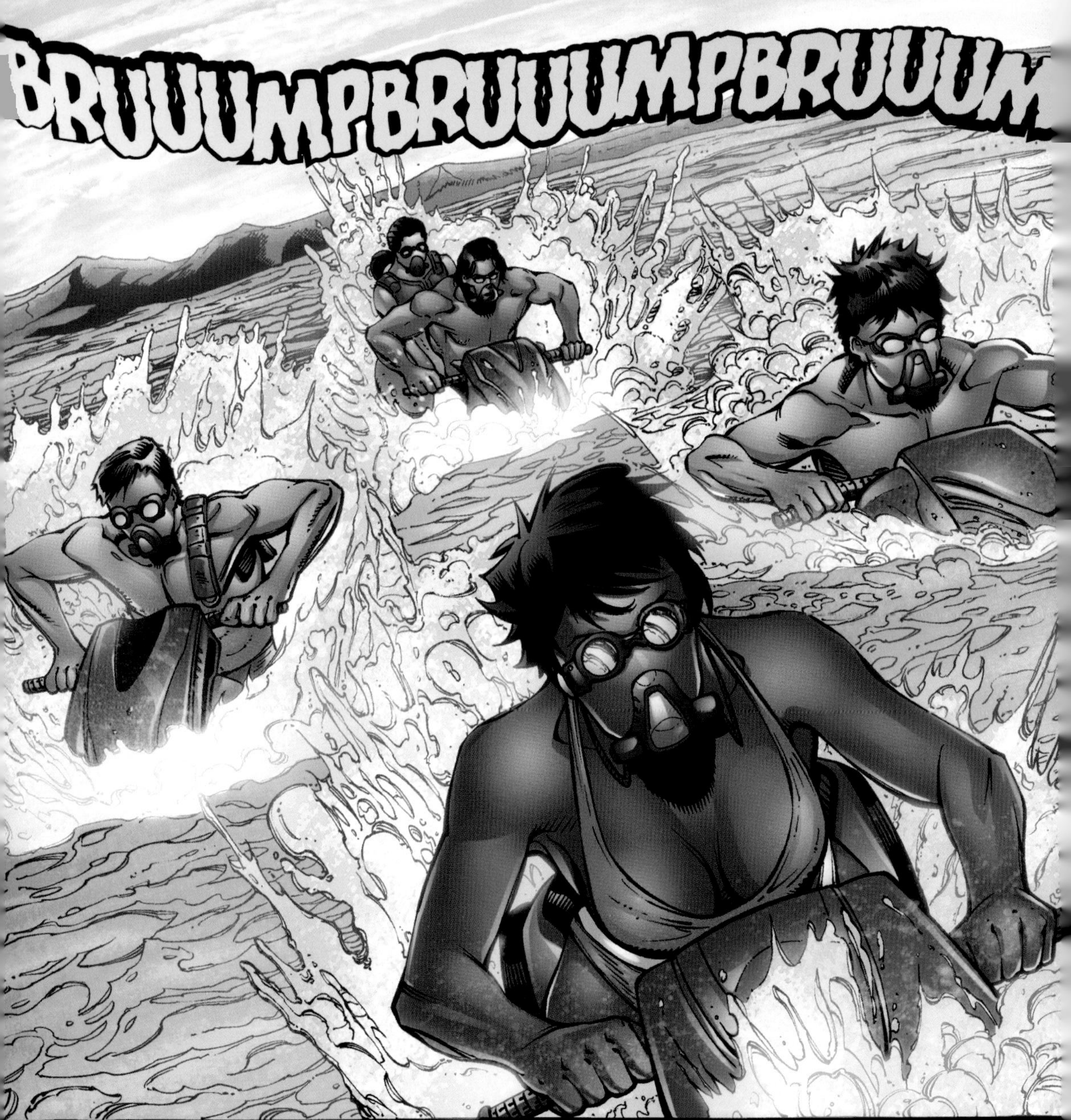
BRUUUMPBRUUUMPBRUUUM

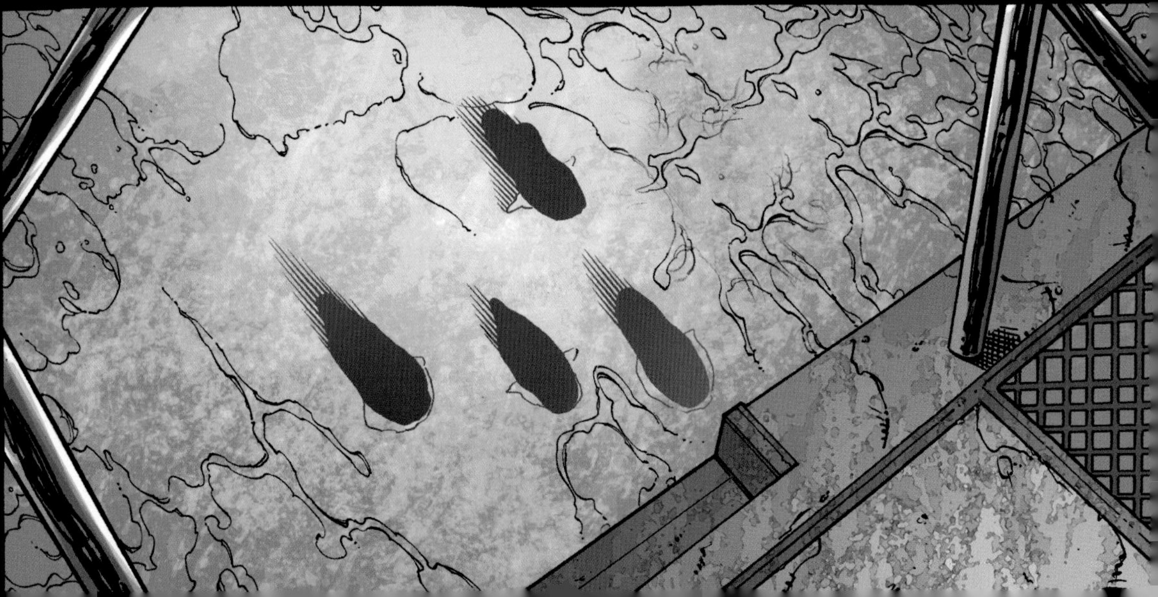

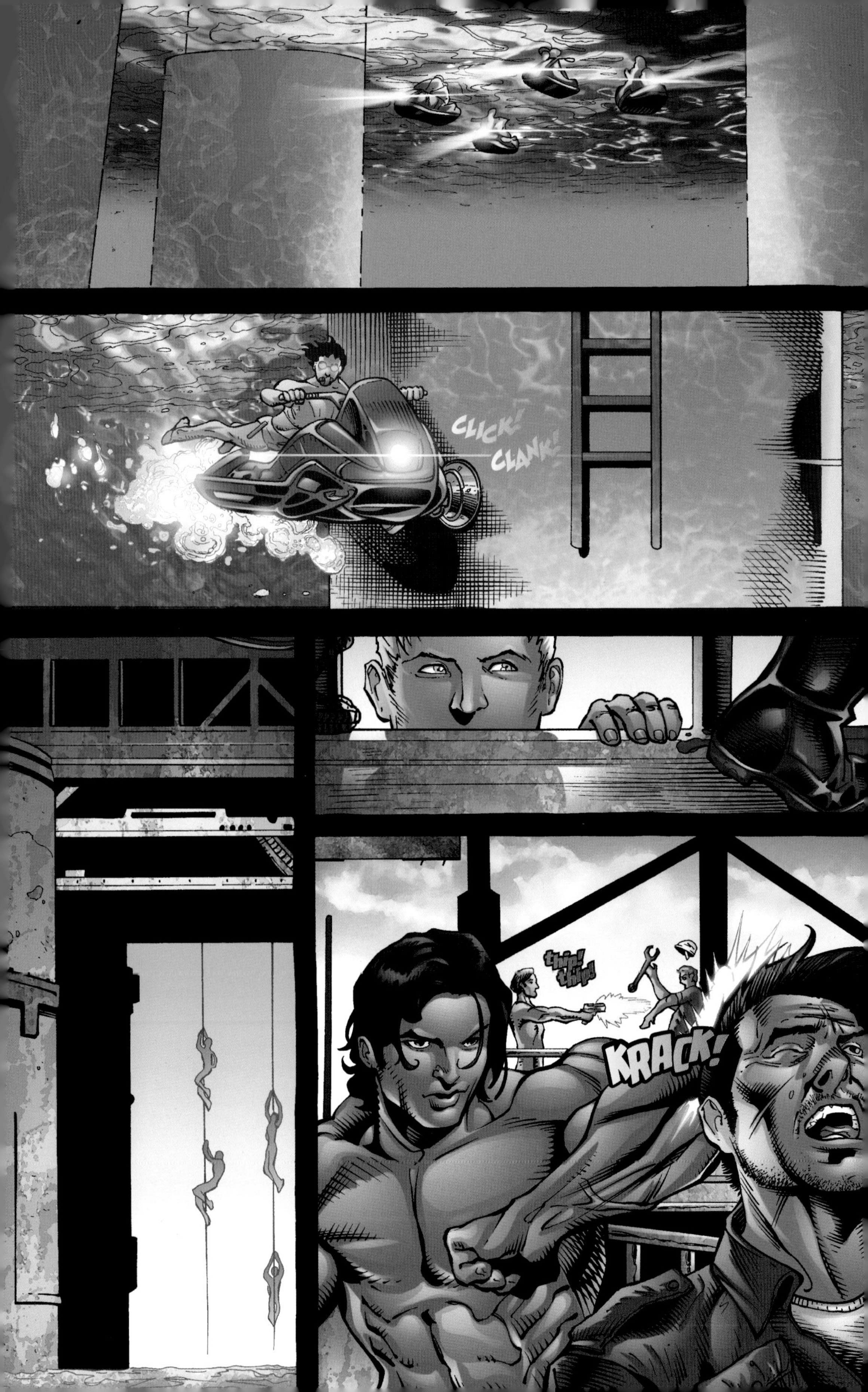
CLICK!
CLANK!
thip! thip!
KRACK!

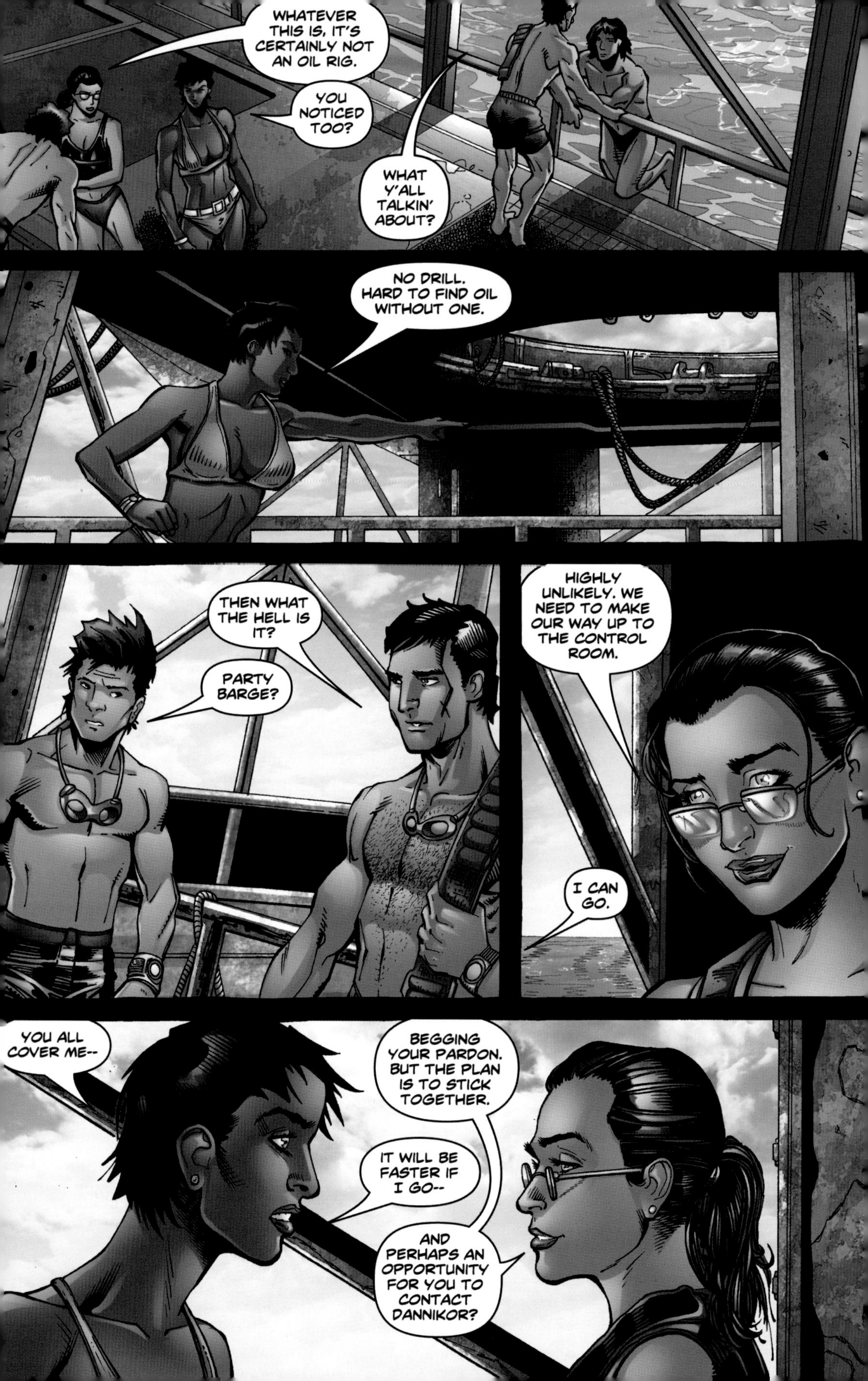
WHATEVER THIS IS, IT'S CERTAINLY NOT AN OIL RIG.
YOU NOTICED TOO?
WHAT Y'ALL TALKIN' ABOUT?
NO DRILL. HARD TO FIND OIL WITHOUT ONE.
THEN WHAT THE HELL IS IT?
PARTY BARGE?
HIGHLY UNLIKELY. WE NEED TO MAKE OUR WAY UP TO THE CONTROL ROOM.
I CAN GO.
YOU ALL COVER ME--
BEGGING YOUR PARDON. BUT THE PLAN IS TO STICK TOGETHER.
IT WILL BE FASTER IF I GO--
AND PERHAPS AN OPPORTUNITY FOR YOU TO CONTACT DANNIKOR?

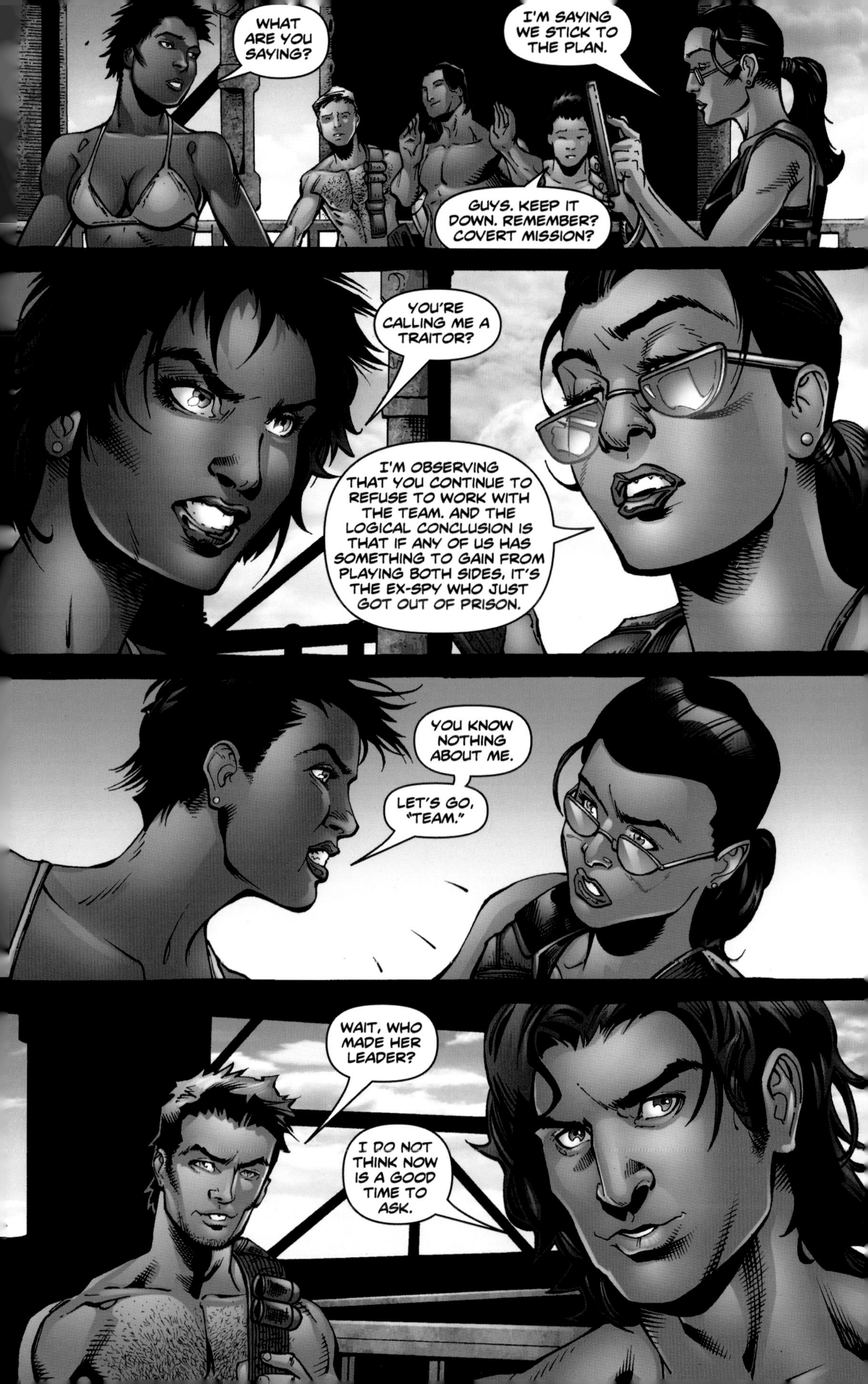
WHAT ARE YOU SAYING?
I'M SAYING WE STICK TO THE PLAN.
GUYS. KEEP IT DOWN. REMEMBER? COVERT MISSION?
YOU'RE CALLING ME A TRAITOR?
I'M OBSERVING THAT YOU CONTINUE TO REFUSE TO WORK WITH THE TEAM. AND THE LOGICAL CONCLUSION IS THAT IF ANY OF US HAS SOMETHING TO GAIN FROM PLAYING BOTH SIDES, IT'S THE EX-SPY WHO JUST GOT OUT OF PRISON.
YOU KNOW NOTHING ABOUT ME.
LET'S GO, "TEAM."
WAIT, WHO MADE HER LEADER?
I DO NOT THINK NOW IS A GOOD TIME TO ASK.

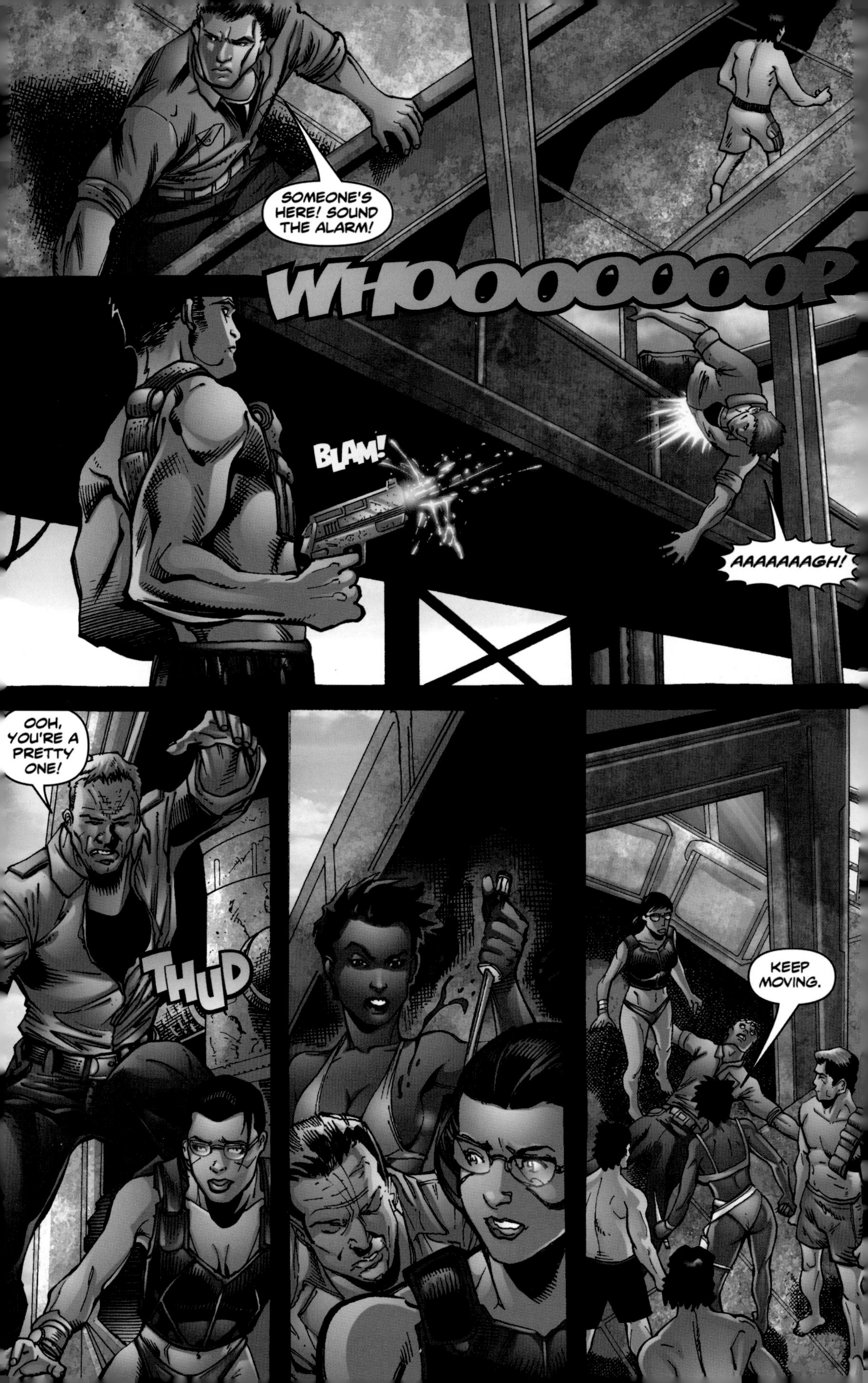
SOMEONE'S HERE! SOUND THE ALARM!
WHOOOOOOOP
BLAM!
AAAAAAAGH!
OOH, YOU'RE A PRETTY ONE!
THUD
KEEP MOVING.

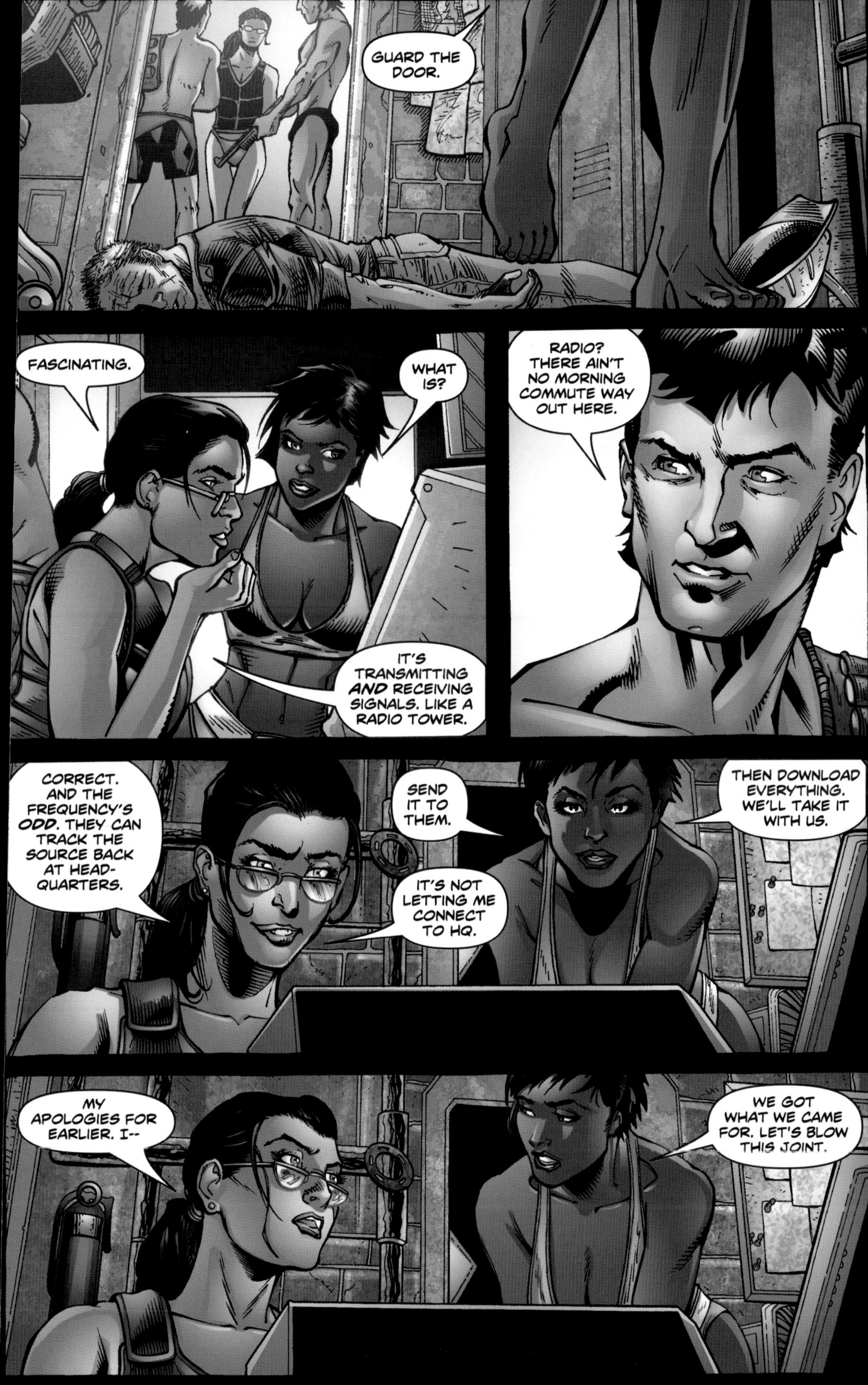

GUARD THE DOOR.
FASCINATING.
WHAT IS?
IT'S TRANSMITTING AND RECEIVING SIGNALS. LIKE A RADIO TOWER.
RADIO? THERE AIN'T NO MORNING COMMUTE WAY OUT HERE.
CORRECT. AND THE FREQUENCY'S ODD. THEY CAN TRACK THE SOURCE BACK AT HEAD-QUARTERS.
SEND IT TO THEM.
IT'S NOT LETTING ME CONNECT TO HQ.
THEN DOWNLOAD EVERYTHING. WE'LL TAKE IT WITH US.
MY APOLOGIES FOR EARLIER. I--
WE GOT WHAT WE CAME FOR. LET'S BLOW THIS JOINT.

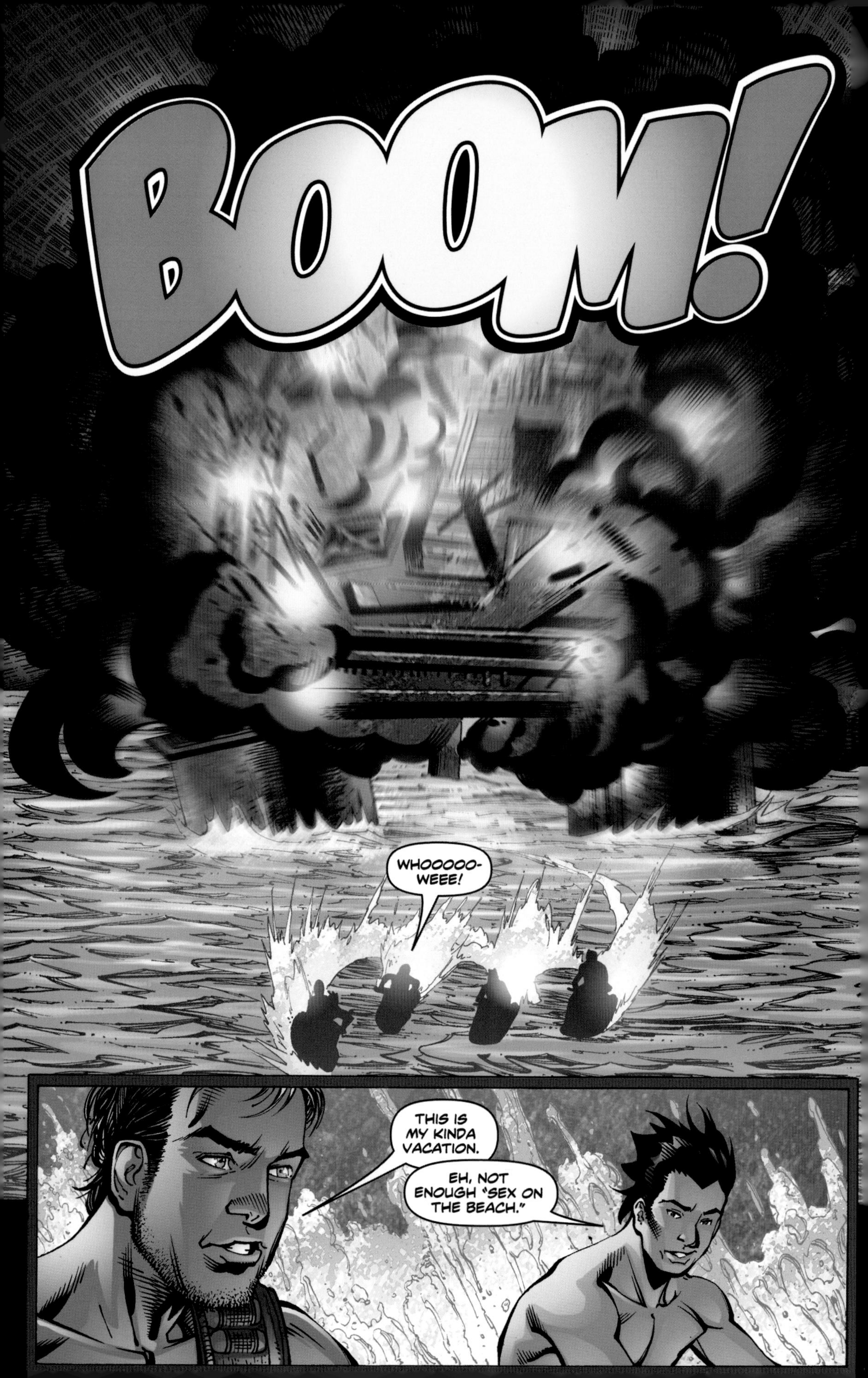
BOOM!
WHOOOOO-WEEE!
THIS IS MY KINDA VACATION.
EH, NOT ENOUGH "SEX ON THE BEACH."

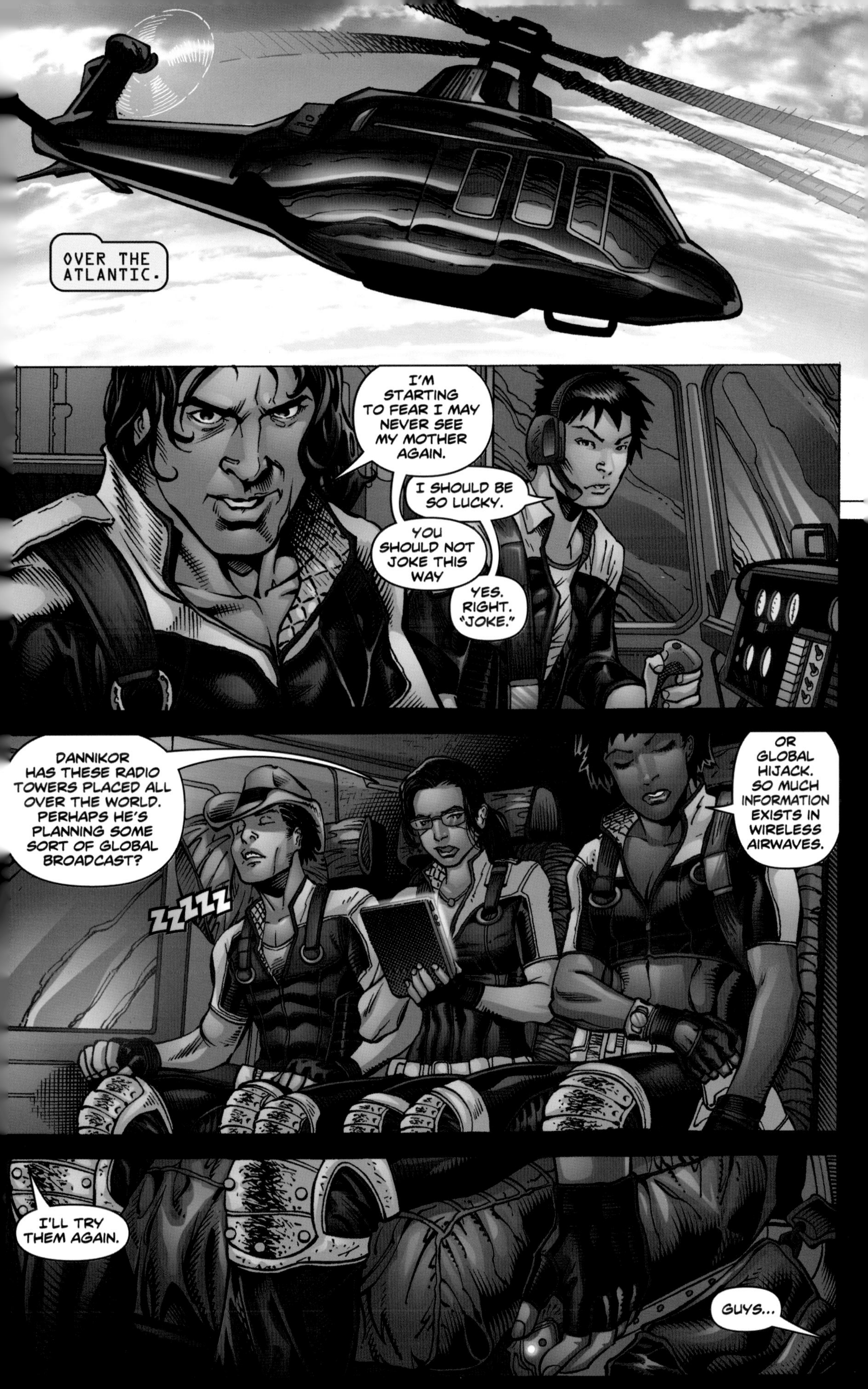
OVER THE ATLANTIC.
I'M STARTING TO FEAR I MAY NEVER SEE MY MOTHER AGAIN.
I SHOULD BE SO LUCKY.
YOU SHOULD NOT JOKE THIS WAY
YES. RIGHT. "JOKE."
DANNIKOR HAS THESE RADIO TOWERS PLACED ALL OVER THE WORLD. PERHAPS HE'S PLANNING SOME SORT OF GLOBAL BROADCAST?
OR GLOBAL HIJACK. SO MUCH INFORMATION EXISTS IN WIRELESS AIRWAVES.
ZZZZZ
I'LL TRY THEM AGAIN.
GUYS...

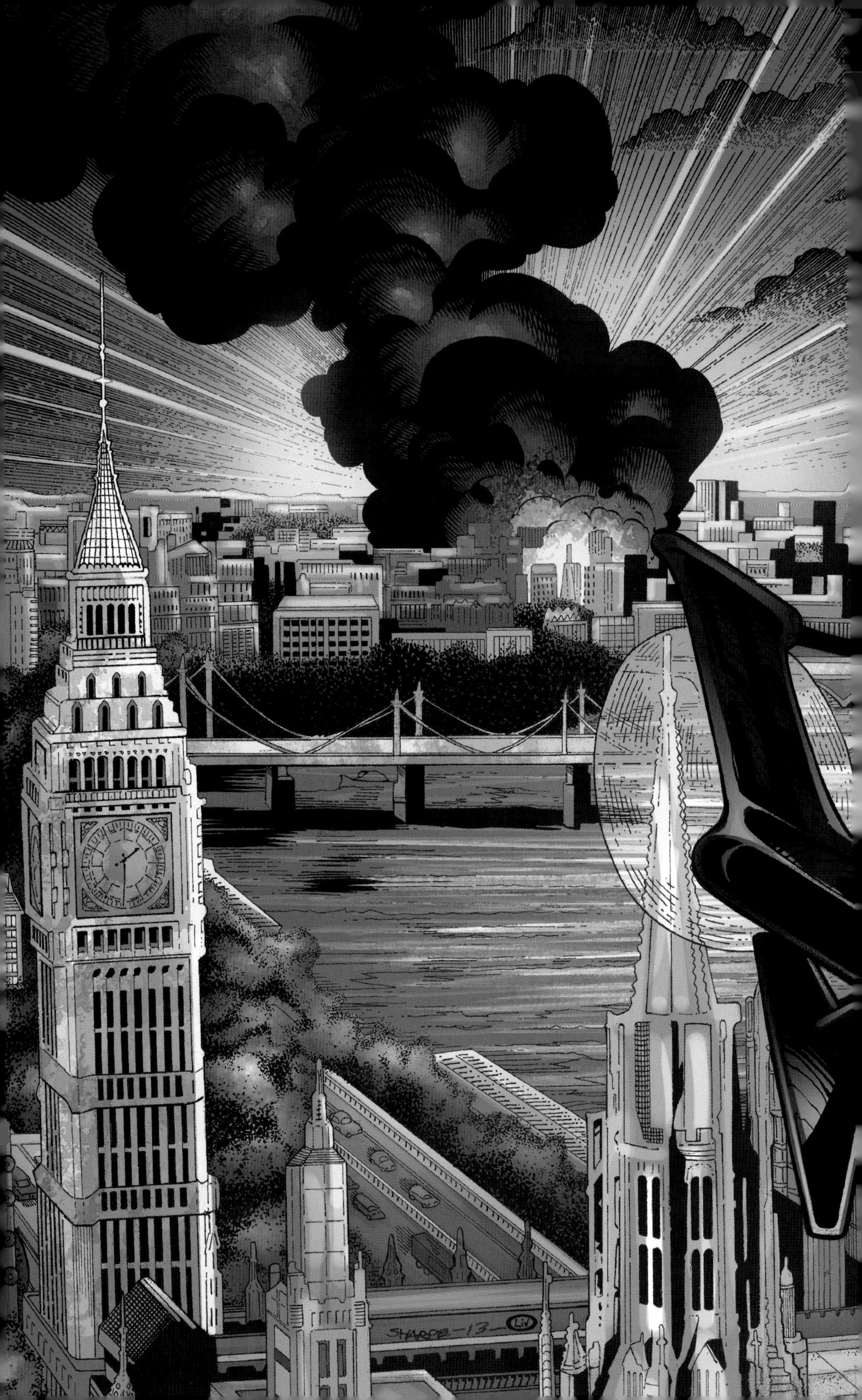
SHARPE-13

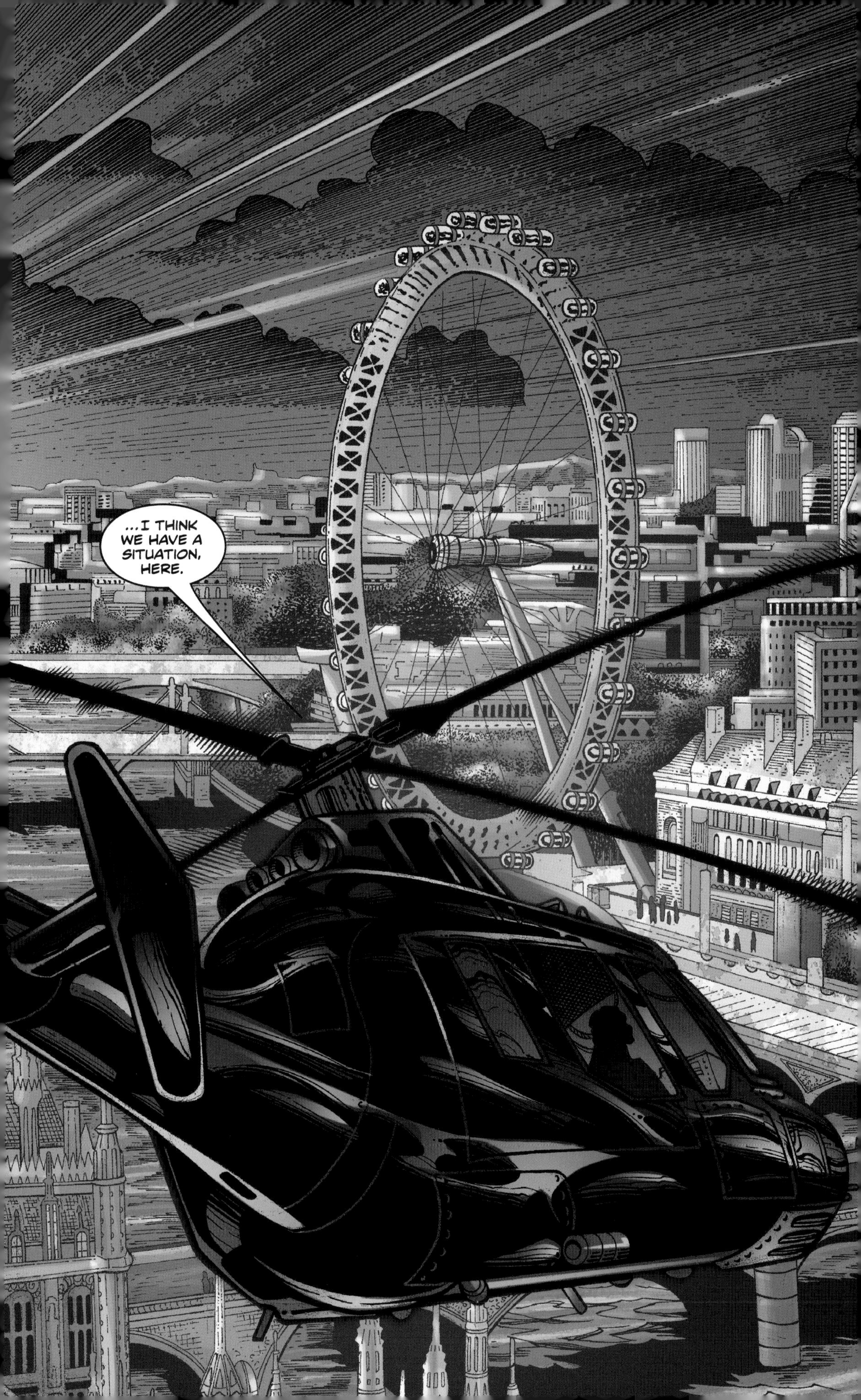
...I THINK WE HAVE A SITUATION, HERE.

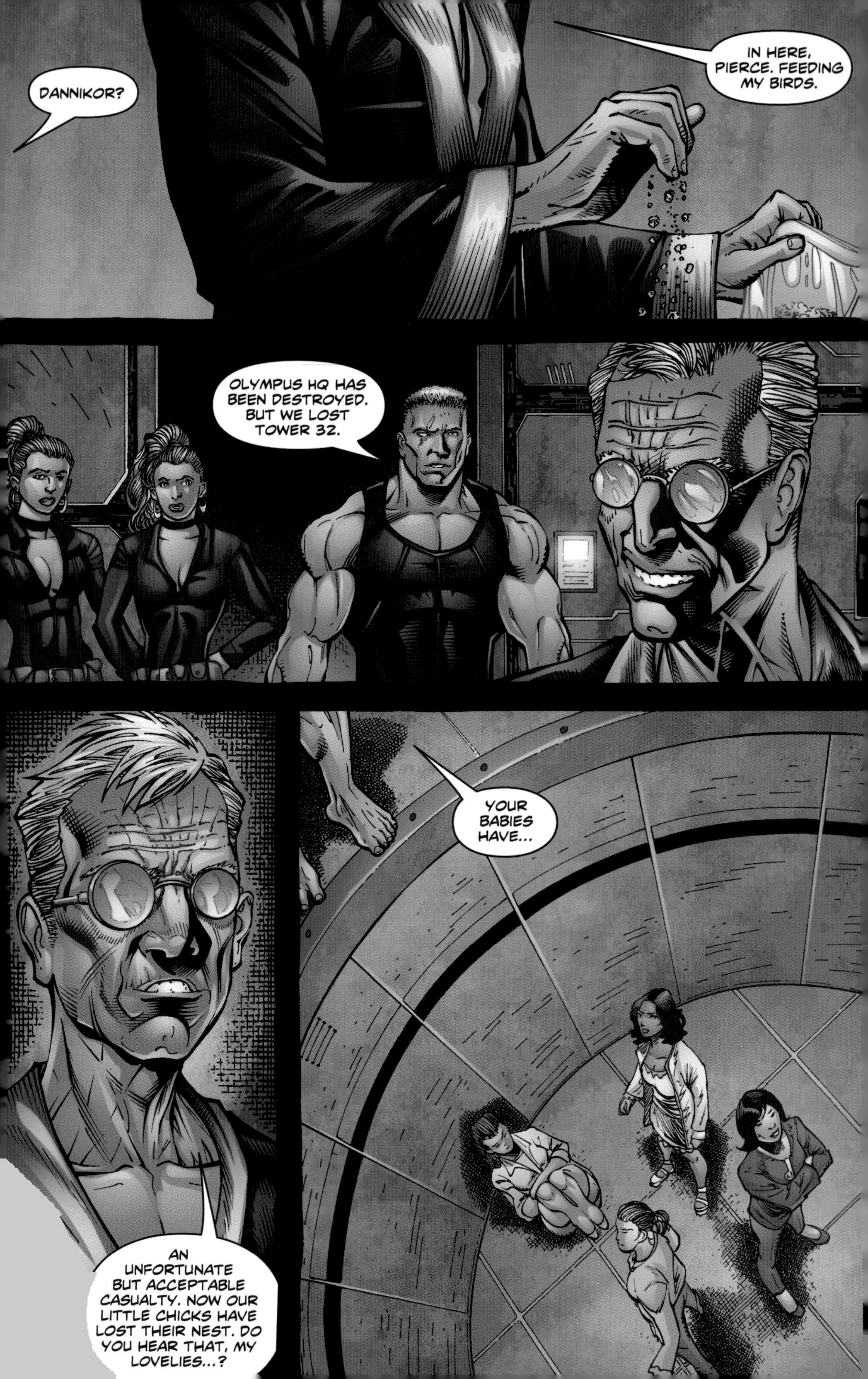
DANNIKOR?
IN HERE, PIERCE. FEEDING MY BIRDS.
OLYMPUS HQ HAS BEEN DESTROYED. BUT WE LOST TOWER 32.
YOUR BABIES HAVE...
AN UNFORTUNATE BUT ACCEPTABLE CASUALTY. NOW OUR LITTLE CHICKS HAVE LOST THEIR NEST. DO YOU HEAR THAT, MY LOVELIES...?

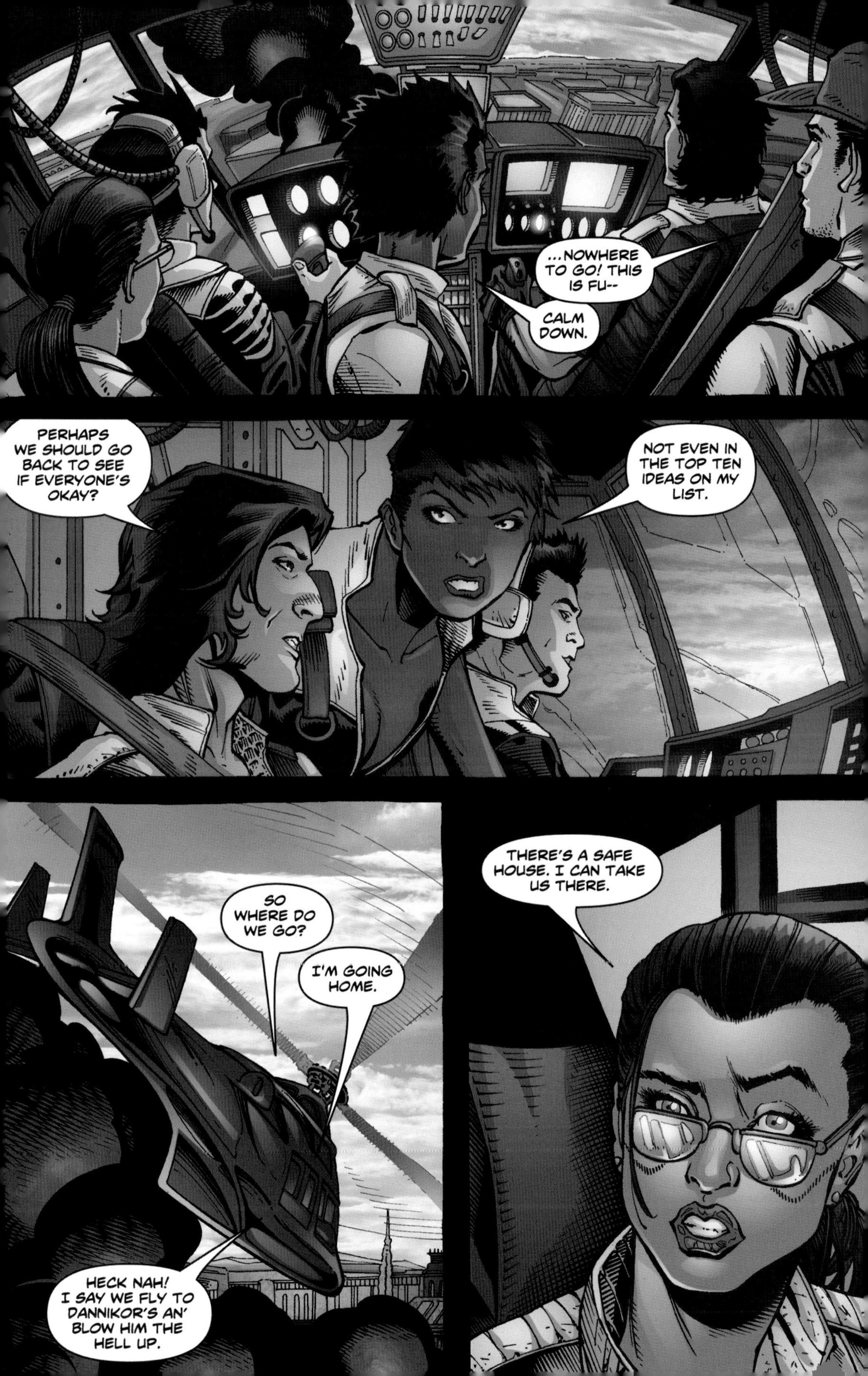
...NOWHERE TO GO! THIS IS FU--
CALM DOWN.
PERHAPS WE SHOULD GO BACK TO SEE IF EVERYONE'S OKAY?
NOT EVEN IN THE TOP TEN IDEAS ON MY LIST.
SO WHERE DO WE GO?
I'M GOING HOME.
HECK NAH! I SAY WE FLY TO DANNIKOR'S AN' BLOW HIM THE HELL UP.
THERE'S A SAFE HOUSE. I CAN TAKE US THERE.

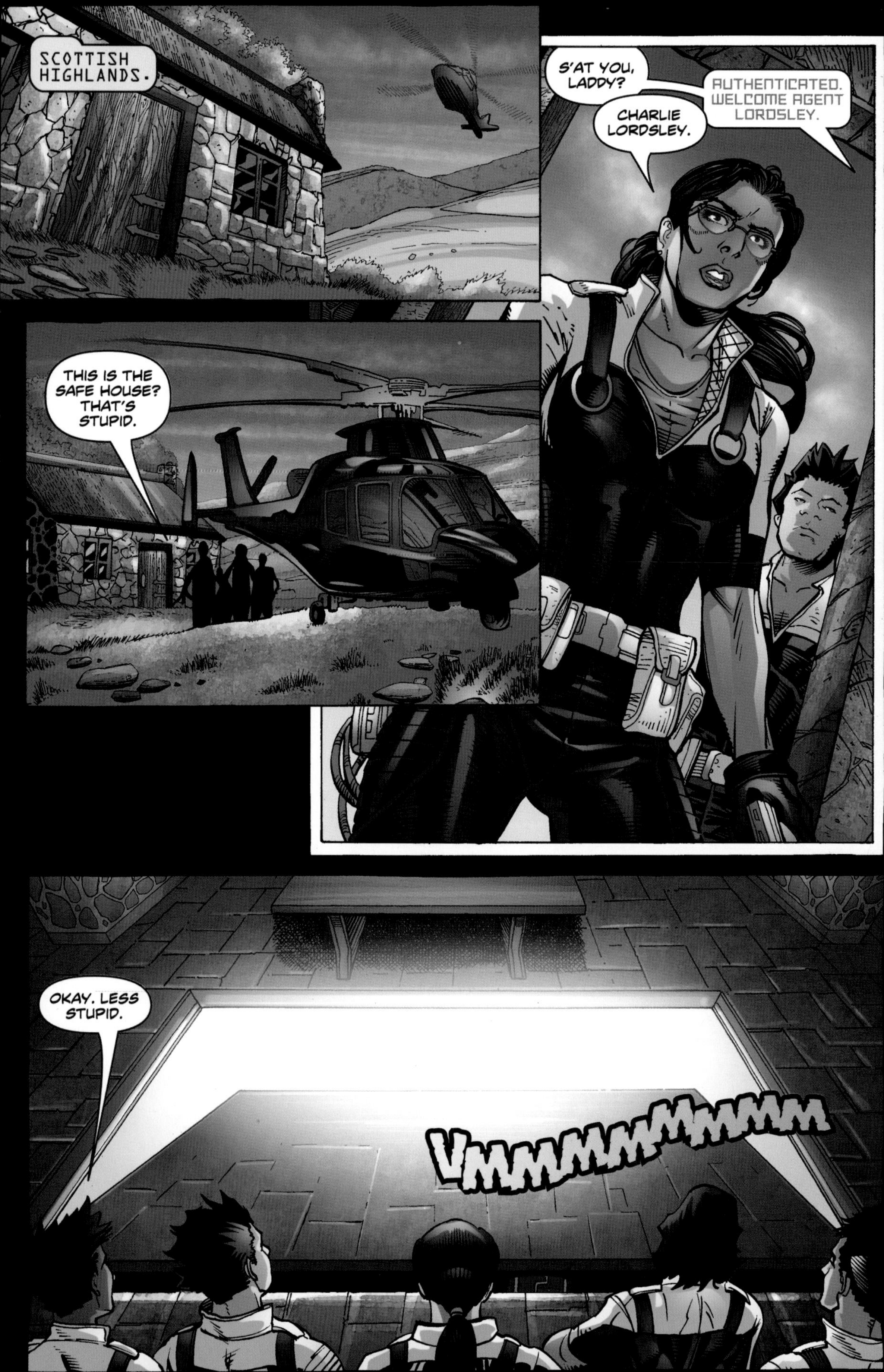
SCOTTISH HIGHLANDS.
THIS IS THE SAFE HOUSE? THAT'S STUPID.
S'AT YOU, LADDY?
CHARLIE LORDSLEY.
AUTHENTICATED. WELCOME AGENT LORDSLEY.
OKAY. LESS STUPID.
VMMMMMMMMM

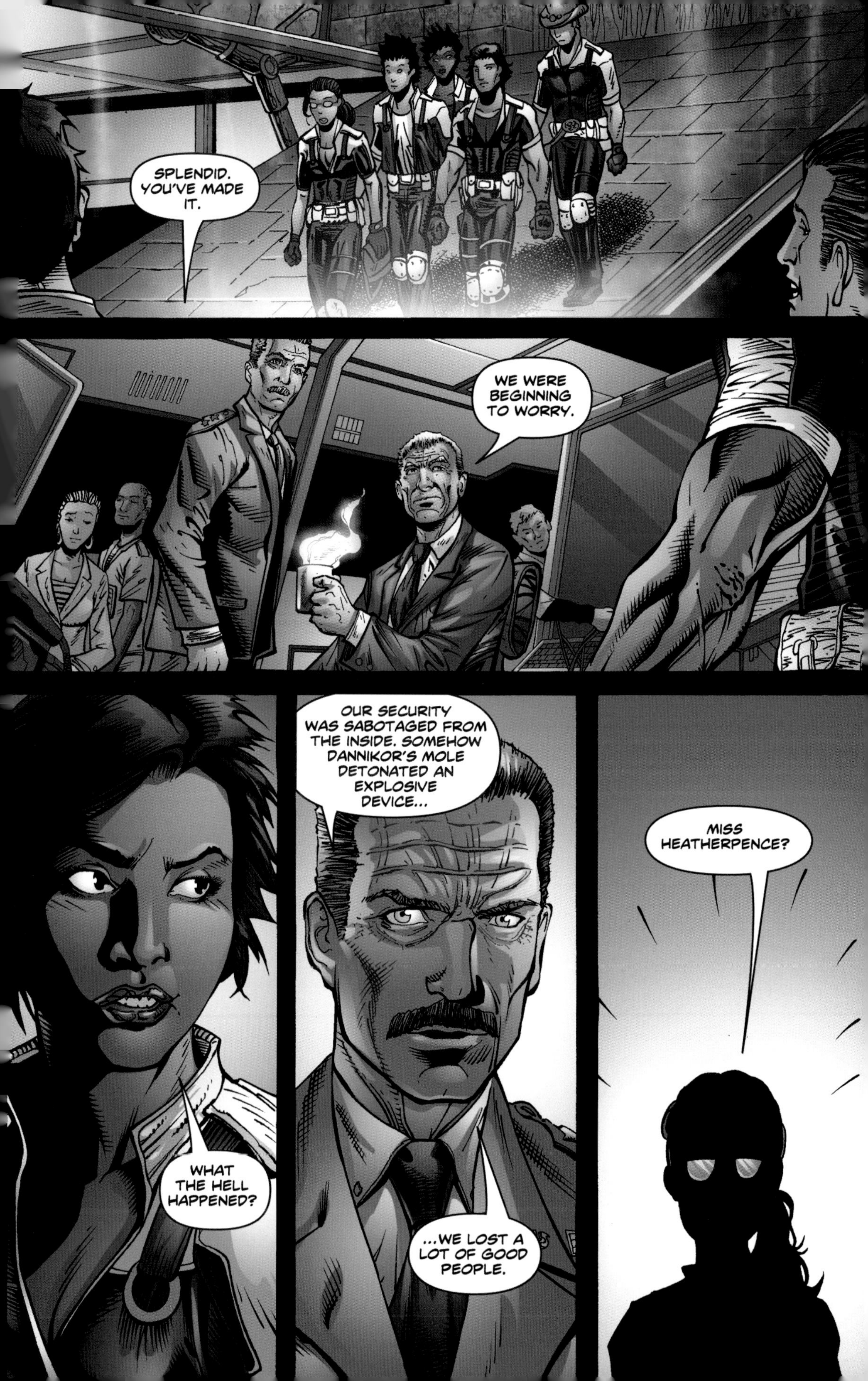
SPLENDID. YOU'VE MADE IT.
WE WERE BEGINNING TO WORRY.
WHAT THE HELL HAPPENED?
OUR SECURITY WAS SABOTAGED FROM THE INSIDE. SOMEHOW DANNIKOR'S MOLE DETONATED AN EXPLOSIVE DEVICE...
...WE LOST A LOT OF GOOD PEOPLE.
MISS HEATHERPENCE?

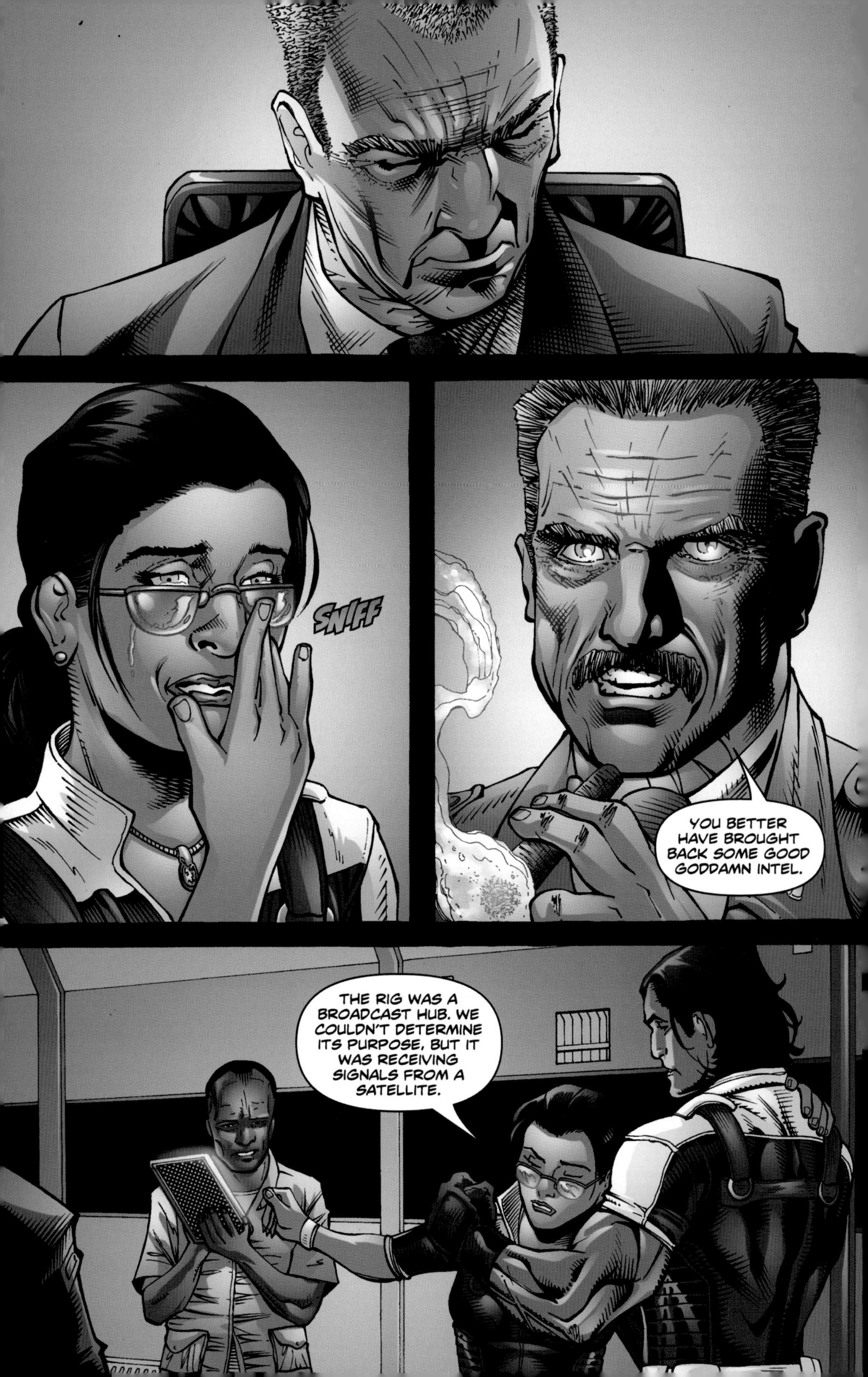
SNIFF
YOU BETTER HAVE BROUGHT BACK SOME GOOD GODDAMN INTEL.
THE RIG WAS A BROADCAST HUB. WE COULDN'T DETERMINE ITS PURPOSE, BUT IT WAS RECEIVING SIGNALS FROM A SATELLITE.

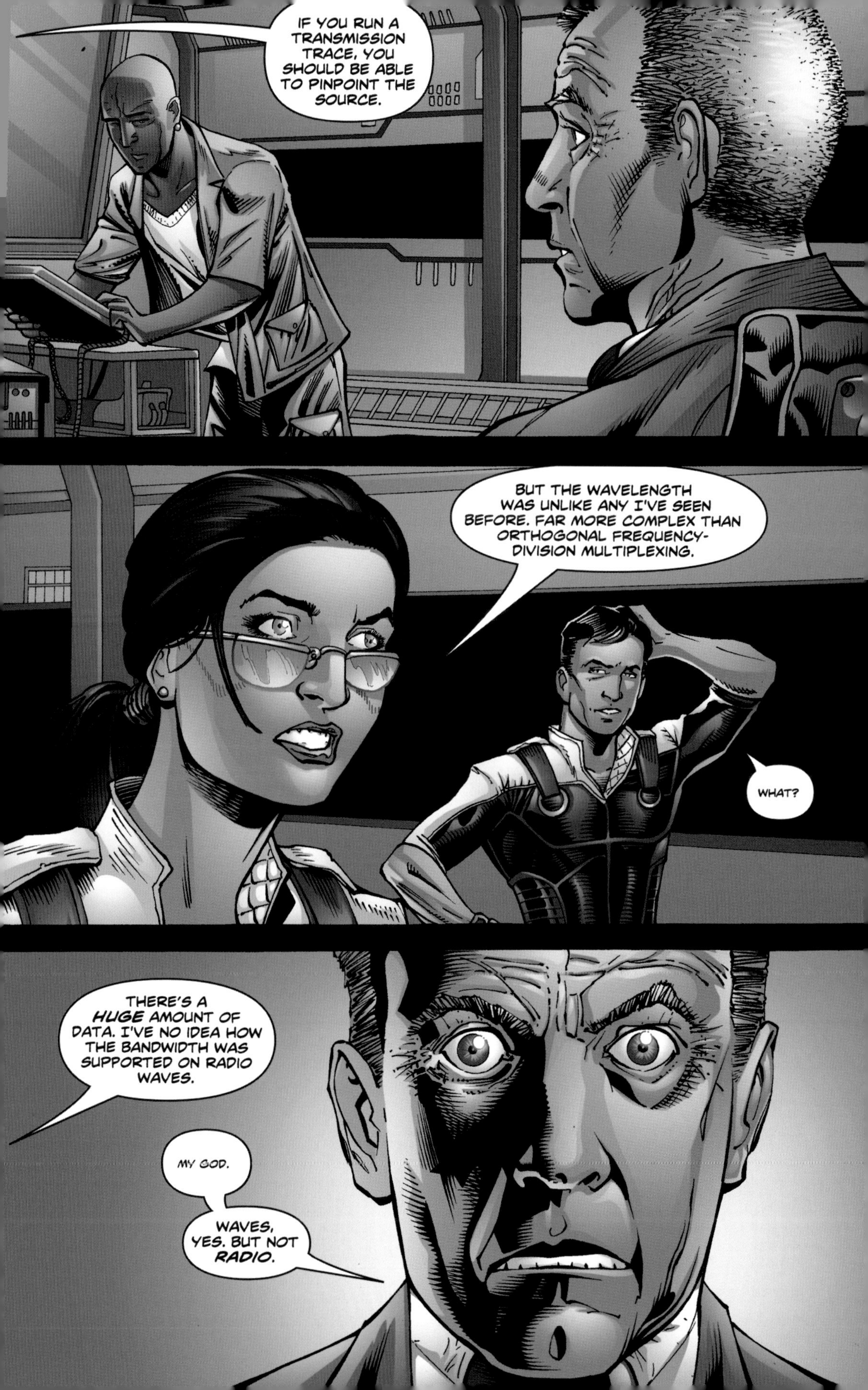
IF YOU RUN A TRANSMISSION TRACE, YOU SHOULD BE ABLE TO PINPOINT THE SOURCE.
BUT THE WAVELENGTH WAS UNLIKE ANY I'VE SEEN BEFORE. FAR MORE COMPLEX THAN ORTHOGONAL FREQUENCY-DIVISION MULTIPLEXING.
WHAT?
THERE'S A *HUGE* AMOUNT OF DATA. I'VE NO IDEA HOW THE BANDWIDTH WAS SUPPORTED ON RADIO WAVES.
MY GOD.
WAVES, YES. BUT NOT *RADIO*.

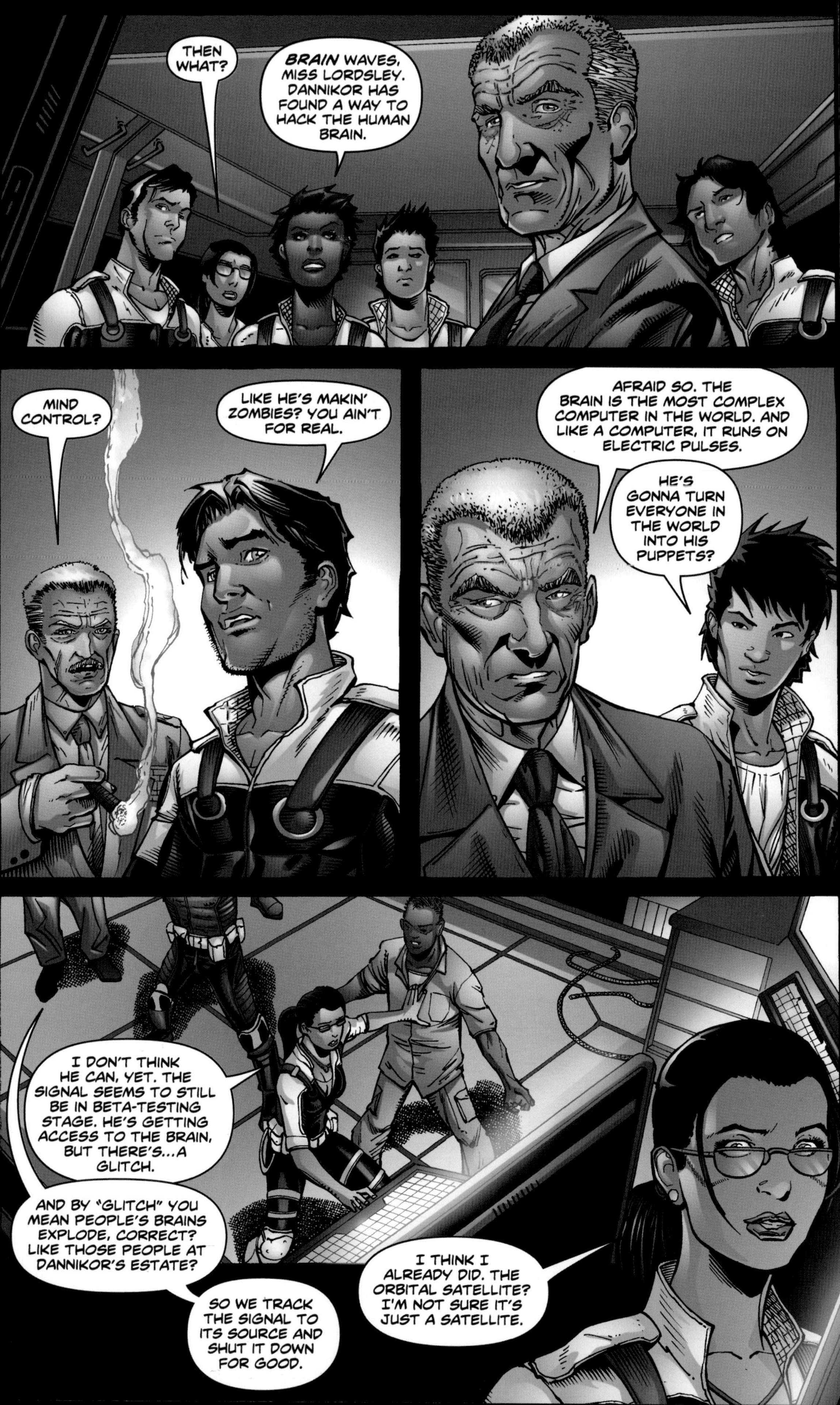

THEN WHAT?
BRAIN WAVES, MISS LORDSLEY. DANNIKOR HAS FOUND A WAY TO HACK THE HUMAN BRAIN.
MIND CONTROL?
LIKE HE'S MAKIN' ZOMBIES? YOU AIN'T FOR REAL.
AFRAID SO. THE BRAIN IS THE MOST COMPLEX COMPUTER IN THE WORLD. AND LIKE A COMPUTER, IT RUNS ON ELECTRIC PULSES.
HE'S GONNA TURN EVERYONE IN THE WORLD INTO HIS PUPPETS?
I DON'T THINK HE CAN, YET. THE SIGNAL SEEMS TO STILL BE IN BETA-TESTING STAGE. HE'S GETTING ACCESS TO THE BRAIN, BUT THERE'S...A GLITCH.
AND BY "GLITCH" YOU MEAN PEOPLE'S BRAINS EXPLODE, CORRECT? LIKE THOSE PEOPLE AT DANNIKOR'S ESTATE?
SO WE TRACK THE SIGNAL TO ITS SOURCE AND SHUT IT DOWN FOR GOOD.
I THINK I ALREADY DID. THE ORBITAL SATELLITE? I'M NOT SURE IT'S JUST A SATELLITE.

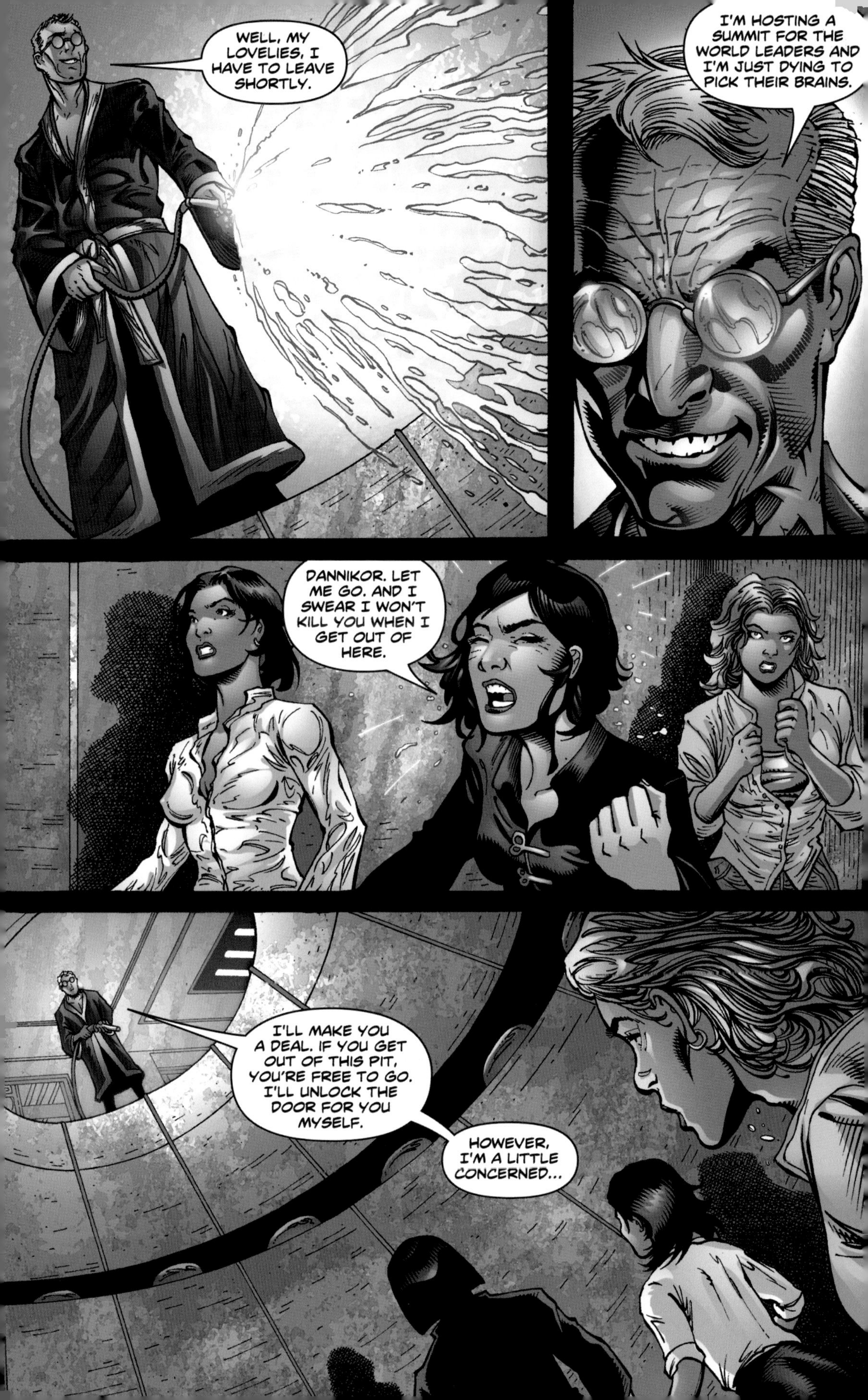
WELL, MY LOVELIES, I HAVE TO LEAVE SHORTLY.
I'M HOSTING A SUMMIT FOR THE WORLD LEADERS AND I'M JUST DYING TO PICK THEIR BRAINS.
DANNIKOR. LET ME GO. AND I SWEAR I WON'T KILL YOU WHEN I GET OUT OF HERE.
I'LL MAKE YOU A DEAL. IF YOU GET OUT OF THIS PIT, YOU'RE FREE TO GO. I'LL UNLOCK THE DOOR FOR YOU MYSELF.
HOWEVER, I'M A LITTLE CONCERNED...

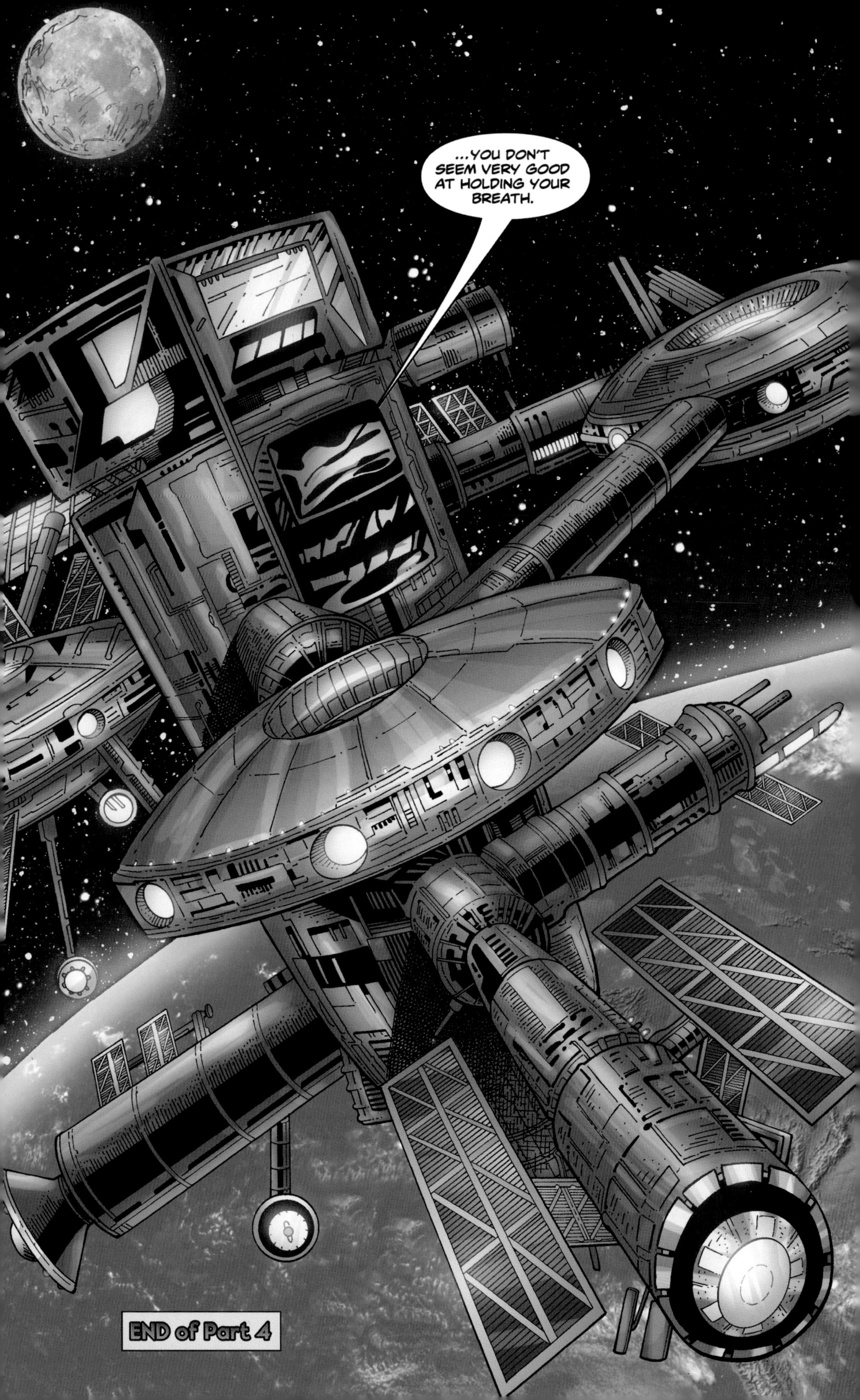
...YOU DON'T SEEM VERY GOOD AT HOLDING YOUR BREATH.
END of Part 4

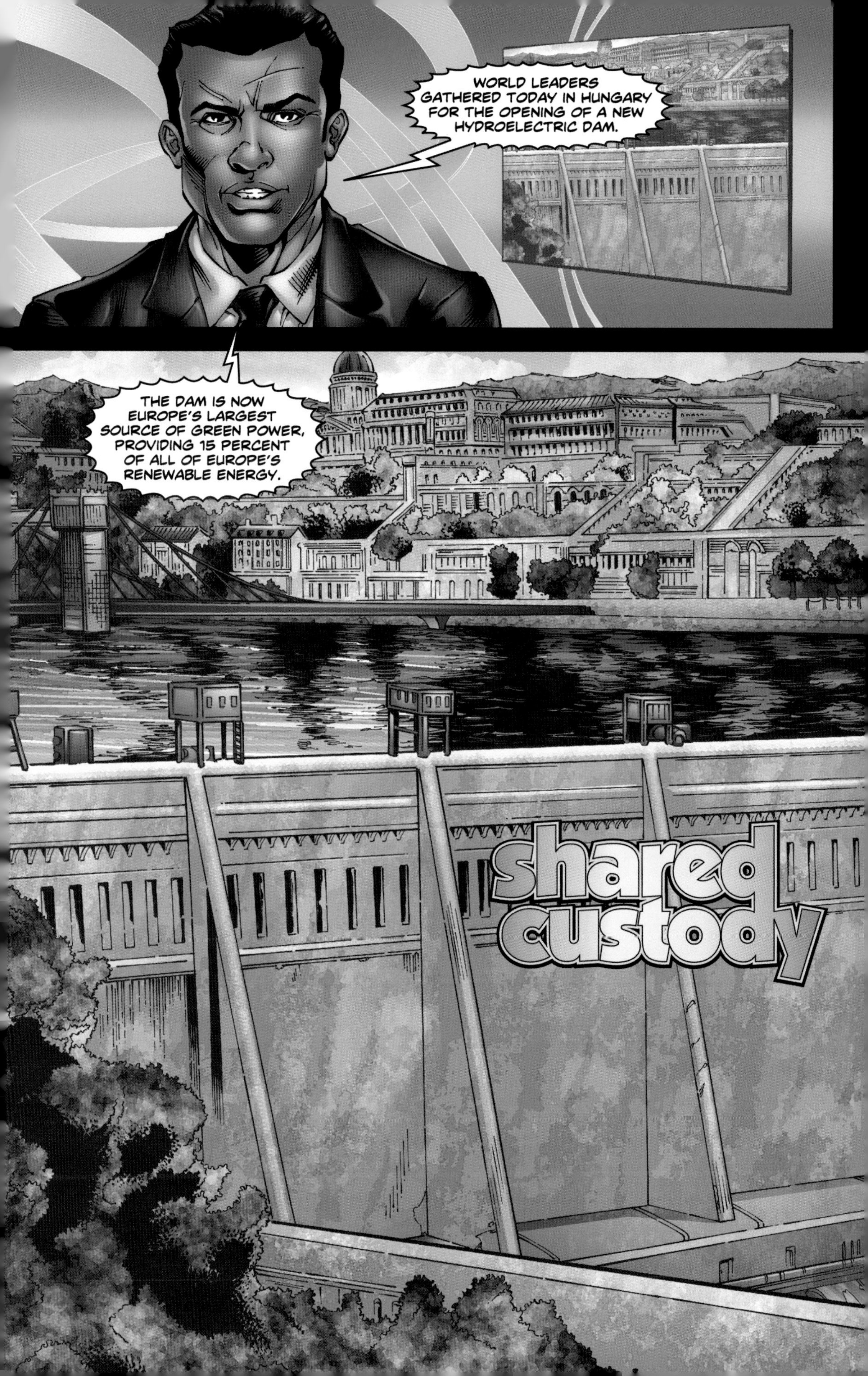
WORLD LEADERS GATHERED TODAY IN HUNGARY FOR THE OPENING OF A NEW HYDROELECTRIC DAM.
THE DAM IS NOW EUROPE'S LARGEST SOURCE OF GREEN POWER, PROVIDING 15 PERCENT OF ALL OF EUROPE'S RENEWABLE ENERGY.
shared custody

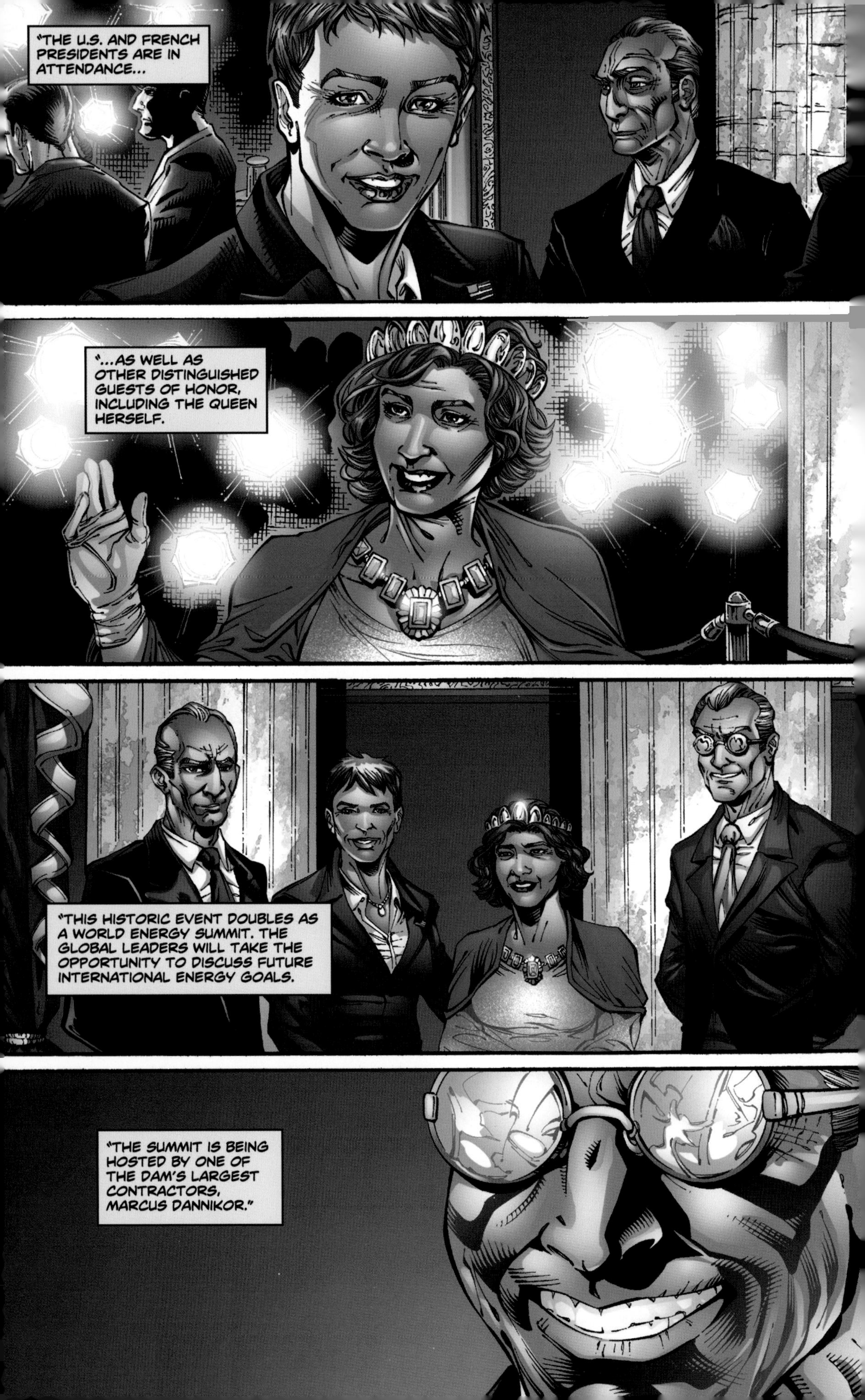
"THE U.S. AND FRENCH PRESIDENTS ARE IN ATTENDANCE...
"...AS WELL AS OTHER DISTINGUISHED GUESTS OF HONOR, INCLUDING THE QUEEN HERSELF.
"THIS HISTORIC EVENT DOUBLES AS A WORLD ENERGY SUMMIT. THE GLOBAL LEADERS WILL TAKE THE OPPORTUNITY TO DISCUSS FUTURE INTERNATIONAL ENERGY GOALS.
"THE SUMMIT IS BEING HOSTED BY ONE OF THE DAM'S LARGEST CONTRACTORS, MARCUS DANNIKOR."

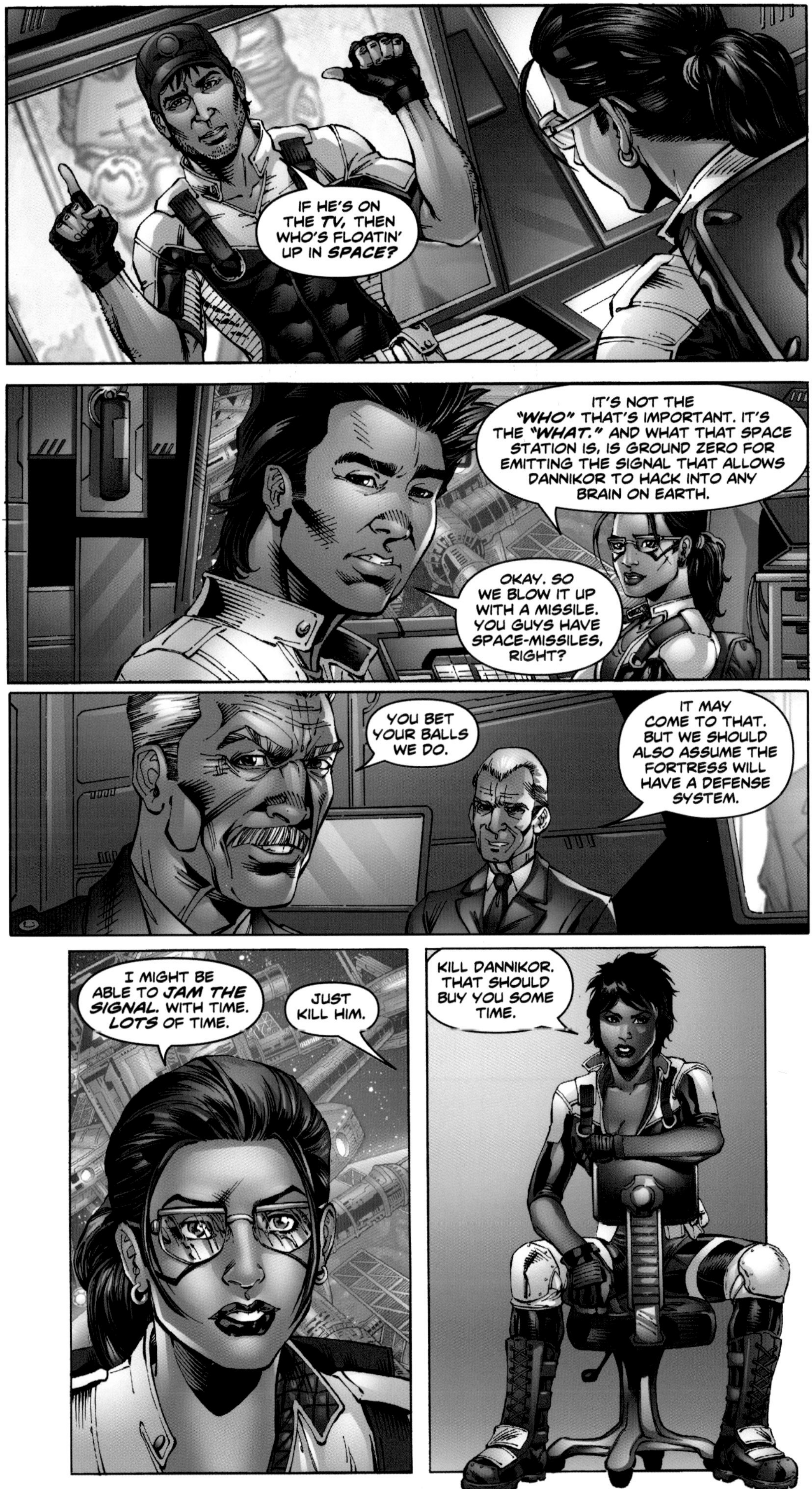
IF HE'S ON THE *TV*, THEN WHO'S FLOATIN' UP IN *SPACE?*
IT'S NOT THE *"WHO"* THAT'S IMPORTANT. IT'S THE *"WHAT."* AND WHAT THAT SPACE STATION IS, IS GROUND ZERO FOR EMITTING THE SIGNAL THAT ALLOWS DANNIKOR TO HACK INTO ANY BRAIN ON EARTH.
OKAY. SO WE BLOW IT UP WITH A MISSILE. YOU GUYS HAVE SPACE-MISSILES, RIGHT?
YOU BET YOUR BALLS WE DO.
IT MAY COME TO THAT. BUT WE SHOULD ALSO ASSUME THE FORTRESS WILL HAVE A DEFENSE SYSTEM.
I MIGHT BE ABLE TO *JAM THE SIGNAL*. WITH TIME. *LOTS* OF TIME.
JUST KILL HIM.
KILL DANNIKOR. THAT SHOULD BUY YOU SOME TIME.

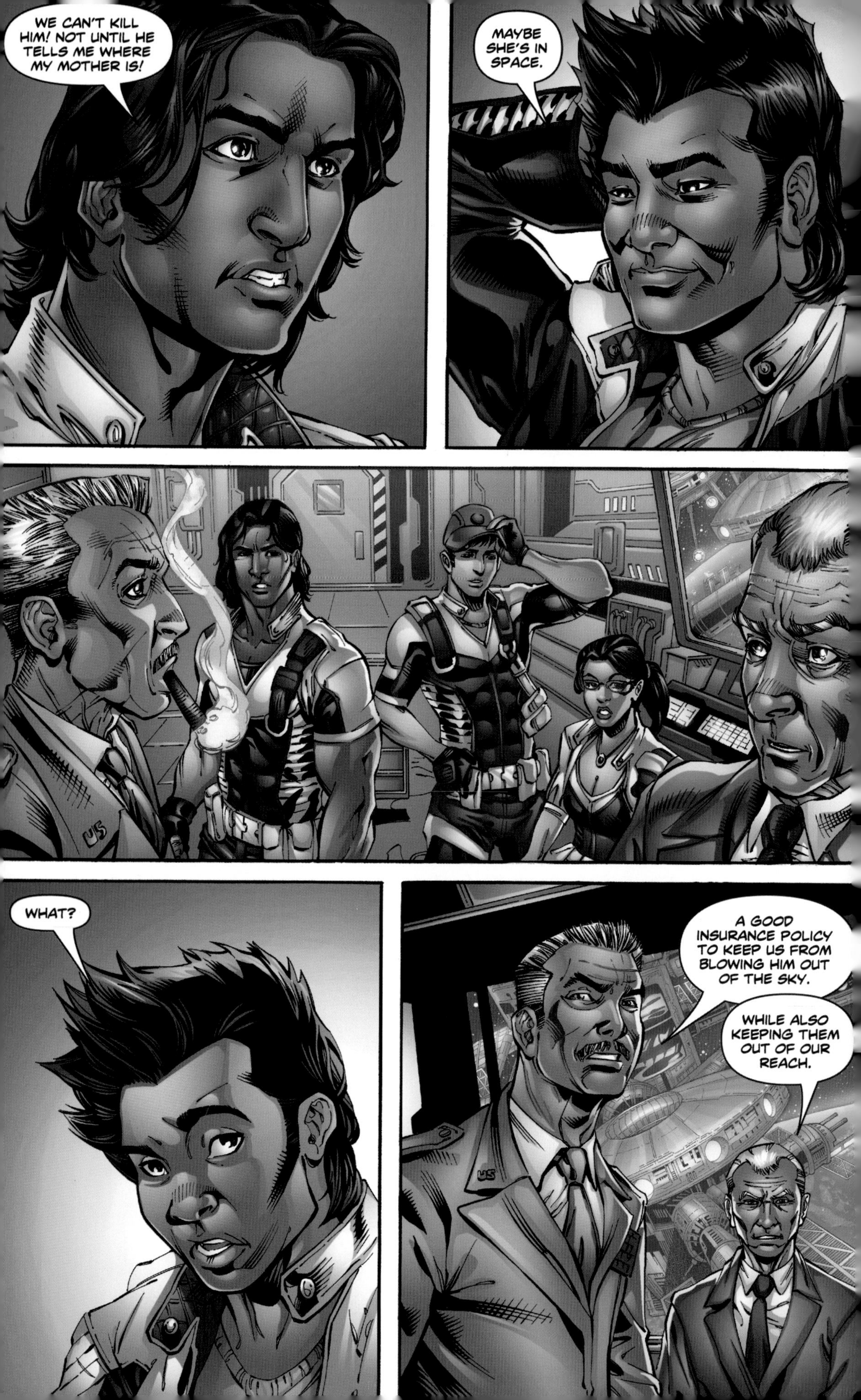
WE CAN'T KILL HIM! NOT UNTIL HE TELLS ME WHERE MY MOTHER IS!
MAYBE SHE'S IN SPACE.
US
WHAT?
A GOOD INSURANCE POLICY TO KEEP US FROM BLOWING HIM OUT OF THE SKY.
WHILE ALSO KEEPING THEM OUT OF OUR REACH.
US

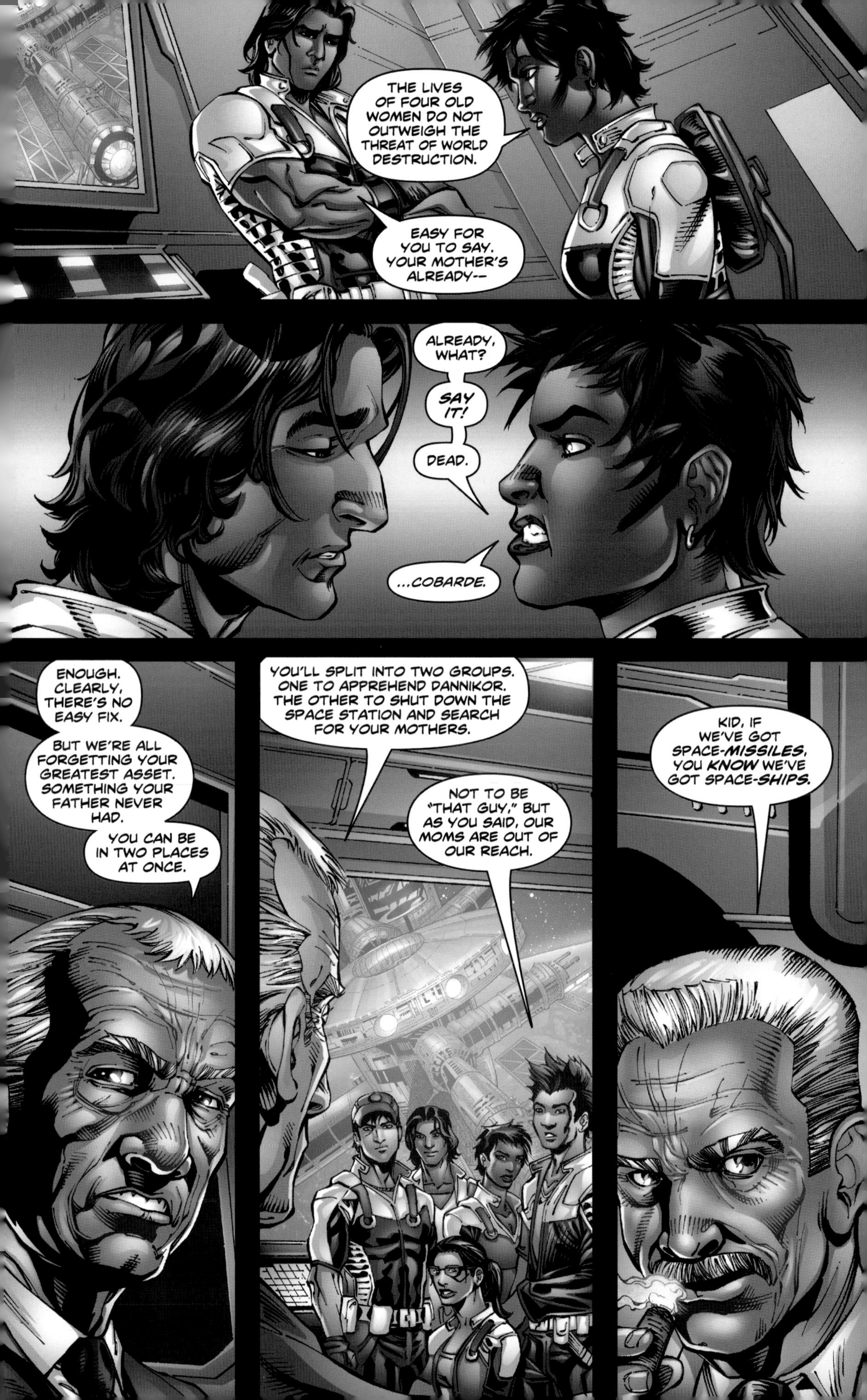
THE LIVES OF FOUR OLD WOMEN DO NOT OUTWEIGH THE THREAT OF WORLD DESTRUCTION.
EASY FOR YOU TO SAY. YOUR MOTHER'S ALREADY--
ALREADY, WHAT?
SAY IT!
DEAD.
...COBARDE.
ENOUGH. CLEARLY, THERE'S NO EASY FIX.
BUT WE'RE ALL FORGETTING YOUR GREATEST ASSET. SOMETHING YOUR FATHER NEVER HAD.
YOU CAN BE IN TWO PLACES AT ONCE.
YOU'LL SPLIT INTO TWO GROUPS. ONE TO APPREHEND DANNIKOR. THE OTHER TO SHUT DOWN THE SPACE STATION AND SEARCH FOR YOUR MOTHERS.
NOT TO BE "THAT GUY," BUT AS YOU SAID, OUR MOMS ARE OUT OF OUR REACH.
KID, IF WE'VE GOT SPACE-MISSILES, YOU KNOW WE'VE GOT SPACE-SHIPS.

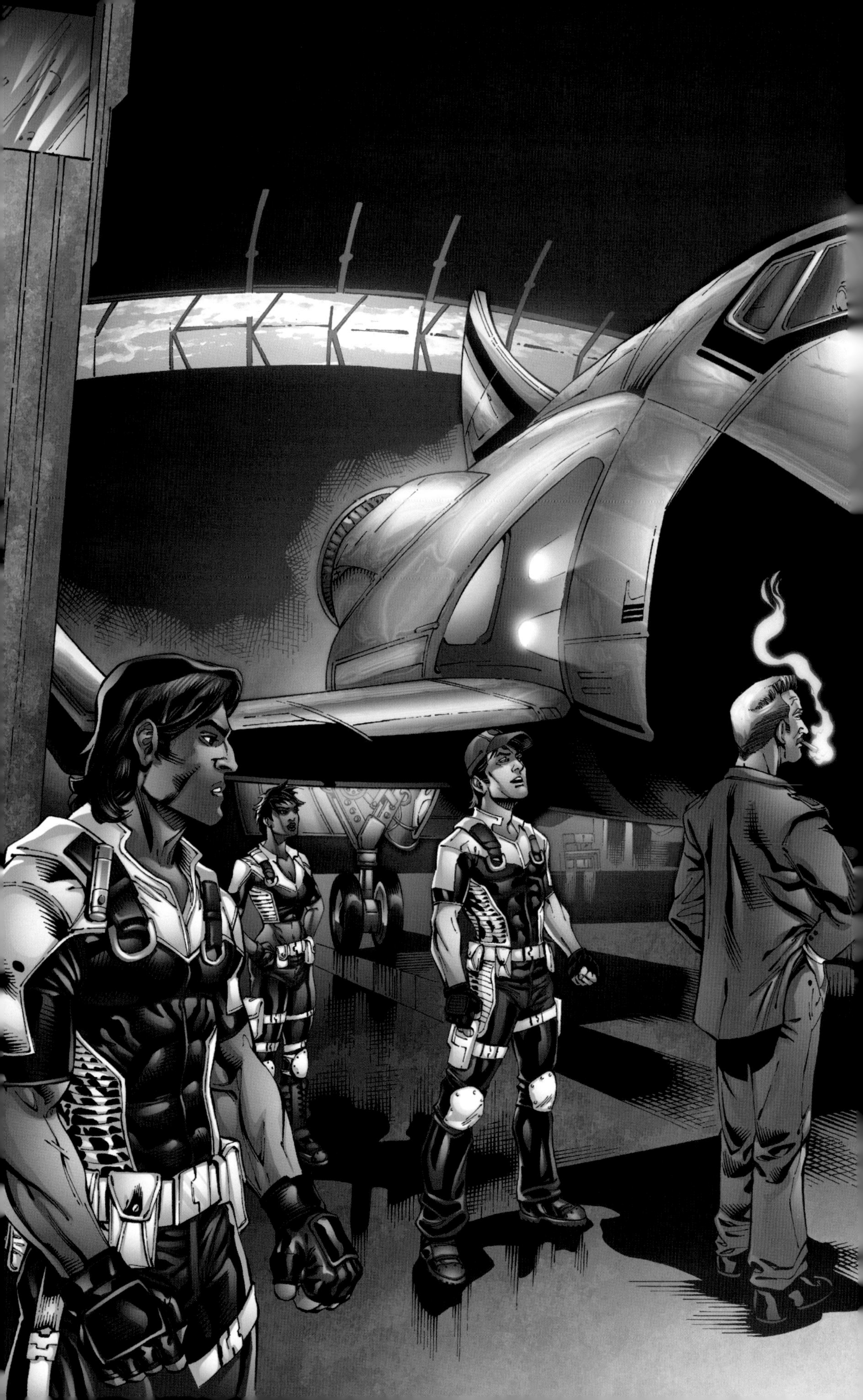

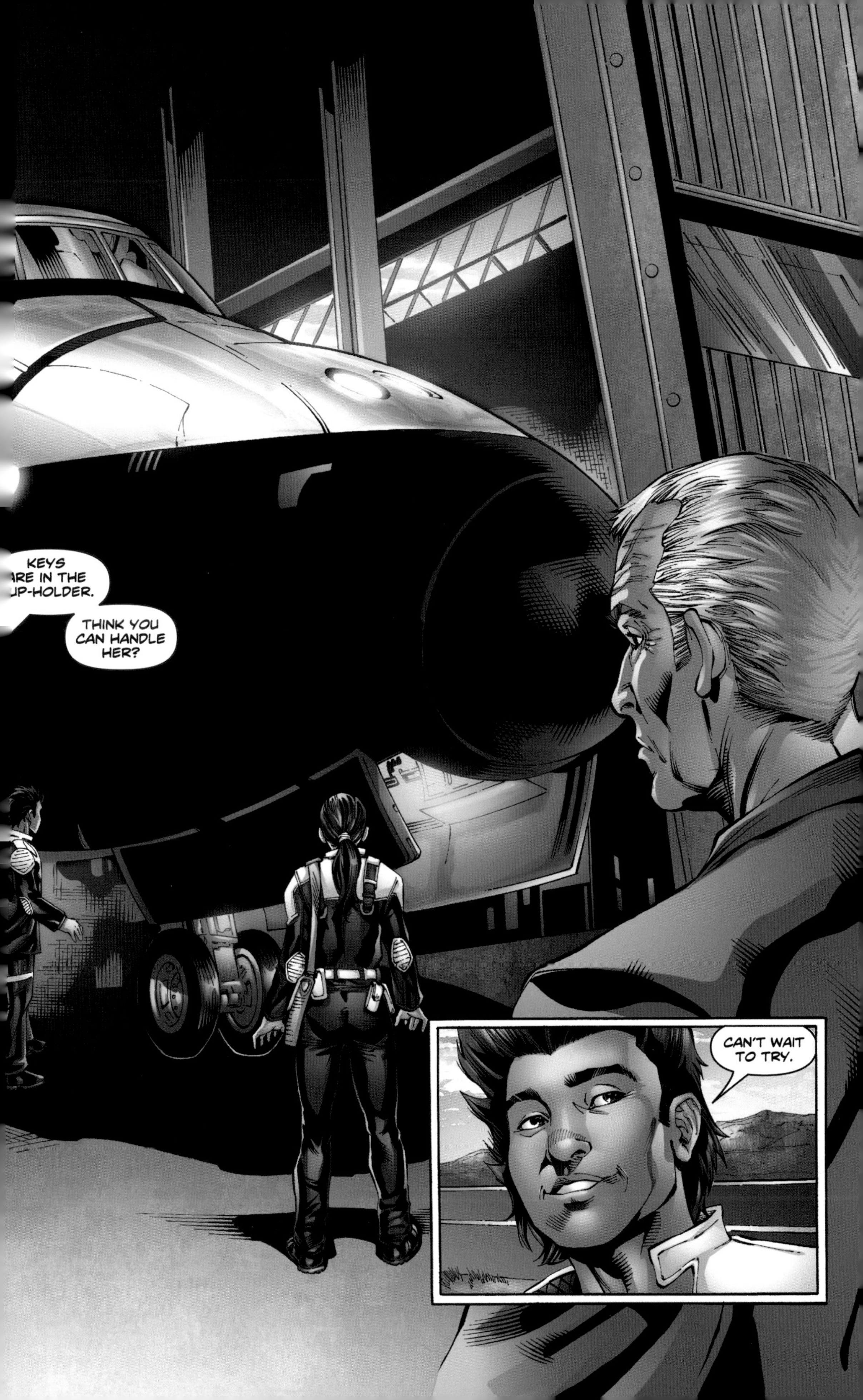
KEYS ARE IN THE UP-HOLDER.
THINK YOU CAN HANDLE HER?
CAN'T WAIT TO TRY.

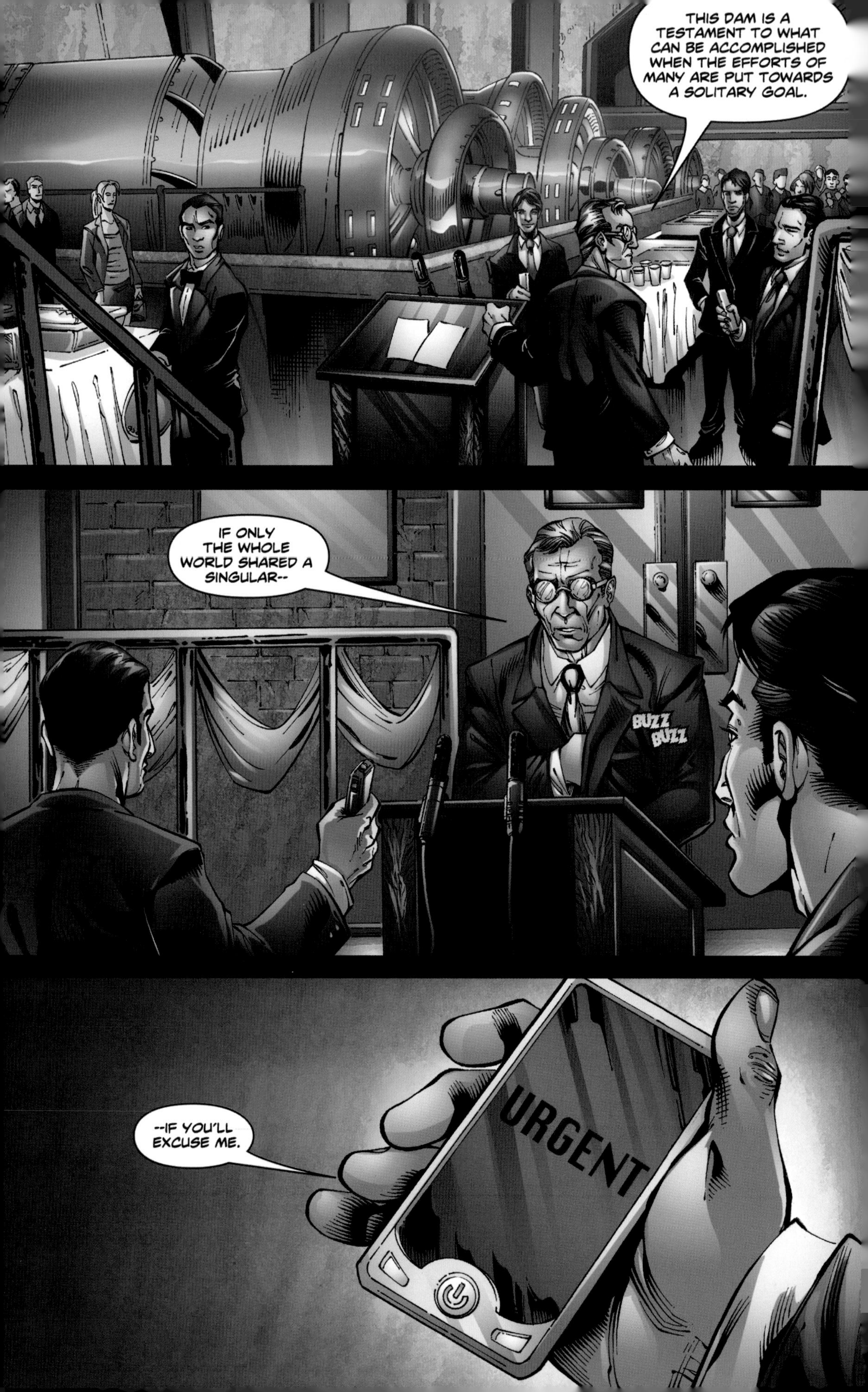
THIS DAM IS A TESTAMENT TO WHAT CAN BE ACCOMPLISHED WHEN THE EFFORTS OF MANY ARE PUT TOWARDS A SOLITARY GOAL.
IF ONLY THE WHOLE WORLD SHARED A SINGULAR--
BUZZ BUZZ
--IF YOU'LL EXCUSE ME.
URGENT

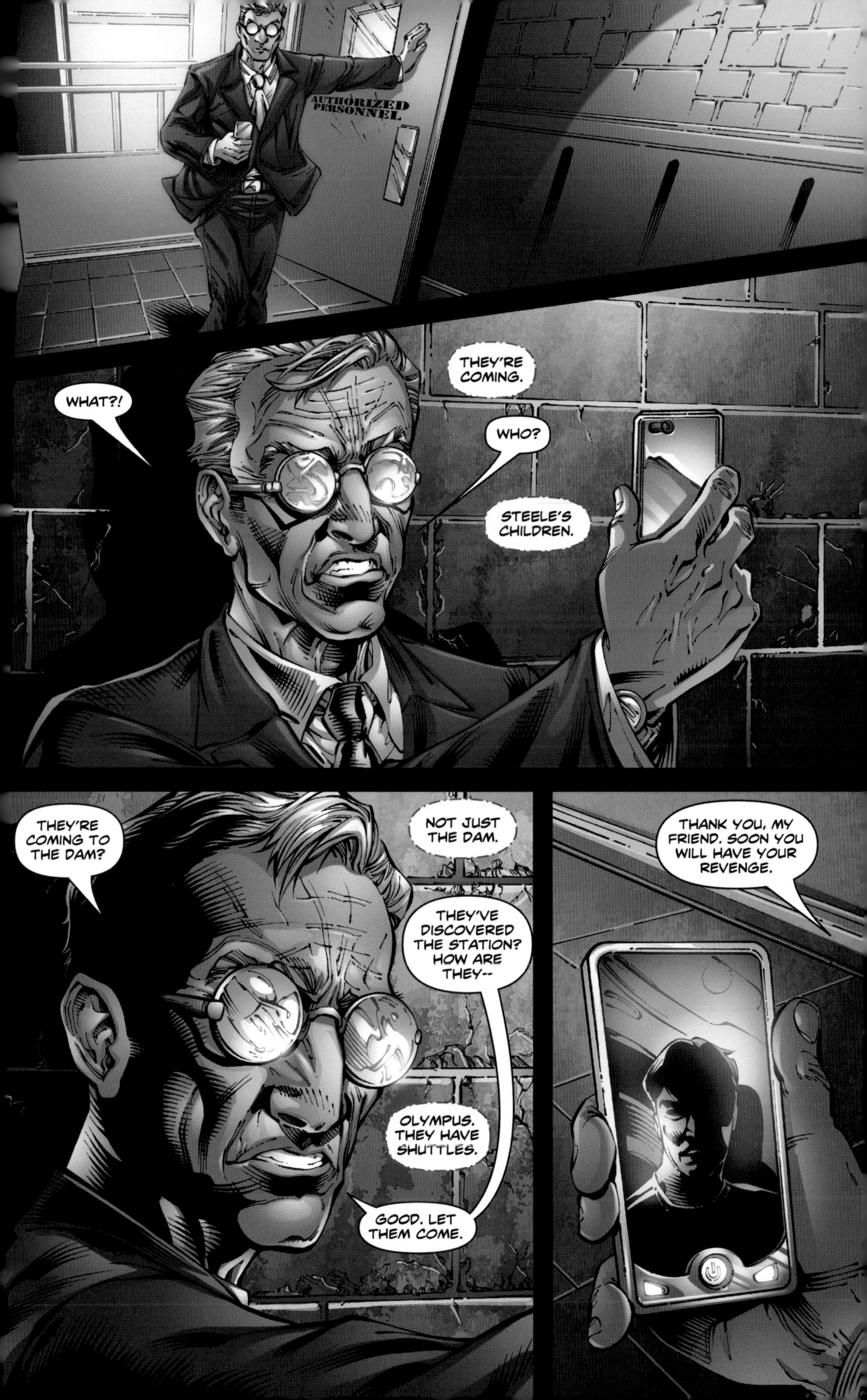
AUTHORIZED PERSONNEL
WHAT?!
THEY'RE COMING.
WHO?
STEELE'S CHILDREN.
THEY'RE COMING TO THE DAM?
NOT JUST THE DAM.
THEY'VE DISCOVERED THE STATION? HOW ARE THEY--
OLYMPUS. THEY HAVE SHUTTLES.
GOOD. LET THEM COME.
THANK YOU, MY FRIEND. SOON YOU WILL HAVE YOUR REVENGE.

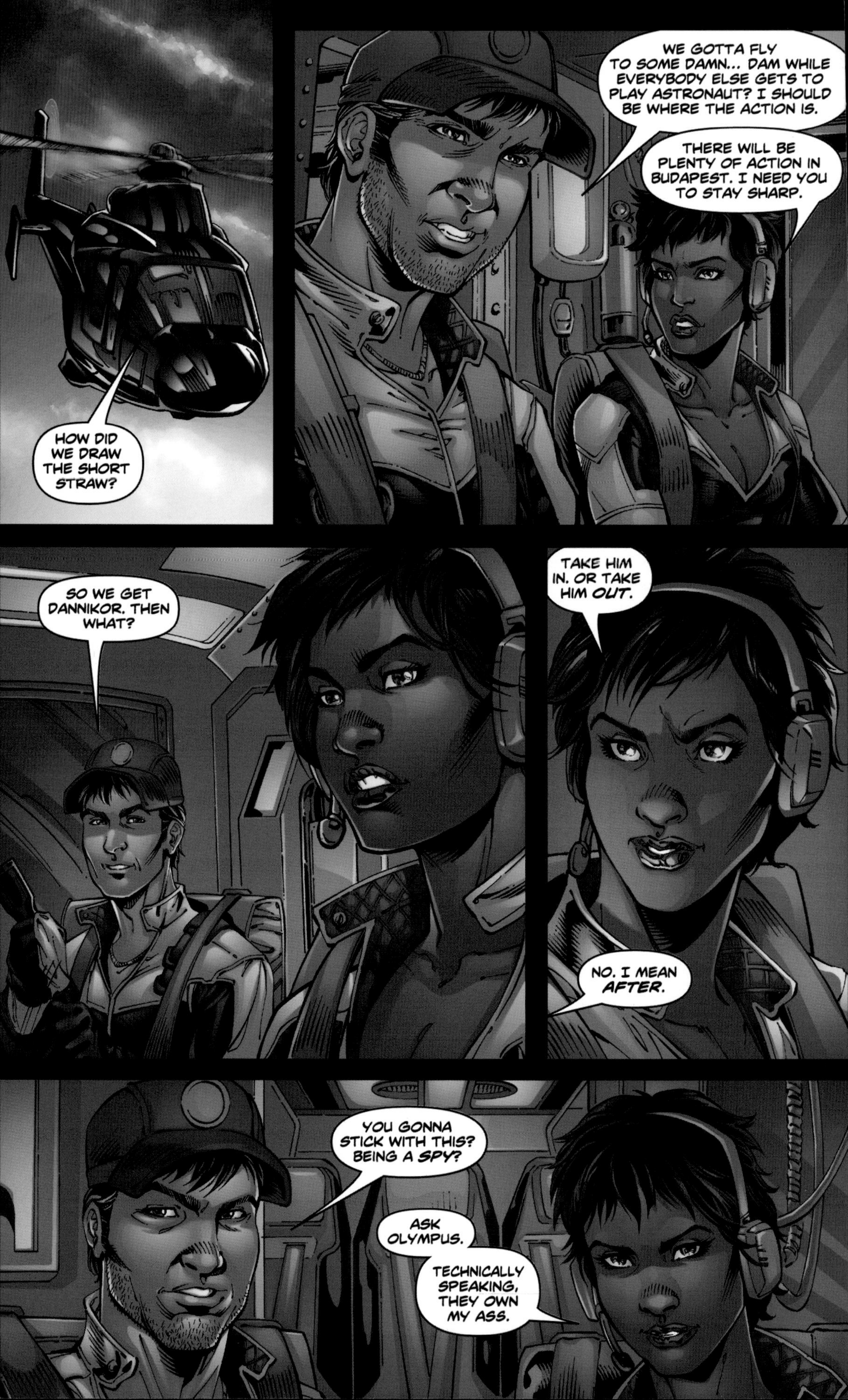
HOW DID WE DRAW THE SHORT STRAW?
WE GOTTA FLY TO SOME DAMN... DAM WHILE EVERYBODY ELSE GETS TO PLAY ASTRONAUT? I SHOULD BE WHERE THE ACTION IS.
THERE WILL BE PLENTY OF ACTION IN BUDAPEST. I NEED YOU TO STAY SHARP.
SO WE GET DANNIKOR. THEN WHAT?
TAKE HIM IN. OR TAKE HIM *OUT*.
NO. I MEAN **AFTER**.
YOU GONNA STICK WITH THIS? BEING A *SPY*?
ASK OLYMPUS.
TECHNICALLY SPEAKING, THEY OWN MY ASS.

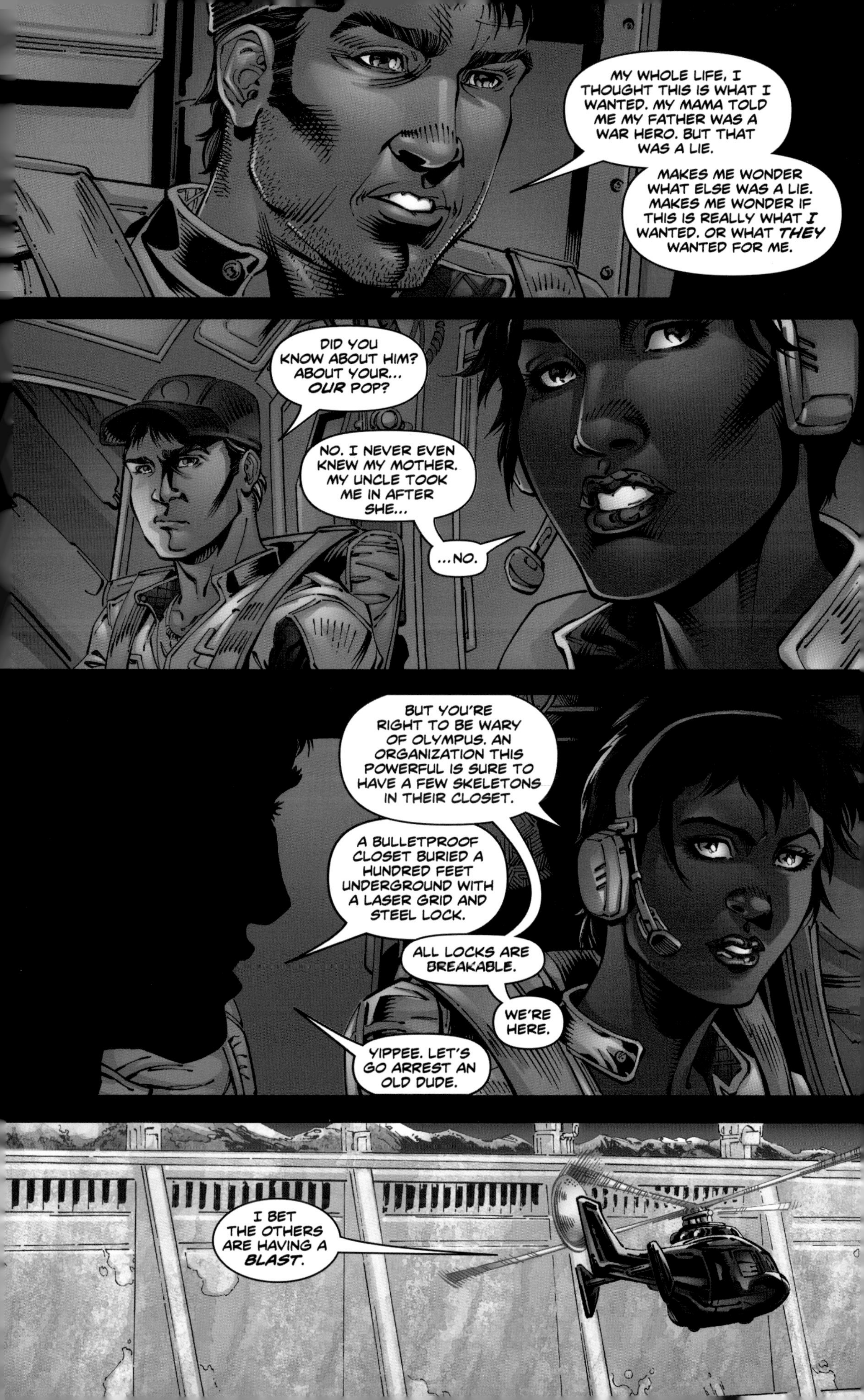
MY WHOLE LIFE, I THOUGHT THIS IS WHAT I WANTED. MY MAMA TOLD ME MY FATHER WAS A WAR HERO. BUT THAT WAS A LIE.
MAKES ME WONDER WHAT ELSE WAS A LIE. MAKES ME WONDER IF THIS IS REALLY WHAT *I* WANTED. OR WHAT *THEY* WANTED FOR ME.
DID YOU KNOW ABOUT HIM? ABOUT YOUR... *OUR* POP?
NO. I NEVER EVEN KNEW MY MOTHER. MY UNCLE TOOK ME IN AFTER SHE...
...NO.
BUT YOU'RE RIGHT TO BE WARY OF OLYMPUS. AN ORGANIZATION THIS POWERFUL IS SURE TO HAVE A FEW SKELETONS IN THEIR CLOSET.
A BULLETPROOF CLOSET BURIED A HUNDRED FEET UNDERGROUND WITH A LASER GRID AND STEEL LOCK.
ALL LOCKS ARE BREAKABLE.
WE'RE HERE.
YIPPEE. LET'S GO ARREST AN OLD DUDE.
I BET THE OTHERS ARE HAVING A *BLAST*.

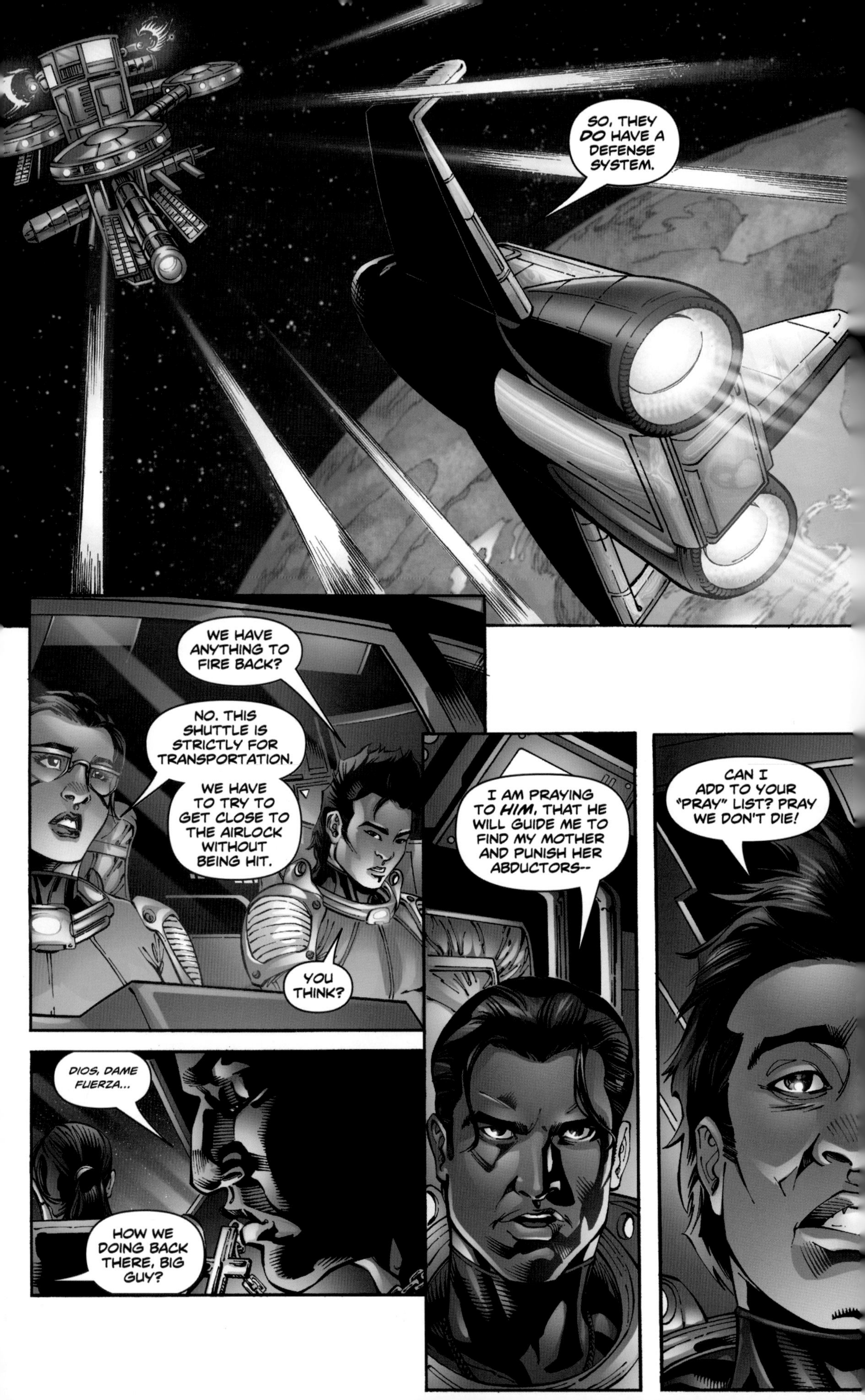
SO, THEY *DO* HAVE A DEFENSE SYSTEM.
WE HAVE ANYTHING TO FIRE BACK?
NO. THIS SHUTTLE IS STRICTLY FOR TRANSPORTATION.
WE HAVE TO TRY TO GET CLOSE TO THE AIRLOCK WITHOUT BEING HIT.
YOU THINK?
I AM PRAYING TO *HIM*, THAT HE WILL GUIDE ME TO FIND MY MOTHER AND PUNISH HER ABDUCTORS--
CAN I ADD TO YOUR "PRAY" LIST? PRAY WE DON'T DIE!
DIOS, DAME FUERZA...
HOW WE DOING BACK THERE, BIG GUY?

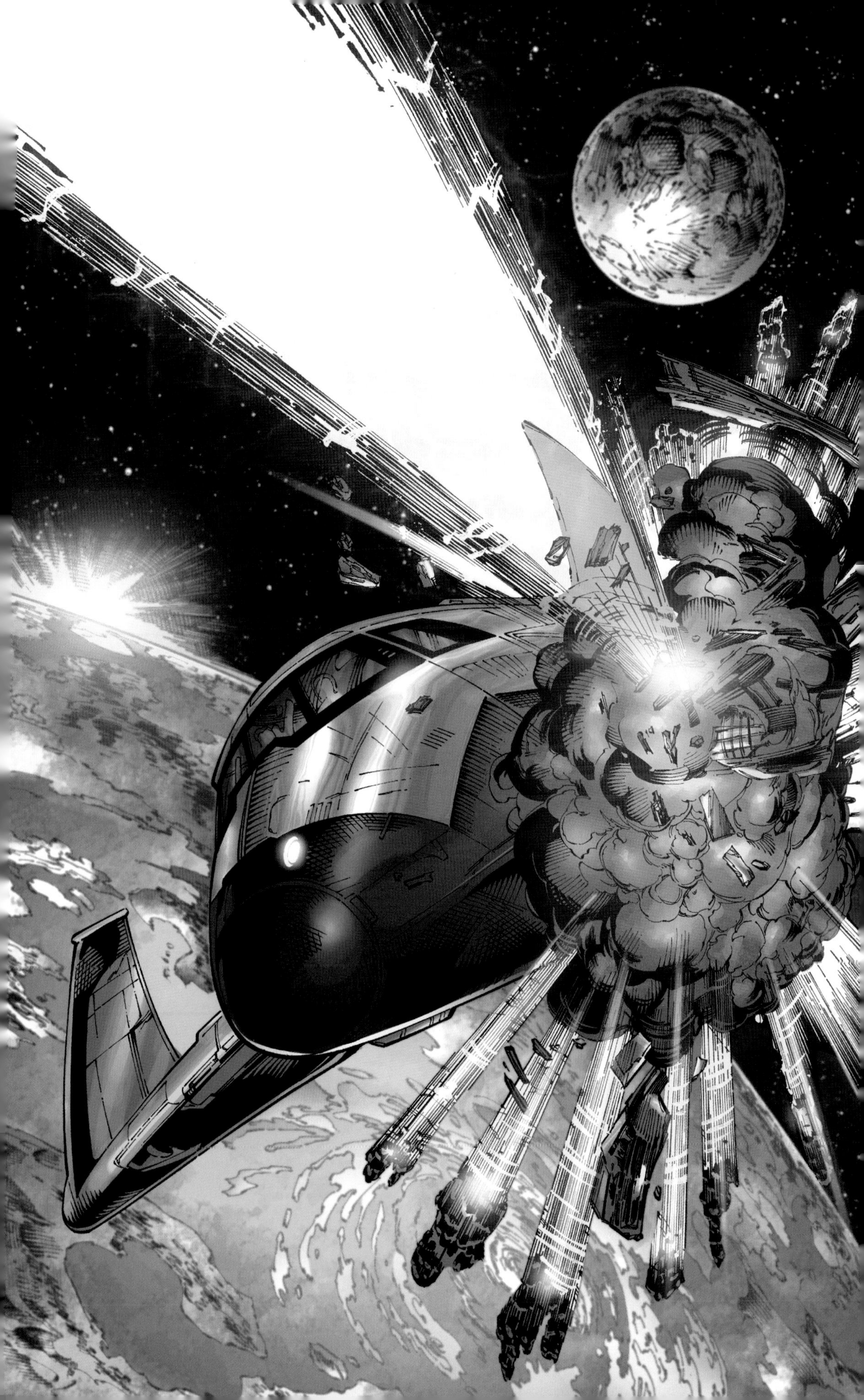

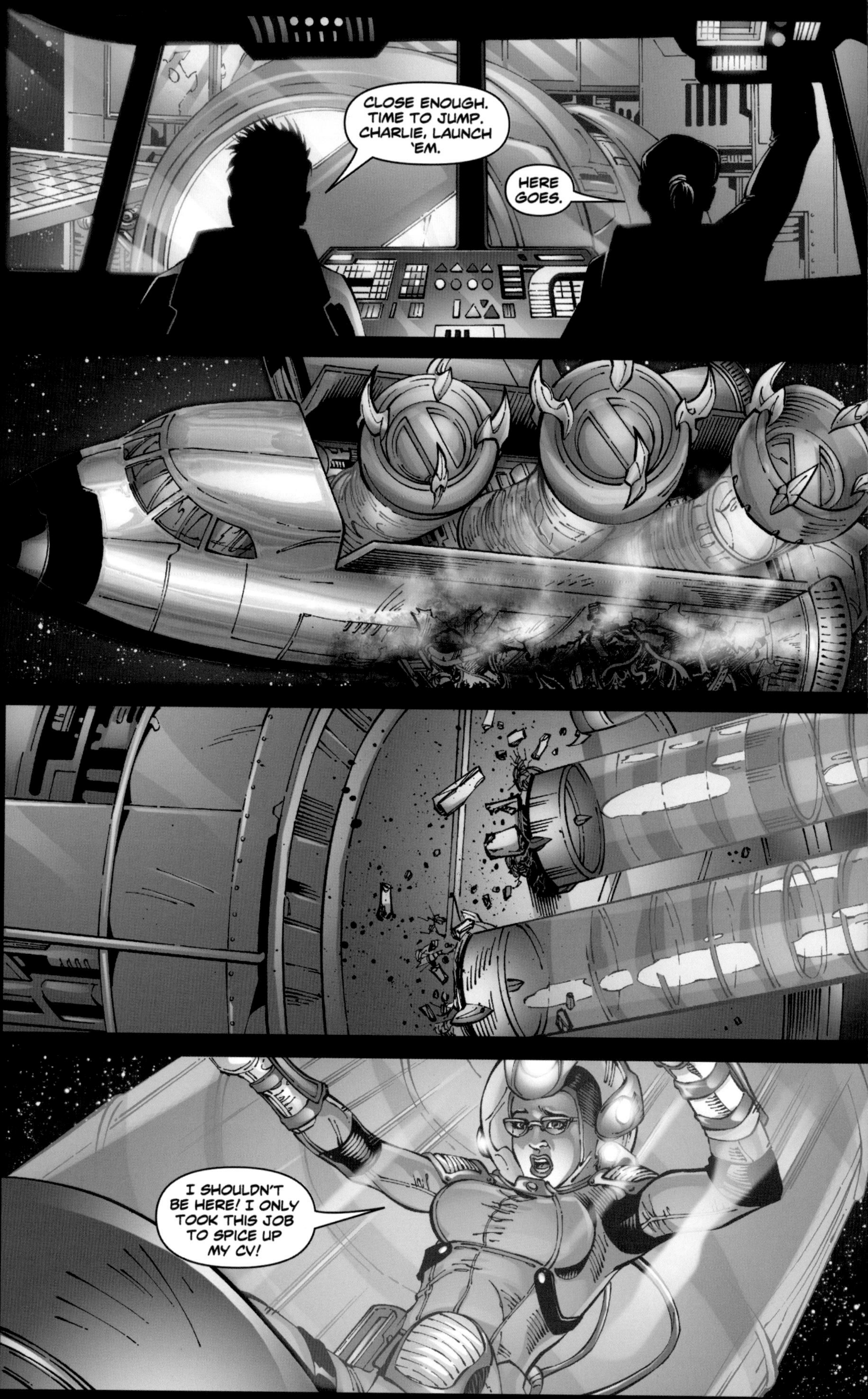
CLOSE ENOUGH. TIME TO JUMP. CHARLIE, LAUNCH 'EM.
HERE GOES.
I SHOULDN'T BE HERE! I ONLY TOOK THIS JOB TO SPICE UP MY CV!

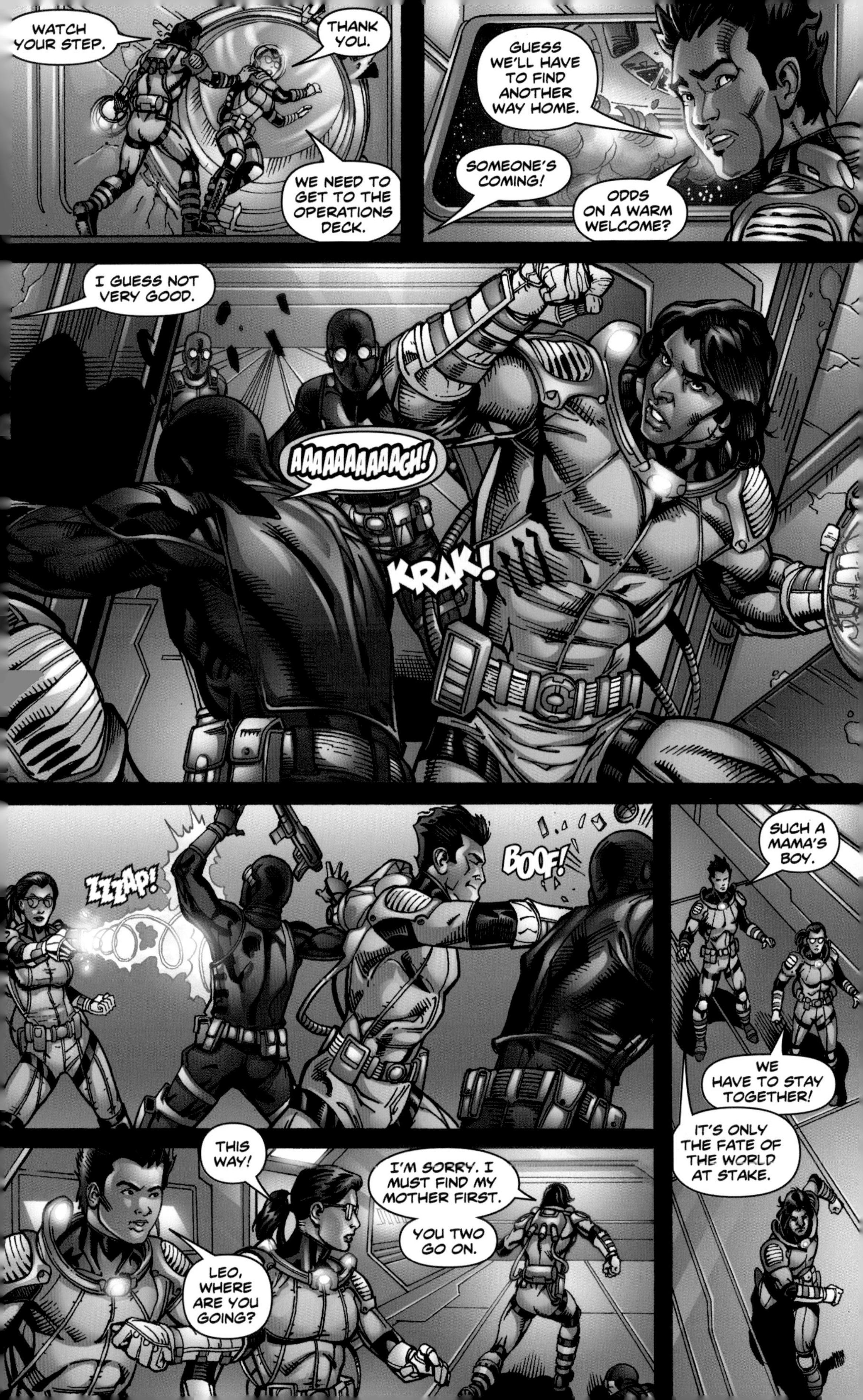
WATCH YOUR STEP.
THANK YOU.
WE NEED TO GET TO THE OPERATIONS DECK.
GUESS WE'LL HAVE TO FIND ANOTHER WAY HOME.
SOMEONE'S COMING!
ODDS ON A WARM WELCOME?
I GUESS NOT VERY GOOD.
AAAAAAAAAAGH!
KRAK!
ZZZAP!
BOOF!
SUCH A MAMA'S BOY.
WE HAVE TO STAY TOGETHER!
IT'S ONLY THE FATE OF THE WORLD AT STAKE.
THIS WAY!
I'M SORRY. I MUST FIND MY MOTHER FIRST.
YOU TWO GO ON.
LEO, WHERE ARE YOU GOING?

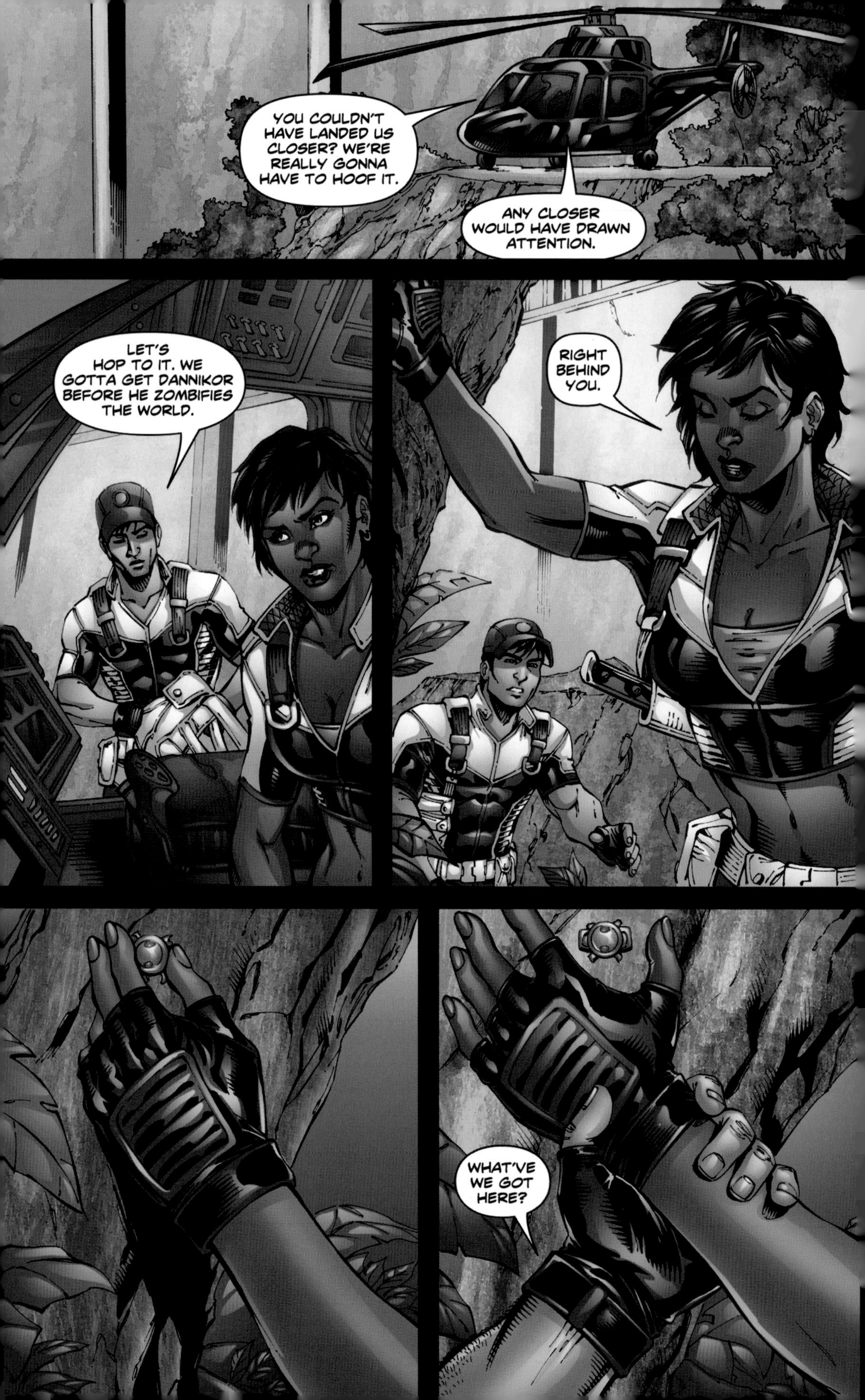
YOU COULDN'T HAVE LANDED US CLOSER? WE'RE REALLY GONNA HAVE TO HOOF IT.
ANY CLOSER WOULD HAVE DRAWN ATTENTION.
LET'S HOP TO IT. WE GOTTA GET DANNIKOR BEFORE HE ZOMBIFIES THE WORLD.
RIGHT BEHIND YOU.
WHAT'VE WE GOT HERE?

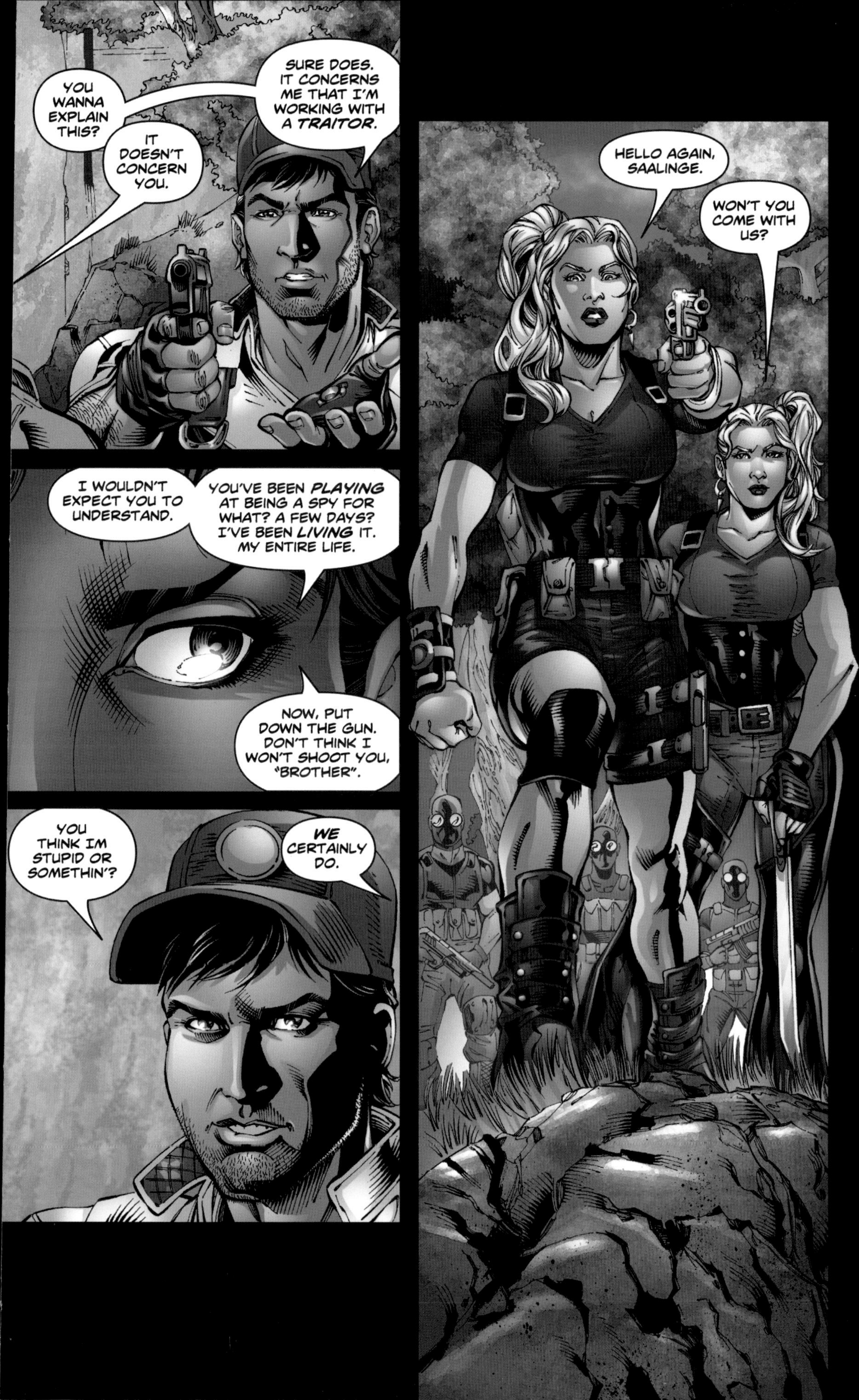
YOU WANNA EXPLAIN THIS?
IT DOESN'T CONCERN YOU.
SURE DOES. IT CONCERNS ME THAT I'M WORKING WITH A *TRAITOR*.
I WOULDN'T EXPECT YOU TO UNDERSTAND.
YOU'VE BEEN *PLAYING* AT BEING A SPY FOR WHAT? A FEW DAYS? I'VE BEEN *LIVING* IT. MY ENTIRE LIFE.
NOW, PUT DOWN THE GUN. DON'T THINK I WON'T SHOOT YOU, "BROTHER".
YOU THINK IM STUPID OR SOMETHIN'?
WE CERTAINLY DO.
HELLO AGAIN, SAALINGE.
WON'T YOU COME WITH US?

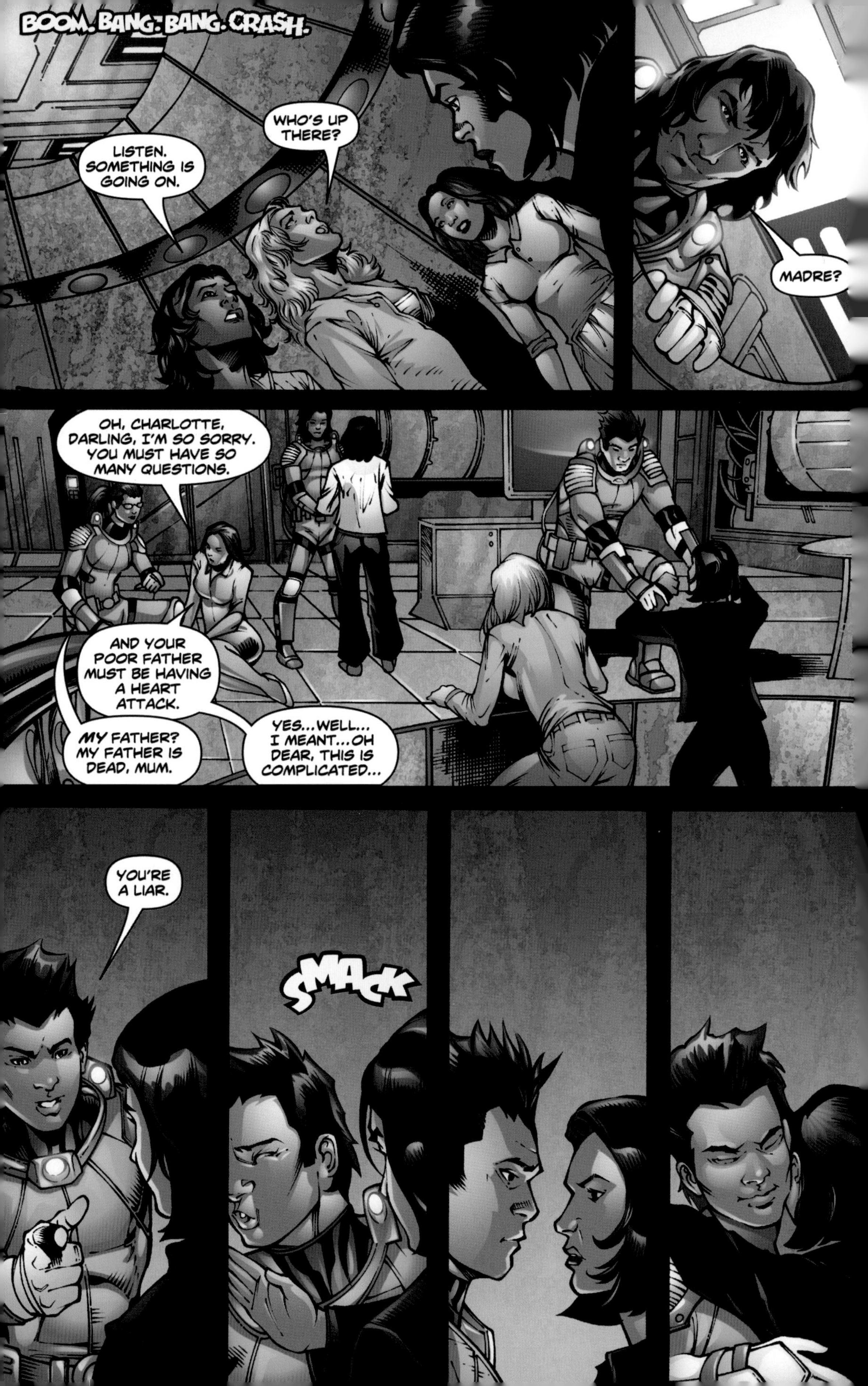
BOOM. BANG. BANG. CRASH.
LISTEN. SOMETHING IS GOING ON.
WHO'S UP THERE?
MADRE?
OH, CHARLOTTE, DARLING, I'M SO SORRY. YOU MUST HAVE SO MANY QUESTIONS.
AND YOUR POOR FATHER MUST BE HAVING A HEART ATTACK.
MY FATHER? MY FATHER IS DEAD, MUM.
YES...WELL... I MEANT...OH DEAR, THIS IS COMPLICATED...
YOU'RE A LIAR.
SMACK

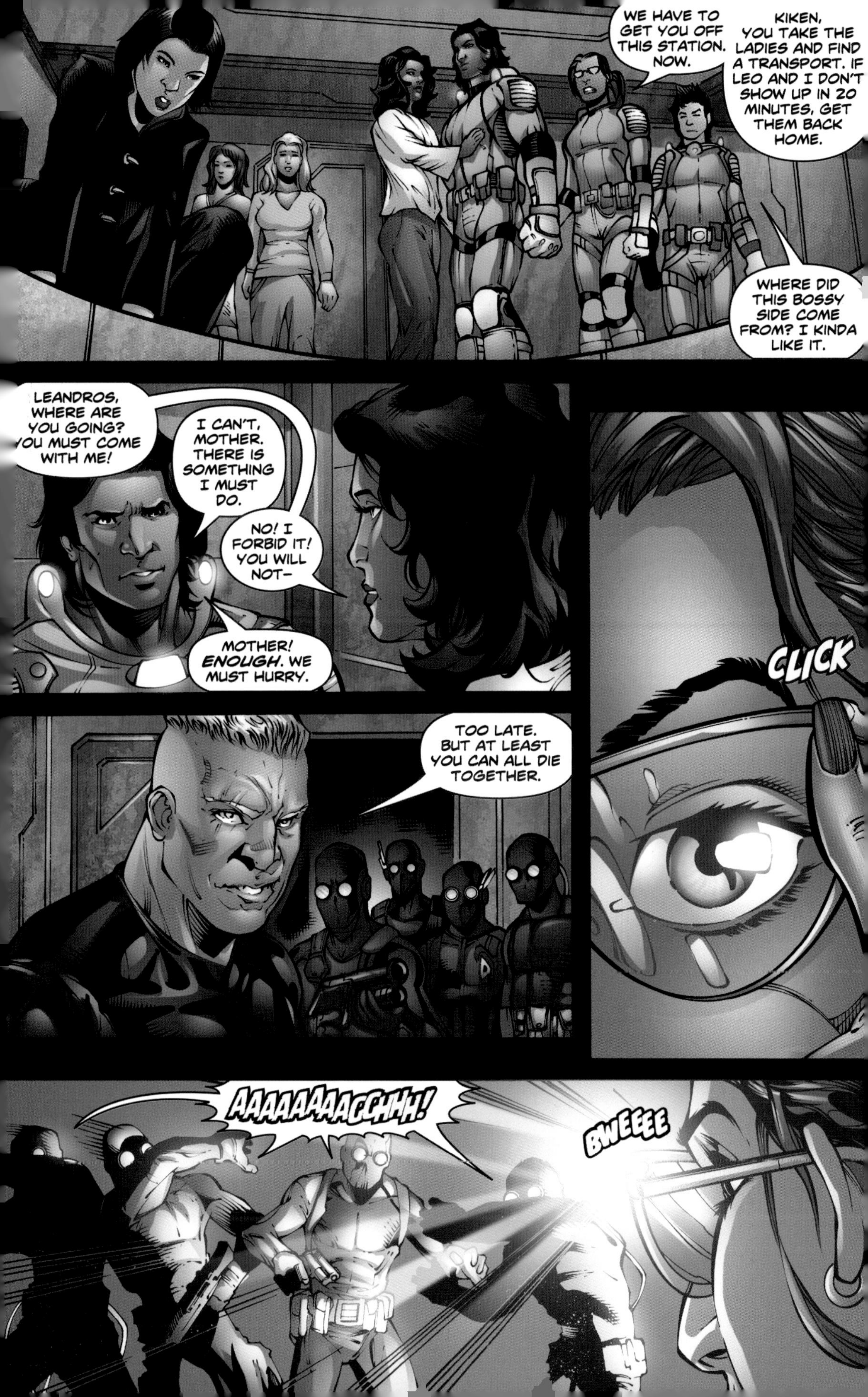
WE HAVE TO GET YOU OFF THIS STATION. NOW.
KIKEN, YOU TAKE THE LADIES AND FIND A TRANSPORT. IF LEO AND I DON'T SHOW UP IN 20 MINUTES, GET THEM BACK HOME.
WHERE DID THIS BOSSY SIDE COME FROM? I KINDA LIKE IT.
LEANDROS, WHERE ARE YOU GOING? YOU MUST COME WITH ME!
I CAN'T, MOTHER. THERE IS SOMETHING I MUST DO.
NO! I FORBID IT! YOU WILL NOT-
MOTHER! ENOUGH. WE MUST HURRY.
CLICK
TOO LATE. BUT AT LEAST YOU CAN ALL DIE TOGETHER.
AAAAAAAACGHHH!
BWEEEE

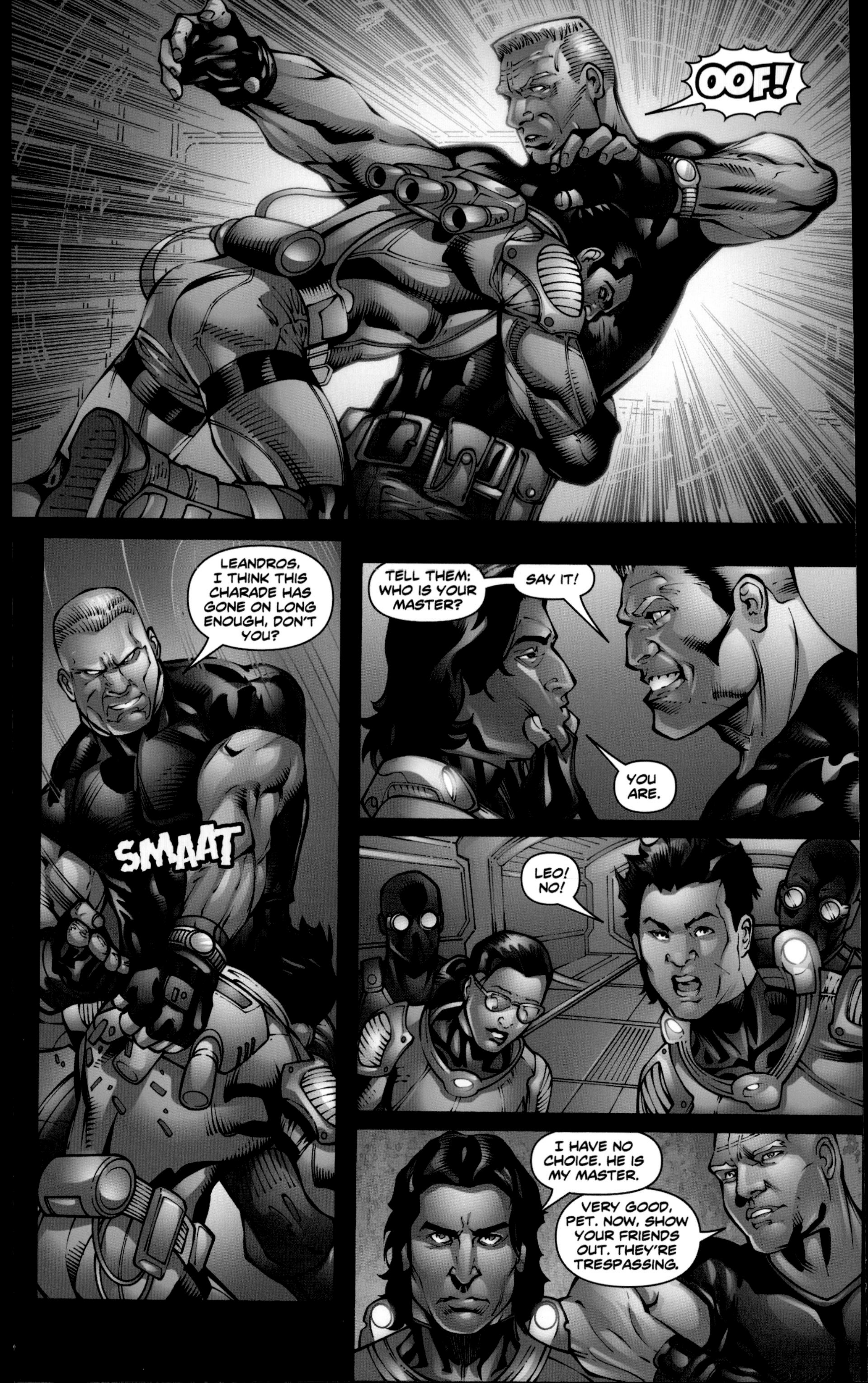
OOF!
LEANDROS, I THINK THIS CHARADE HAS GONE ON LONG ENOUGH, DON'T YOU?
SMAAT
TELL THEM: WHO IS YOUR MASTER?
SAY IT!
YOU ARE.
LEO! NO!
I HAVE NO CHOICE. HE IS MY MASTER.
VERY GOOD, PET. NOW, SHOW YOUR FRIENDS OUT. THEY'RE TRESPASSING.

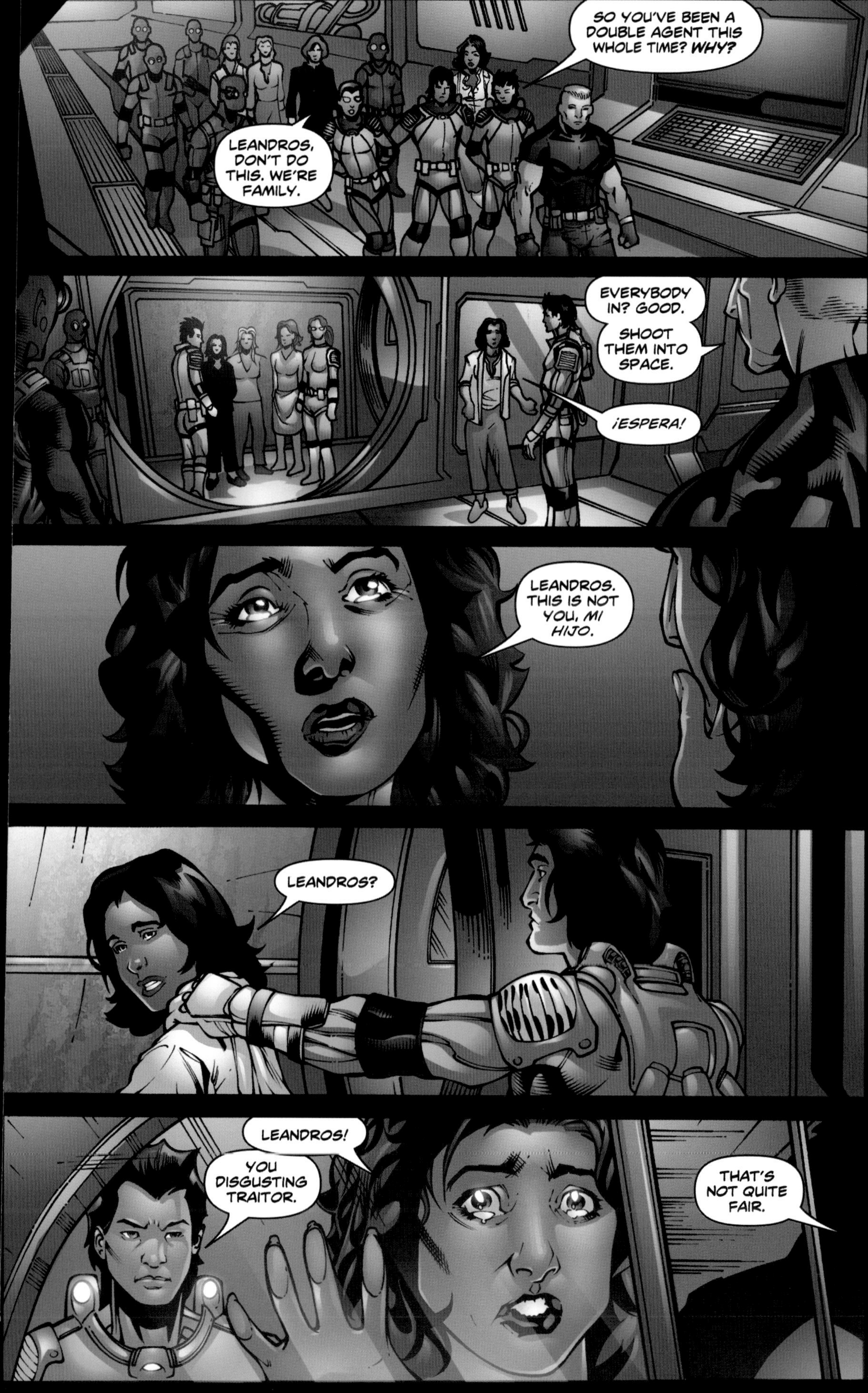
SO YOU'VE BEEN A DOUBLE AGENT THIS WHOLE TIME? *WHY?*
LEANDROS, DON'T DO THIS. WE'RE FAMILY.
EVERYBODY IN? GOOD.
SHOOT THEM INTO SPACE.
¡ESPERA!
LEANDROS. THIS IS NOT YOU, *MI HIJO.*
LEANDROS?
LEANDROS!
YOU DISGUSTING TRAITOR.
THAT'S NOT QUITE FAIR.

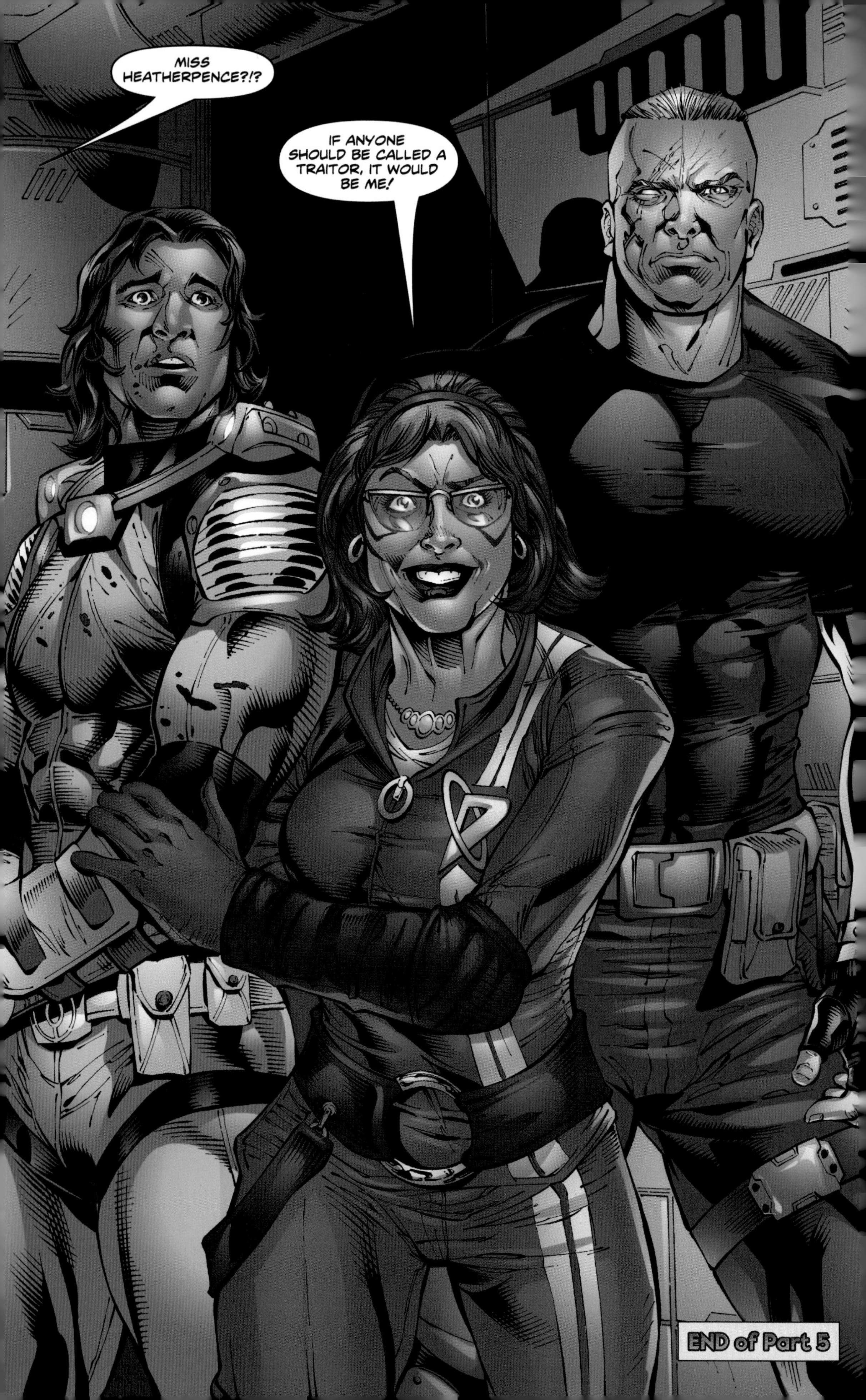
MISS HEATHERPENCE?!?
IF ANYONE SHOULD BE CALLED A TRAITOR, IT WOULD BE ME!
END of Part 5

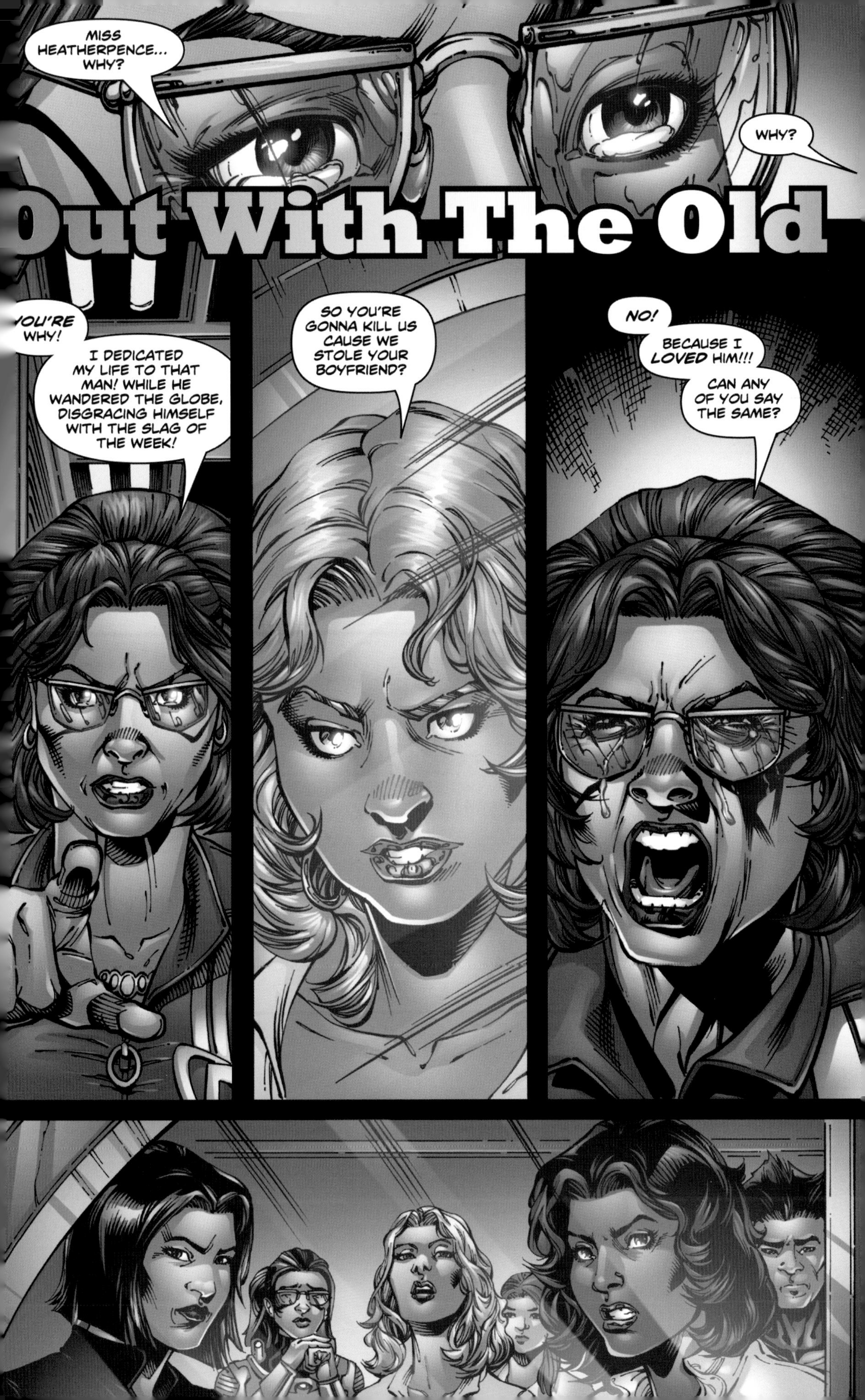

MISS HEATHERPENCE... WHY?
WHY?
Out With The Old
YOU'RE WHY!
I DEDICATED MY LIFE TO THAT MAN! WHILE HE WANDERED THE GLOBE, DISGRACING HIMSELF WITH THE SLAG OF THE WEEK!
SO YOU'RE GONNA KILL US CAUSE WE STOLE YOUR BOYFRIEND?
NO!
BECAUSE I LOVED HIM!!!
CAN ANY OF YOU SAY THE SAME?

"I GAVE HIM EVERYTHING.

"TOO MUCH."

WE CAN'T KEEP IT, JOANNE.

WE'D BE TOO EXPOSED.

PEOPLE WANTING TO HURT ME WOULD COME AFTER IT. AND YOU.

I UNDER-STAND.

HE SAID IT WAS SOMETHING WE COULD NEVER HAVE. OUR SACRIFICE FOR THE GREATER GOOD.

AND THEN I FOUND OUT ABOUT YOU.

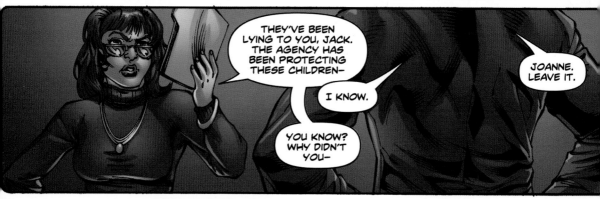

THEY'VE BEEN LYING TO YOU, JACK. THE AGENCY HAS BEEN PROTECTING THESE CHILDREN—

I KNOW.

JOANNE. LEAVE IT.

YOU KNOW? WHY DIDN'T YOU—

MISS HEATHERPENCE, IF YOU REALLY LOVED HIM, WHY BETRAY EVERYTHING HE BELIEVED IN? WHY HELP THE MAN WHO KILLED HIM?

YOU THINK DANNIKOR KILLED STEELE?

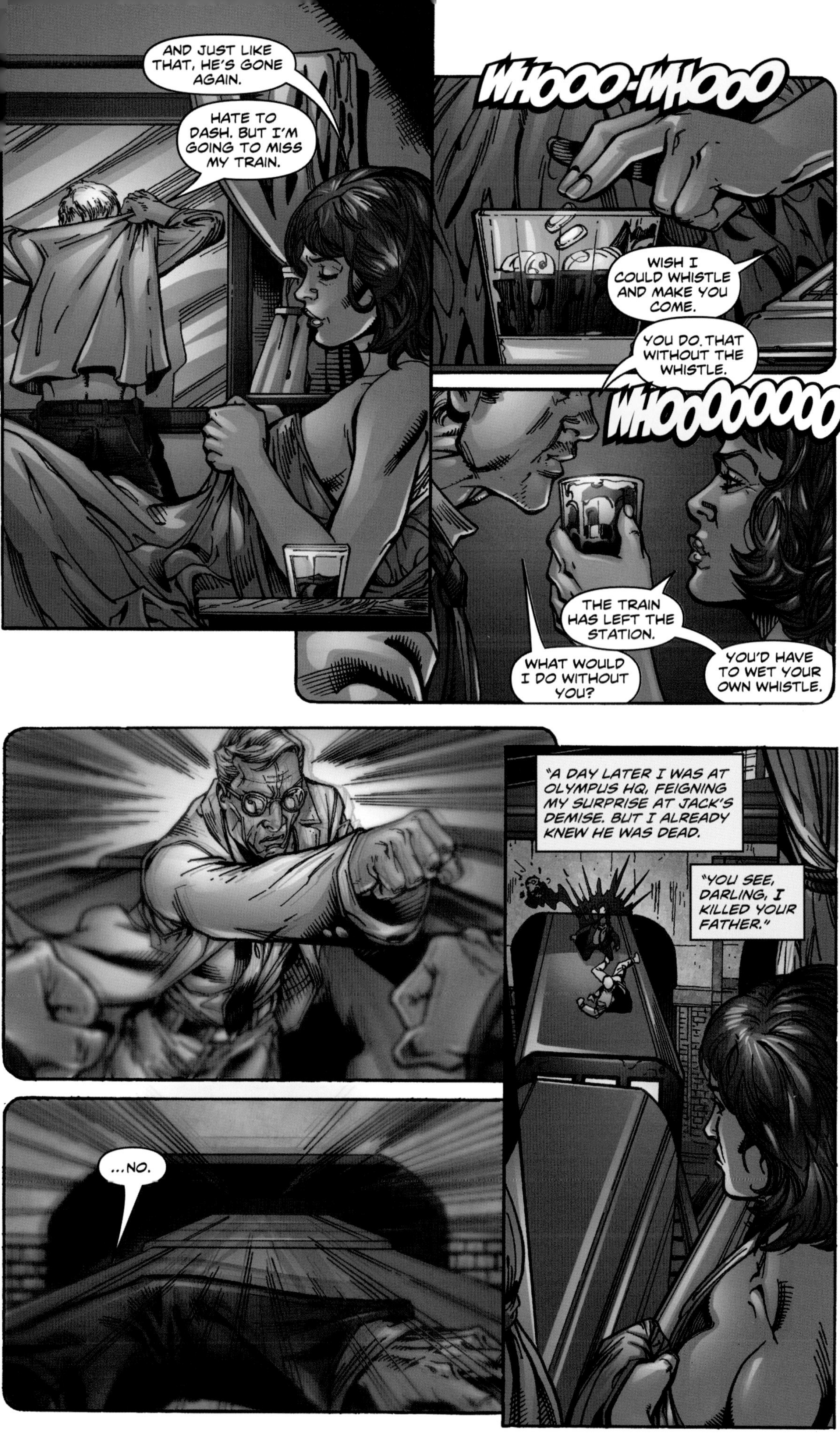
AND JUST LIKE THAT, HE'S GONE AGAIN.
HATE TO DASH. BUT I'M GOING TO MISS MY TRAIN.
WHOOO-WHOOO
WISH I COULD WHISTLE AND MAKE YOU COME.
YOU DO. THAT WITHOUT THE WHISTLE.
WHOOOOOOOO
THE TRAIN HAS LEFT THE STATION.
WHAT WOULD I DO WITHOUT YOU?
YOU'D HAVE TO WET YOUR OWN WHISTLE.
...NO.
"A DAY LATER I WAS AT OLYMPUS HQ, FEIGNING MY SURPRISE AT JACK'S DEMISE. BUT I ALREADY KNEW HE WAS DEAD.
"YOU SEE, DARLING, I KILLED YOUR FATHER."

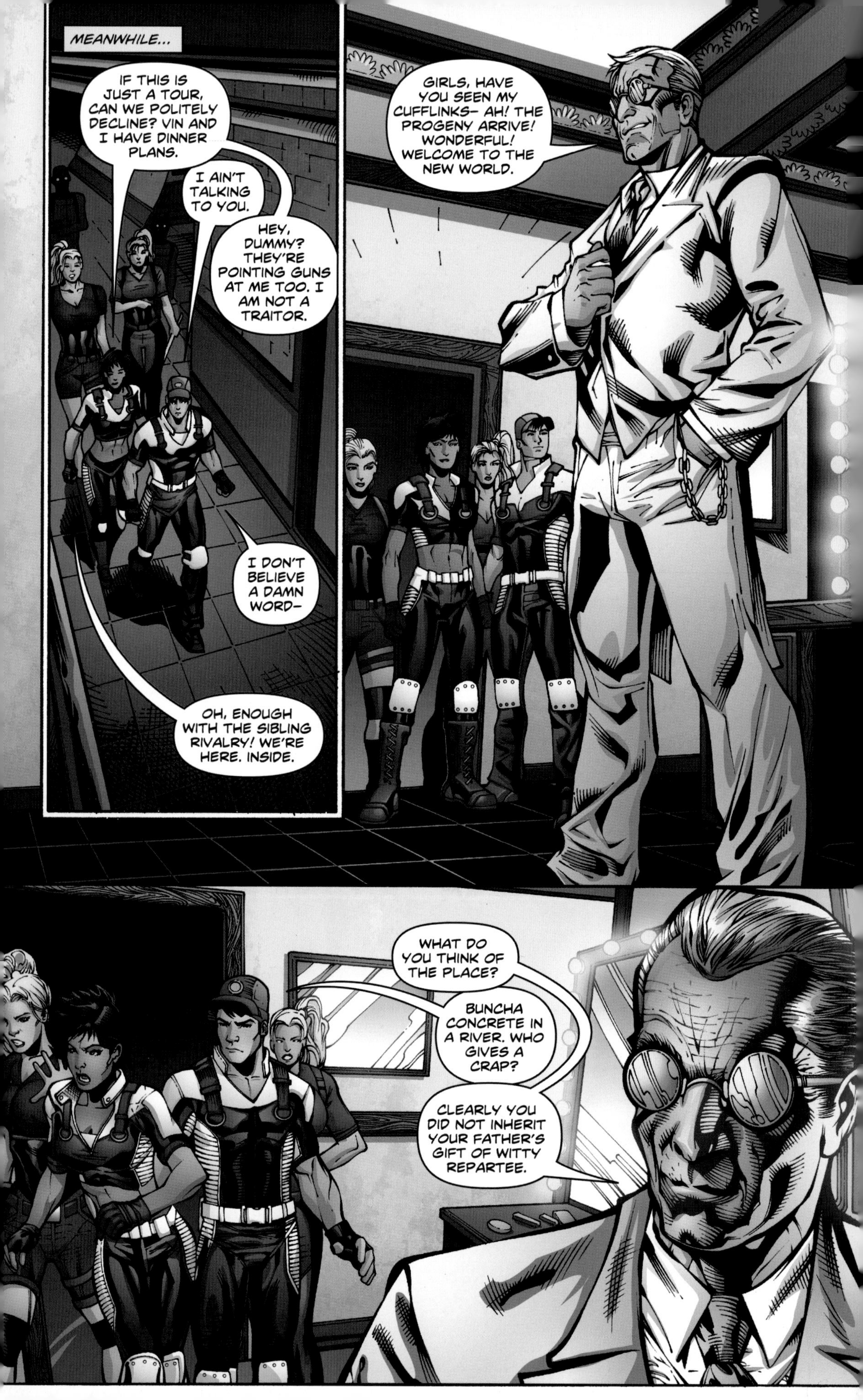
MEANWHILE...
IF THIS IS JUST A TOUR, CAN WE POLITELY DECLINE? VIN AND I HAVE DINNER PLANS.
I AIN'T TALKING TO YOU.
HEY, DUMMY? THEY'RE POINTING GUNS AT ME TOO. I AM NOT A TRAITOR.
I DON'T BELIEVE A DAMN WORD–
OH, ENOUGH WITH THE SIBLING RIVALRY! WE'RE HERE. INSIDE.
GIRLS, HAVE YOU SEEN MY CUFFLINKS– AH! THE PROGENY ARRIVE! WONDERFUL! WELCOME TO THE NEW WORLD.
WHAT DO YOU THINK OF THE PLACE?
BUNCHA CONCRETE IN A RIVER. WHO GIVES A CRAP?
CLEARLY YOU DID NOT INHERIT YOUR FATHER'S GIFT OF WITTY REPARTEE.

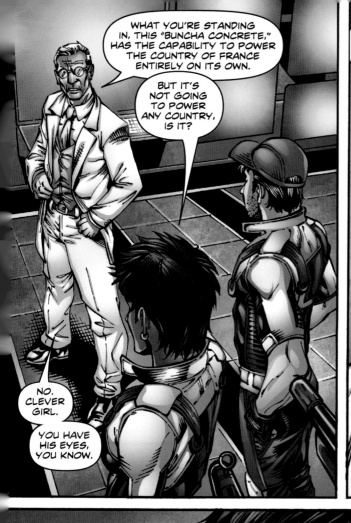

WHAT YOU'RE STANDING IN, THIS "BUNCHA CONCRETE," HAS THE CAPABILITY TO POWER THE COUNTRY OF FRANCE ENTIRELY ON ITS OWN.

BUT IT'S NOT GOING TO POWER ANY COUNTRY, IS IT?

NO. CLEVER GIRL.

YOU HAVE HIS EYES, YOU KNOW.

WHAT FEW PEOPLE OUTSIDE OF THIS ROOM REALIZE IS THAT I HAVE CONSTRUCTED THIS DAM TO POWER MY NEW GLOBAL NETWORK. WHAT I'M CALLING MY "MINDNET."

THE WORLD IS ALREADY CONNECTED. CELLPHONES, COMPUTERS, SOCIAL MEDIA ALL ALLOW PEOPLE TO COMMUNICATE FROM ANYWHERE TO ANYWHERE ON EARTH. I'M JUST TAKING IT TO THE NEXT LEVEL.

TAKING CONTROL OF EVERY MIND ON THE PLANET IS NOT THE NEXT LEVEL. IT'S EVIL.

EVIL IS SUCH AN ARCHAIC CONCEPT. THIS IS SIMPLY TECHNOLOGICAL DARWINISM, CHILD.

GIRLS, KEEP THEM HERE UNTIL AFTER THE LAUNCH. I HAVE SPECIAL PLANS FOR THEM. JACK STEELE'S CHILDREN WORSHIPPING ME IS MY OWN HAPPY ENDING.

NOW, PLEASE EXCUSE ME. I'M GOING TO MAKE THE LEADERS OF THE WORLD KILL EACH OTHER.

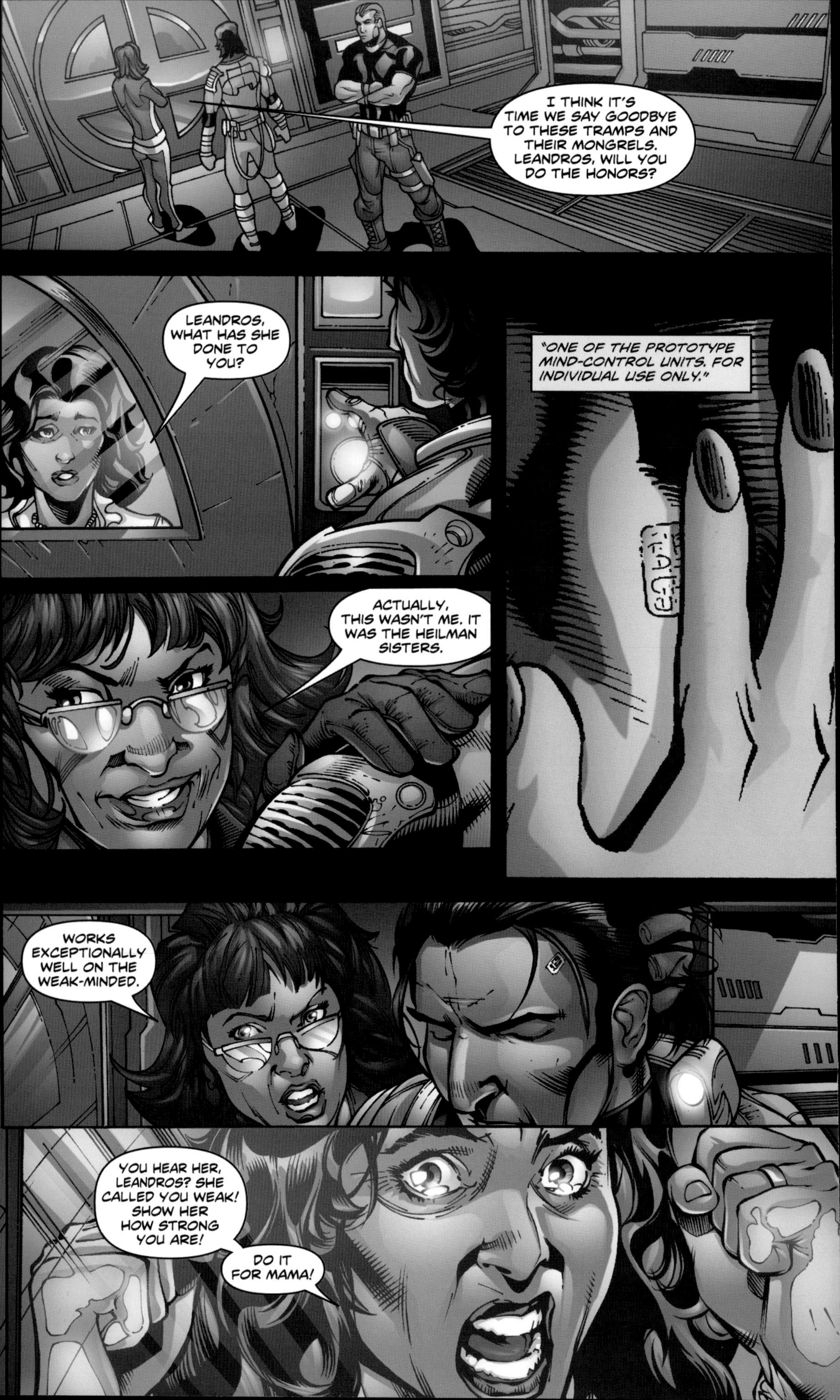

I THINK IT'S TIME WE SAY GOODBYE TO THESE TRAMPS AND THEIR MONGRELS. LEANDROS, WILL YOU DO THE HONORS?
LEANDROS, WHAT HAS SHE DONE TO YOU?
ACTUALLY, THIS WASN'T ME. IT WAS THE HEILMAN SISTERS.
"ONE OF THE PROTOTYPE MIND-CONTROL UNITS. FOR INDIVIDUAL USE ONLY."
WORKS EXCEPTIONALLY WELL ON THE WEAK-MINDED.
YOU HEAR HER, LEANDROS? SHE CALLED YOU WEAK! SHOW HER HOW STRONG YOU ARE!
DO IT FOR MAMA!

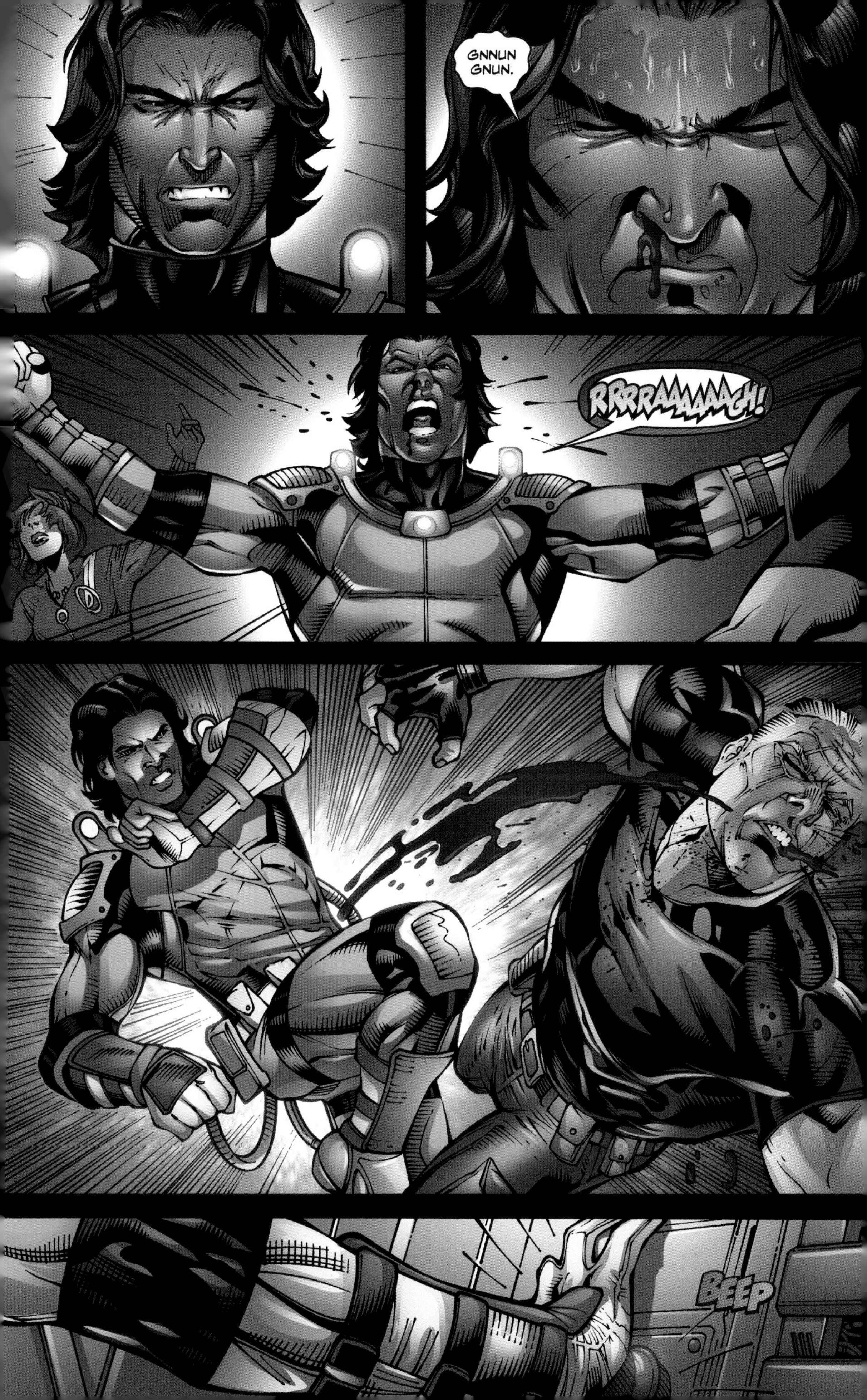
GNNUN GNUN.
RRRRAAAAAAGH!
BEEP

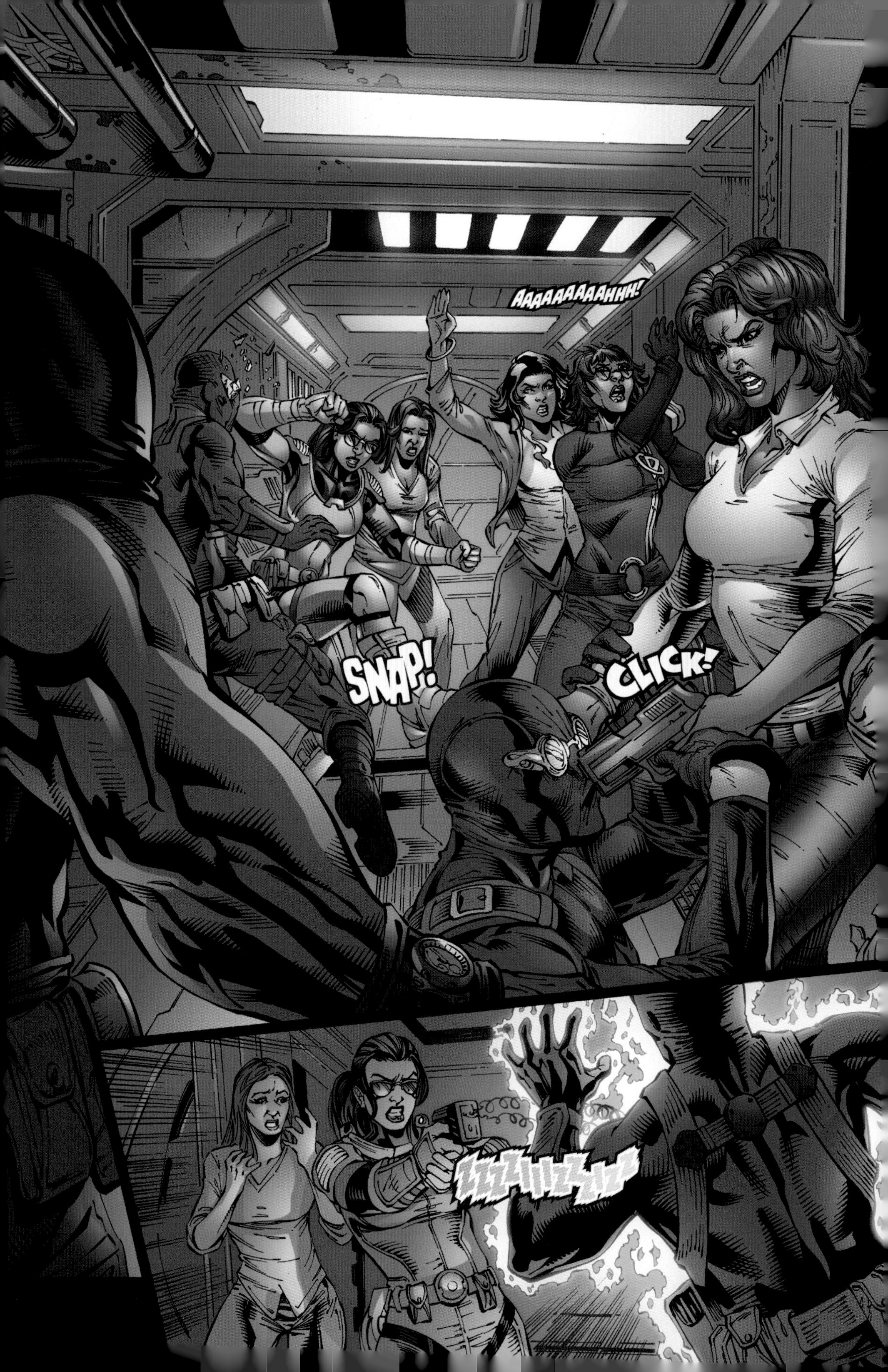
AAAAAAAAAHHH!
SNAP!
CLICK!
ZZZZIIIZZZZZZ

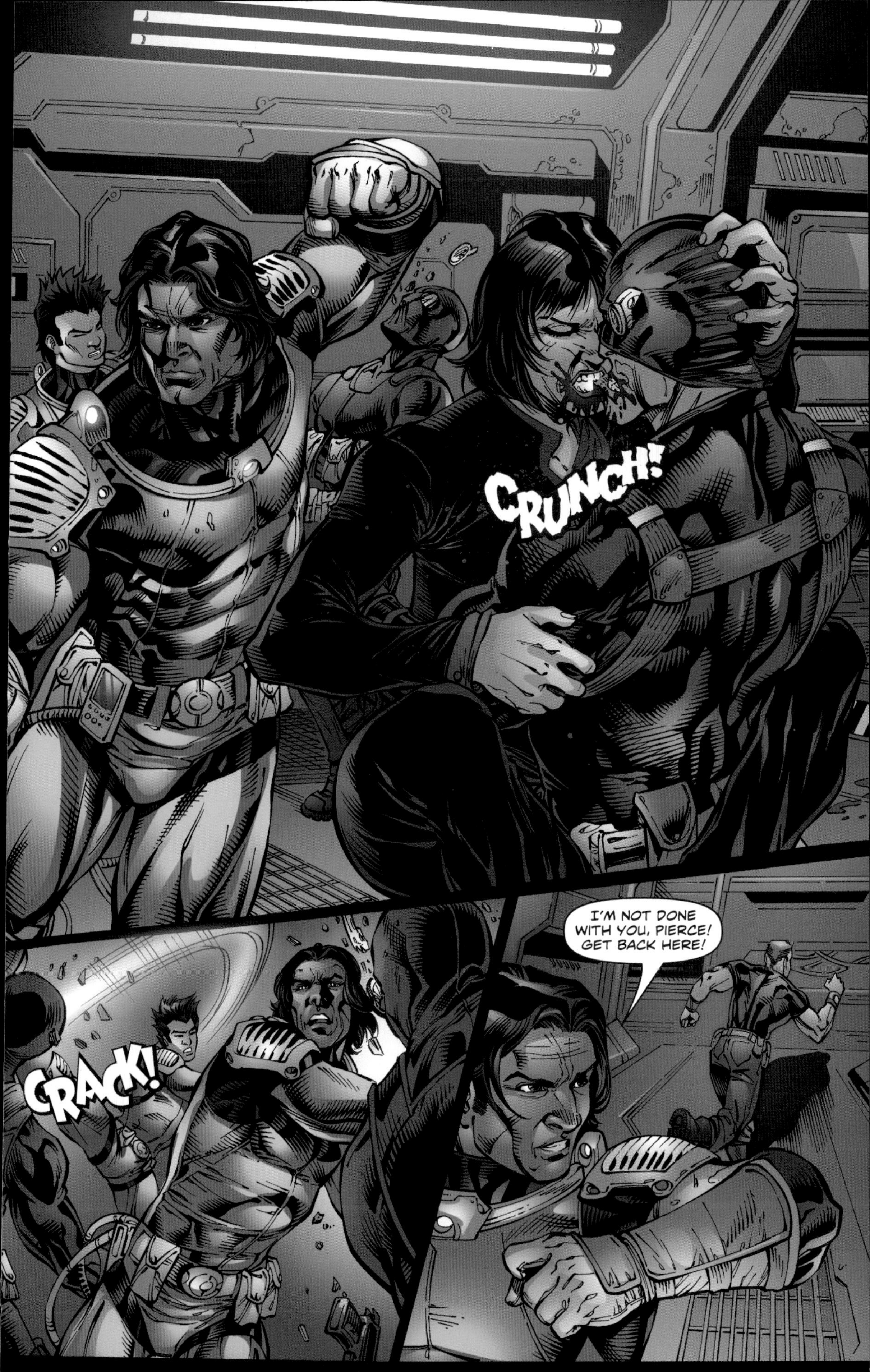
CRUNCH!
CRACK!
I'M NOT DONE WITH YOU, PIERCE! GET BACK HERE!

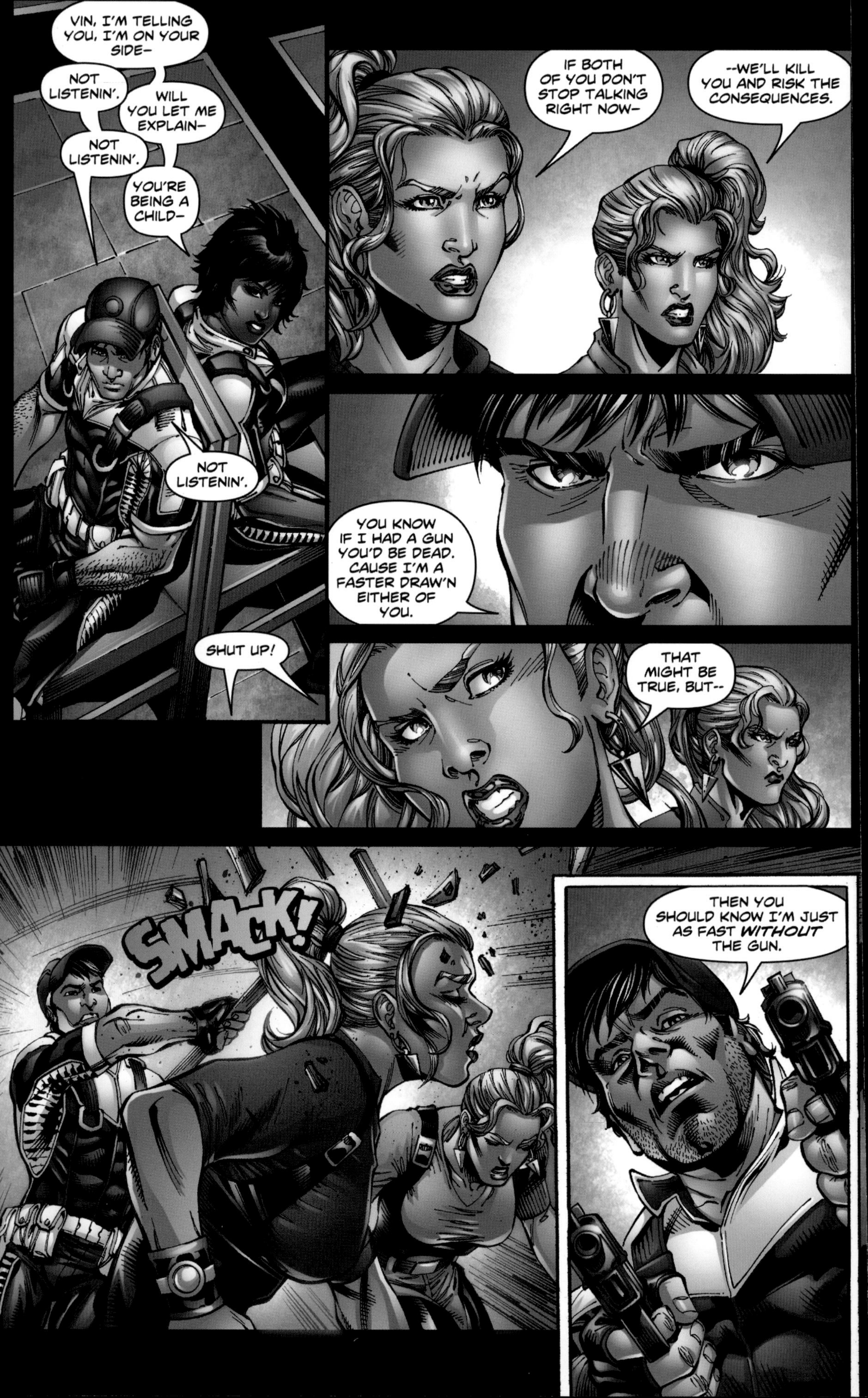
VIN, I'M TELLING YOU, I'M ON YOUR SIDE–
NOT LISTENIN'.
WILL YOU LET ME EXPLAIN–
NOT LISTENIN'.
YOU'RE BEING A CHILD–
NOT LISTENIN'.
IF BOTH OF YOU DON'T STOP TALKING RIGHT NOW–
--WE'LL KILL YOU AND RISK THE CONSEQUENCES.
YOU KNOW IF I HAD A GUN YOU'D BE DEAD. CAUSE I'M A FASTER DRAW'N EITHER OF YOU.
SHUT UP!
THAT MIGHT BE TRUE, BUT--
SMACK!
THEN YOU SHOULD KNOW I'M JUST AS FAST *WITHOUT* THE GUN.

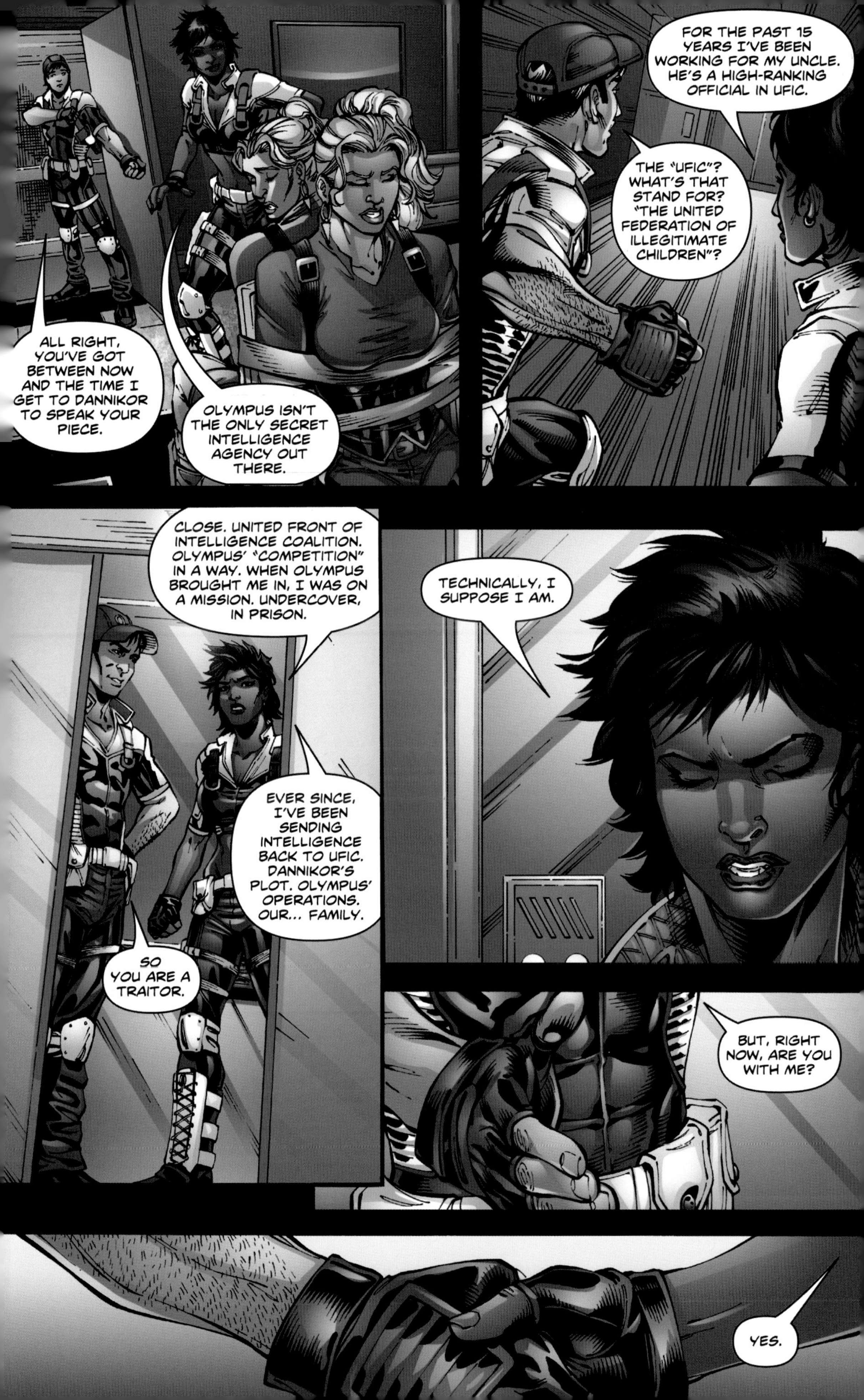
ALL RIGHT, YOU'VE GOT BETWEEN NOW AND THE TIME I GET TO DANNIKOR TO SPEAK YOUR PIECE.
OLYMPUS ISN'T THE ONLY SECRET INTELLIGENCE AGENCY OUT THERE.
FOR THE PAST 15 YEARS I'VE BEEN WORKING FOR MY UNCLE. HE'S A HIGH-RANKING OFFICIAL IN UFIC.
THE "UFIC"? WHAT'S THAT STAND FOR? "THE UNITED FEDERATION OF ILLEGITIMATE CHILDREN"?
CLOSE. UNITED FRONT OF INTELLIGENCE COALITION. OLYMPUS' "COMPETITION" IN A WAY. WHEN OLYMPUS BROUGHT ME IN, I WAS ON A MISSION. UNDERCOVER, IN PRISON.
EVER SINCE, I'VE BEEN SENDING INTELLIGENCE BACK TO UFIC. DANNIKOR'S PLOT. OLYMPUS' OPERATIONS. OUR... FAMILY.
SO YOU ARE A TRAITOR.
TECHNICALLY, I SUPPOSE I AM.
BUT, RIGHT NOW, ARE YOU WITH ME?
YES.

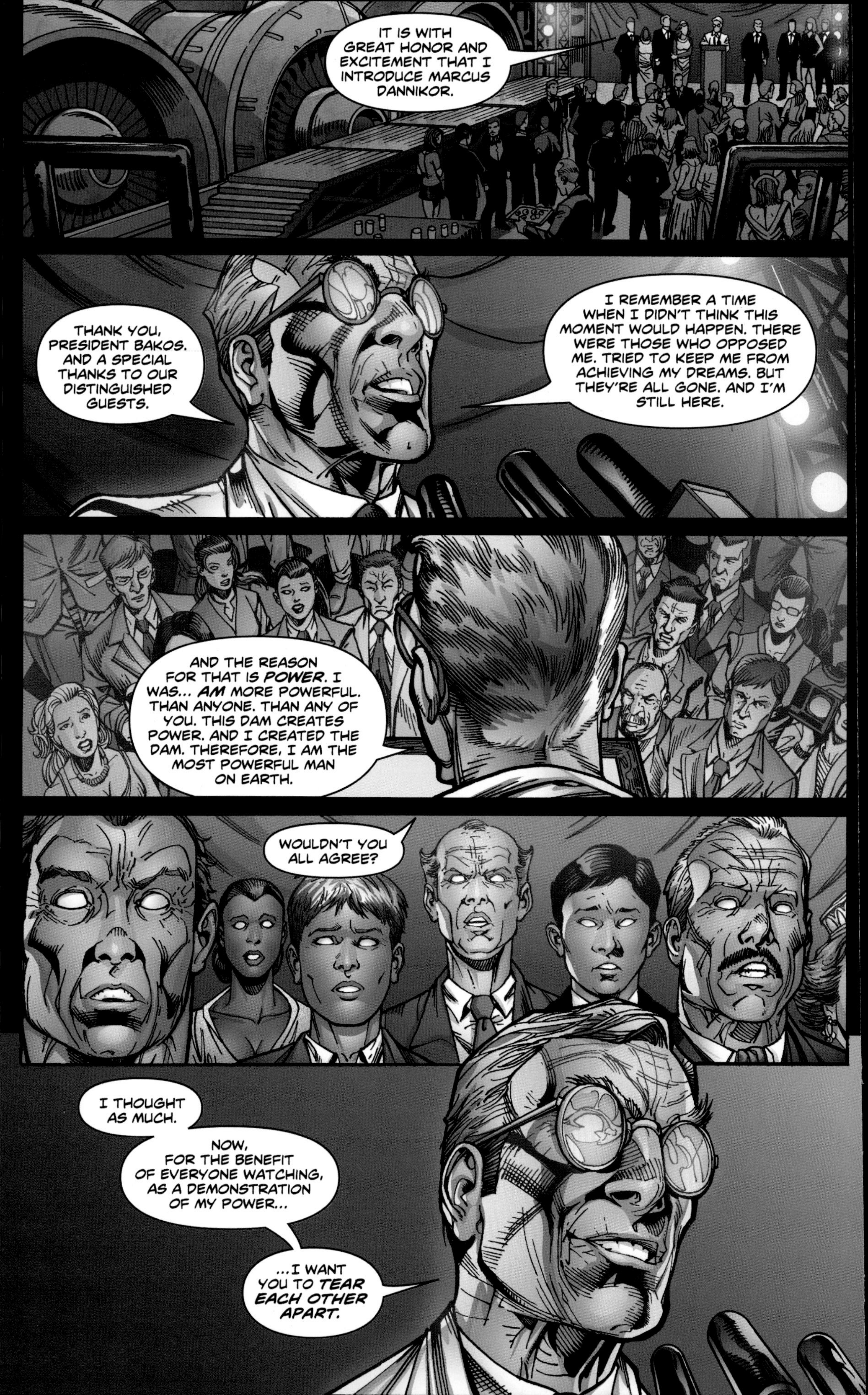
IT IS WITH GREAT HONOR AND EXCITEMENT THAT I INTRODUCE MARCUS DANNIKOR.
THANK YOU, PRESIDENT BAKOS. AND A SPECIAL THANKS TO OUR DISTINGUISHED GUESTS.
I REMEMBER A TIME WHEN I DIDN'T THINK THIS MOMENT WOULD HAPPEN. THERE WERE THOSE WHO OPPOSED ME. TRIED TO KEEP ME FROM ACHIEVING MY DREAMS. BUT THEY'RE ALL GONE. AND I'M STILL HERE.
AND THE REASON FOR THAT IS *POWER*. I WAS... *AM* MORE POWERFUL. THAN ANYONE. THAN ANY OF YOU. THIS DAM CREATES POWER. AND I CREATED THE DAM. THEREFORE, I AM THE MOST POWERFUL MAN ON EARTH.
WOULDN'T YOU ALL AGREE?
I THOUGHT AS MUCH.
NOW, FOR THE BENEFIT OF EVERYONE WATCHING, AS A DEMONSTRATION OF MY POWER...
...I WANT YOU TO *TEAR EACH OTHER APART*.

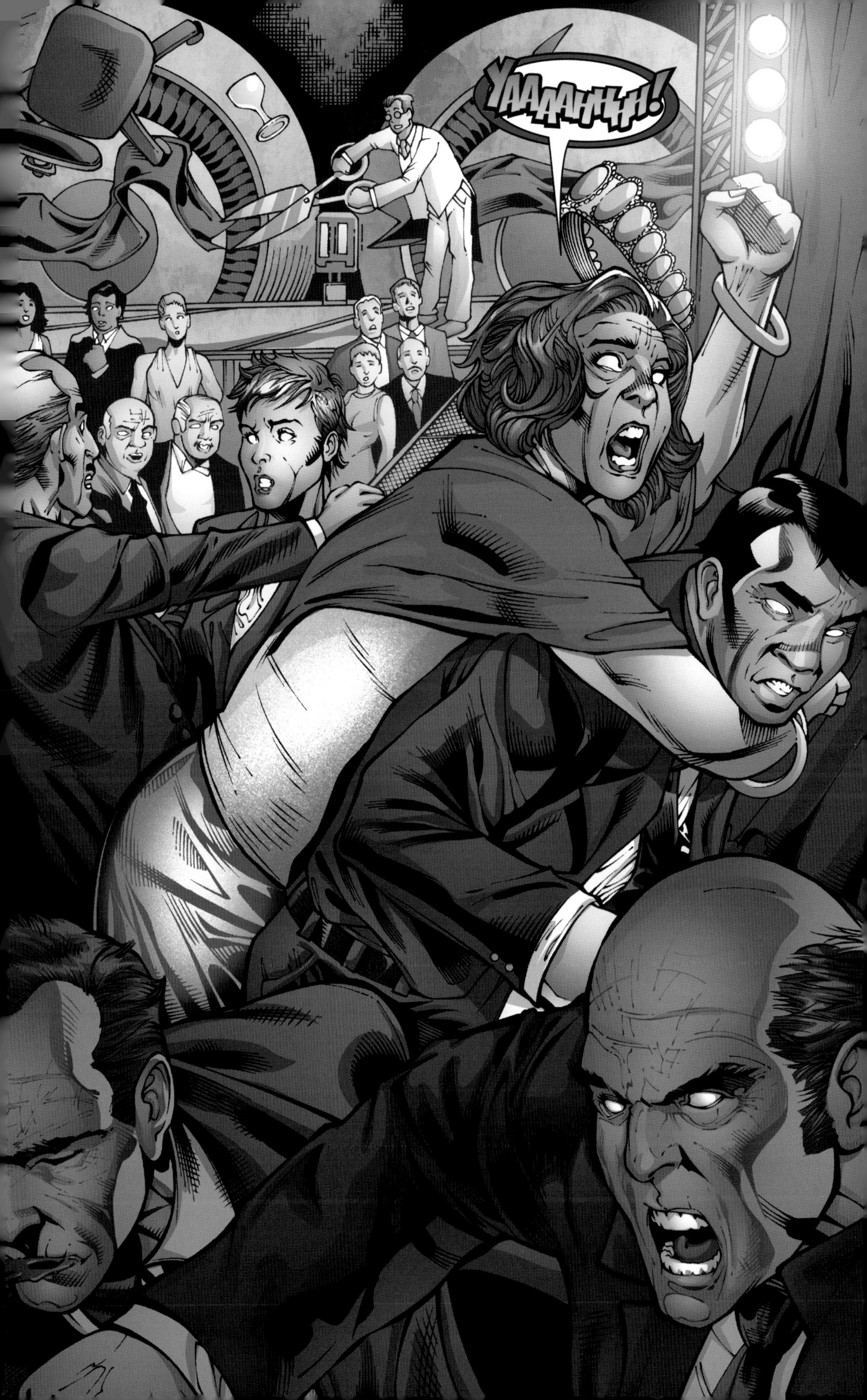
YAAAAHHHH!

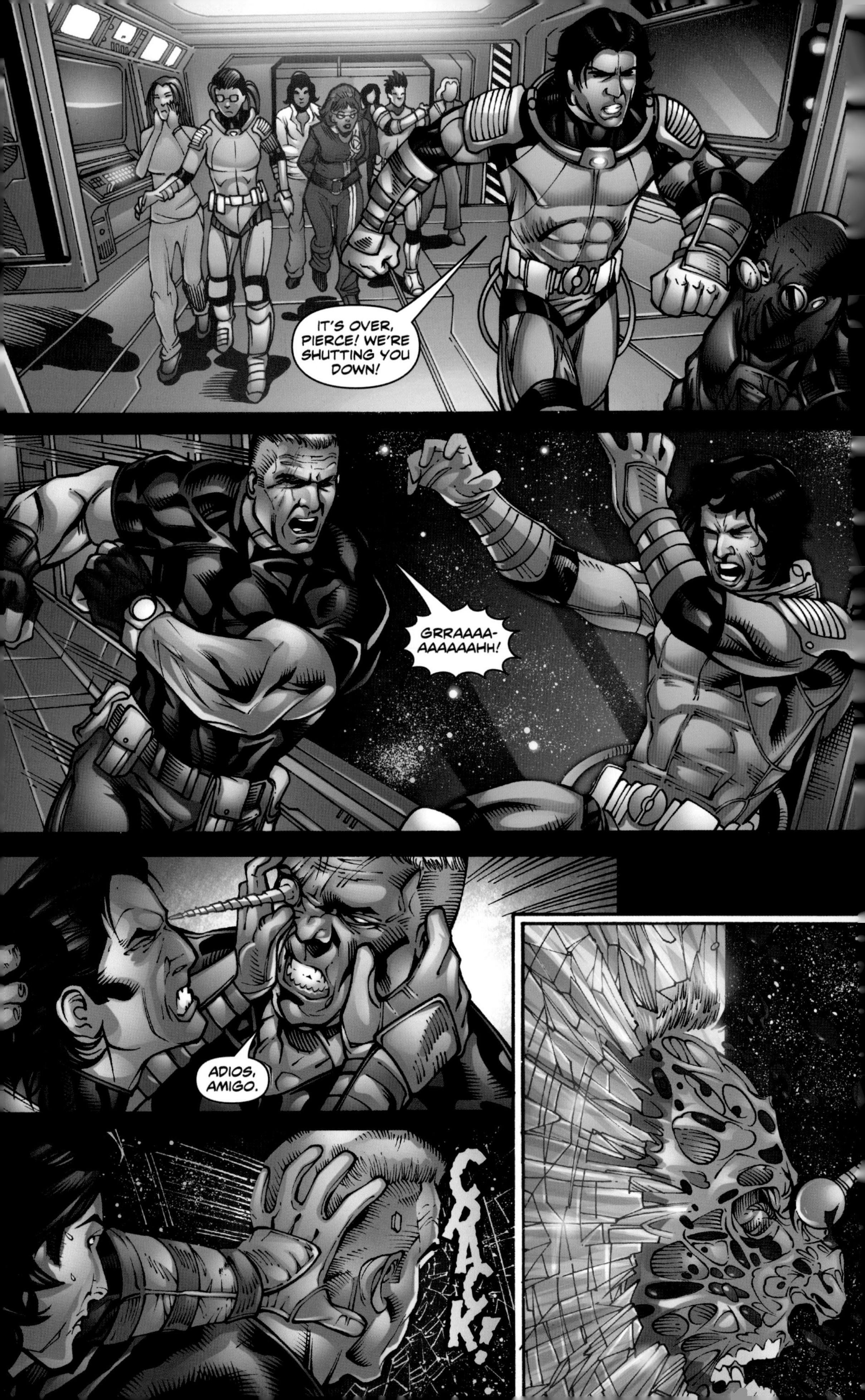
IT'S OVER, PIERCE! WE'RE SHUTTING YOU DOWN!
GRRAAAA-AAAAAAHH!
ADIOS, AMIGO.
CRACK!

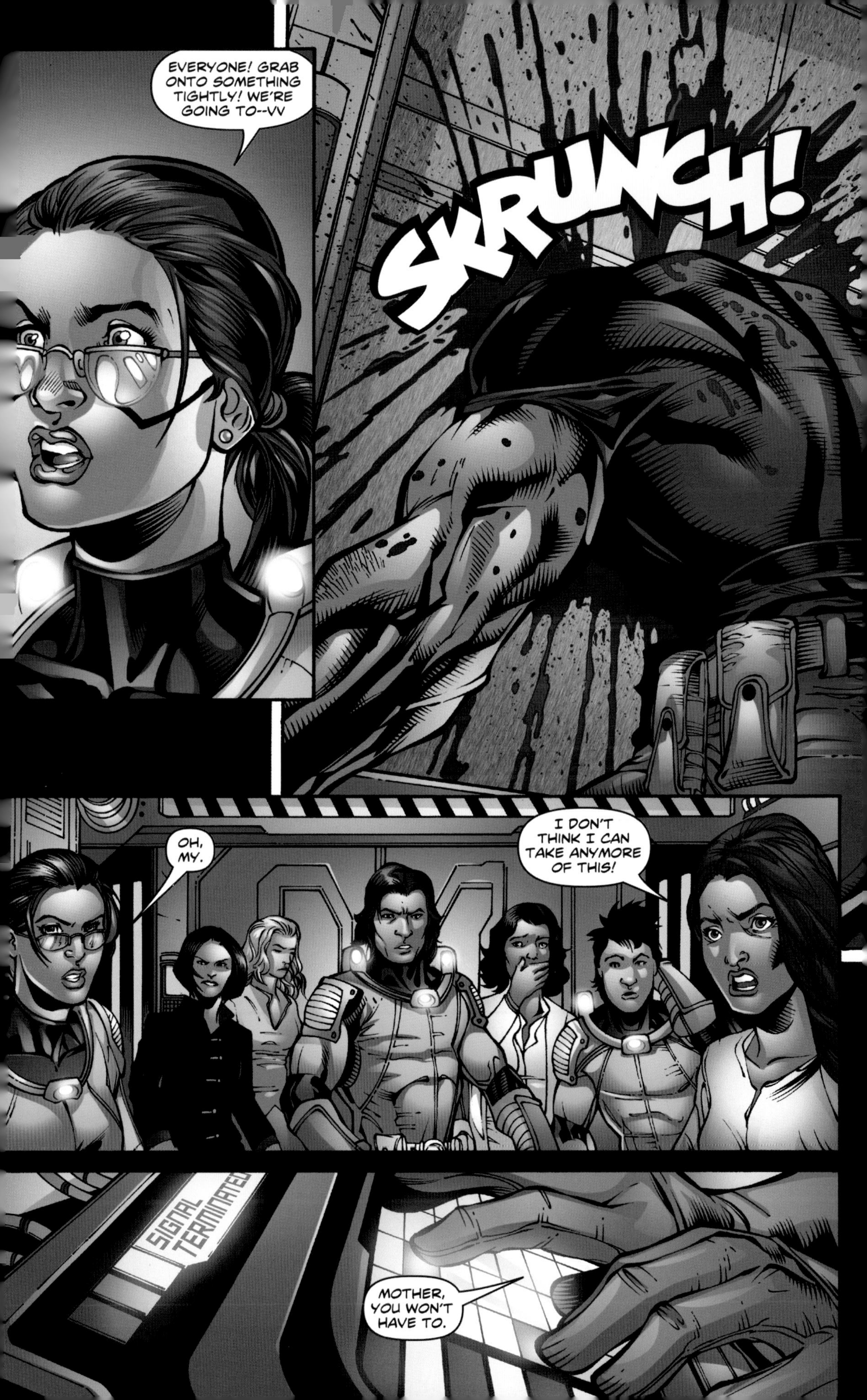
EVERYONE! GRAB ONTO SOMETHING TIGHTLY! WE'RE GOING TO--VV
SKRUNCH!
OH, MY.
I DON'T THINK I CAN TAKE ANYMORE OF THIS!
SIGNAL TERMINATED
MOTHER, YOU WON'T HAVE TO.

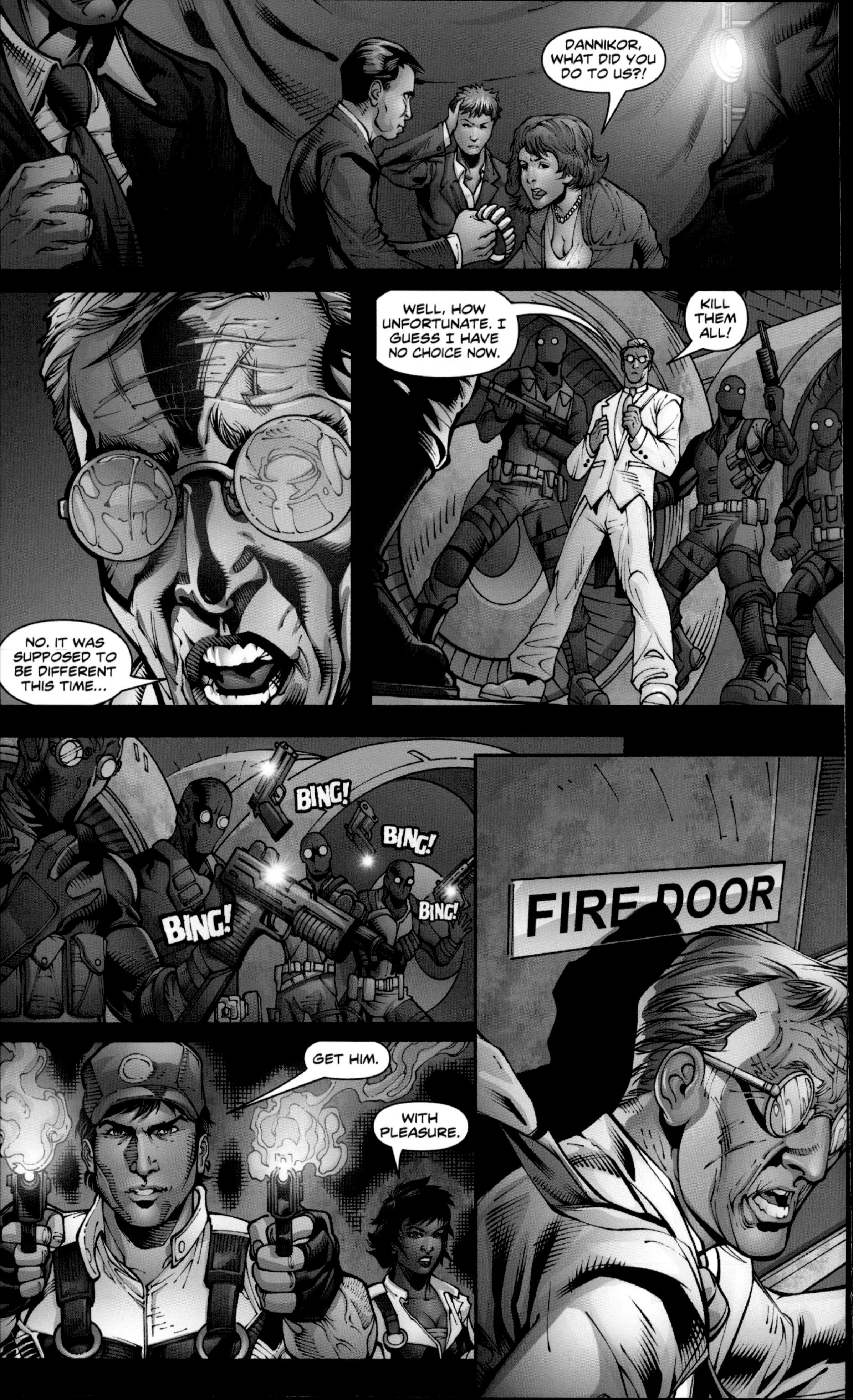
DANNIKOR, WHAT DID YOU DO TO US?!
NO. IT WAS SUPPOSED TO BE DIFFERENT THIS TIME...
WELL, HOW UNFORTUNATE. I GUESS I HAVE NO CHOICE NOW.
KILL THEM ALL!
BING!
BING!
BING!
BING!
FIRE DOOR
GET HIM.
WITH PLEASURE.

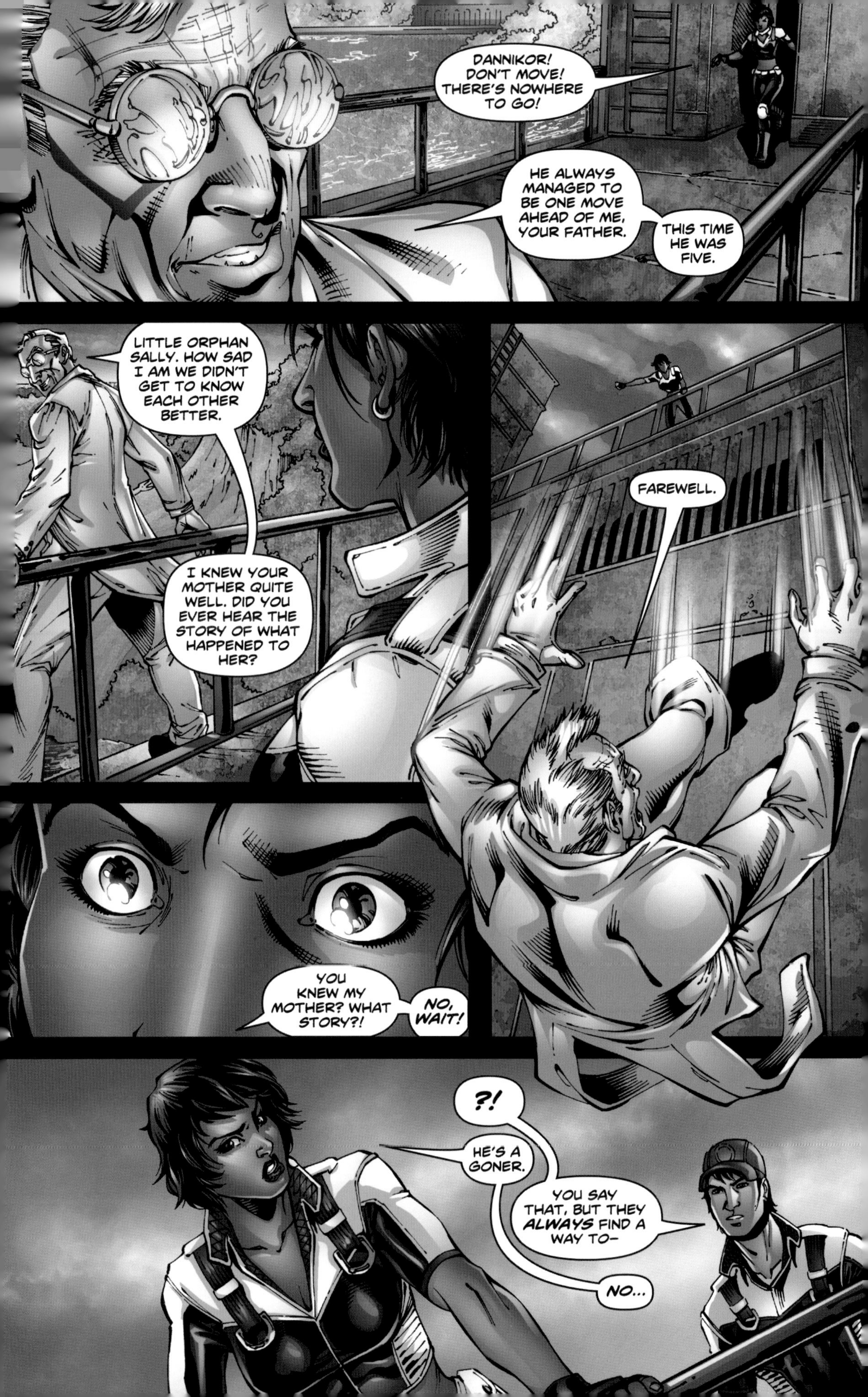
DANNIKOR! DON'T MOVE! THERE'S NOWHERE TO GO!
HE ALWAYS MANAGED TO BE ONE MOVE AHEAD OF ME, YOUR FATHER.
THIS TIME HE WAS FIVE.
LITTLE ORPHAN SALLY. HOW SAD I AM WE DIDN'T GET TO KNOW EACH OTHER BETTER.
I KNEW YOUR MOTHER QUITE WELL. DID YOU EVER HEAR THE STORY OF WHAT HAPPENED TO HER?
FAREWELL.
YOU KNEW MY MOTHER? WHAT STORY?!
NO, WAIT!
?!
HE'S A GONER.
YOU SAY THAT, BUT THEY ALWAYS FIND A WAY TO–
NO...

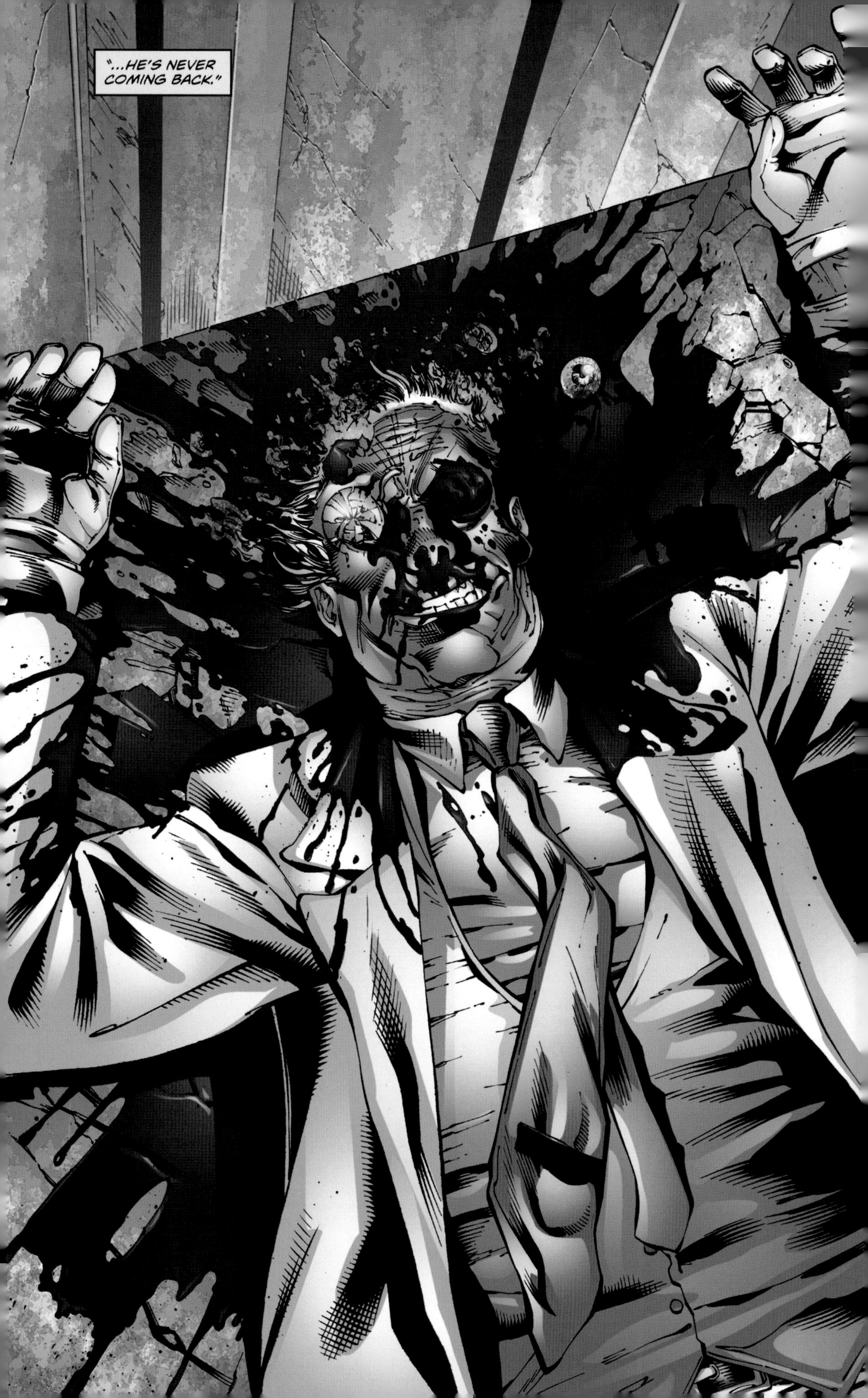
"...HE'S NEVER COMING BACK."

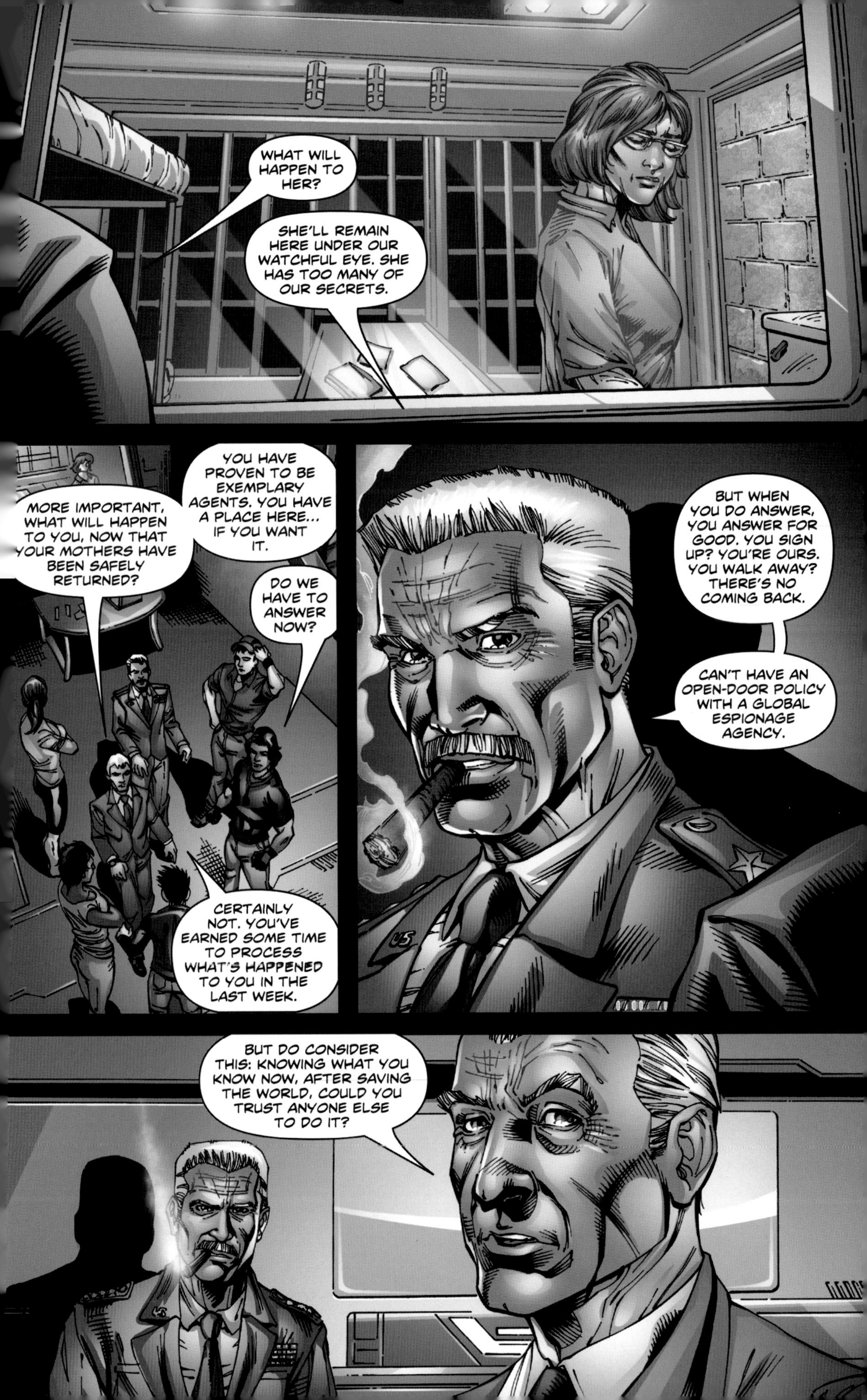
WHAT WILL HAPPEN TO HER?
SHE'LL REMAIN HERE UNDER OUR WATCHFUL EYE. SHE HAS TOO MANY OF OUR SECRETS.
MORE IMPORTANT, WHAT WILL HAPPEN TO YOU, NOW THAT YOUR MOTHERS HAVE BEEN SAFELY RETURNED?
YOU HAVE PROVEN TO BE EXEMPLARY AGENTS. YOU HAVE A PLACE HERE... IF YOU WANT IT.
DO WE HAVE TO ANSWER NOW?
CERTAINLY NOT. YOU'VE EARNED SOME TIME TO PROCESS WHAT'S HAPPENED TO YOU IN THE LAST WEEK.
BUT WHEN YOU DO ANSWER, YOU ANSWER FOR GOOD. YOU SIGN UP? YOU'RE OURS. YOU WALK AWAY? THERE'S NO COMING BACK.
CAN'T HAVE AN OPEN-DOOR POLICY WITH A GLOBAL ESPIONAGE AGENCY.
BUT DO CONSIDER THIS: KNOWING WHAT YOU KNOW NOW, AFTER SAVING THE WORLD, COULD YOU TRUST ANYONE ELSE TO DO IT?

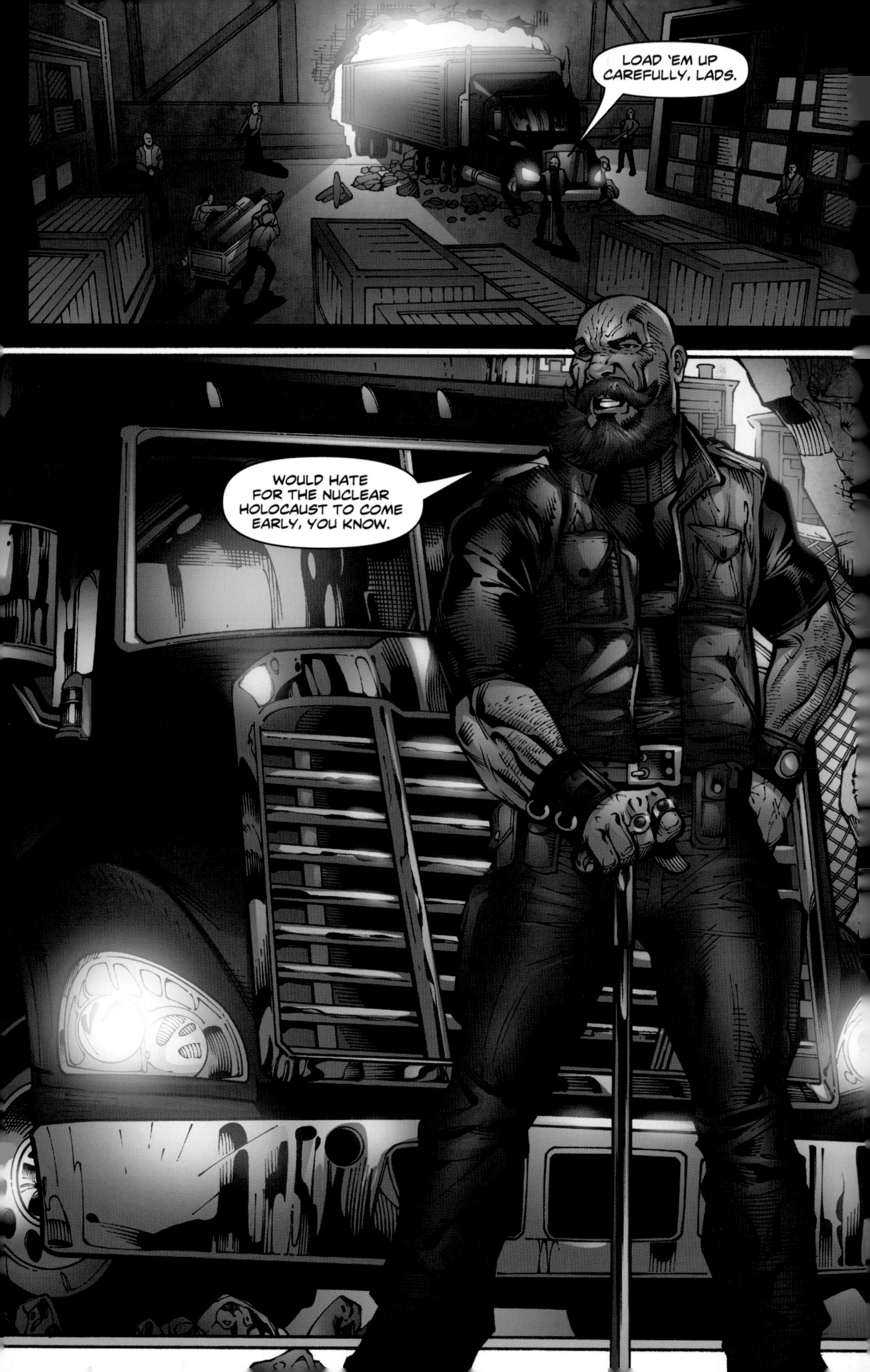
LOAD 'EM UP CAREFULLY, LADS.
WOULD HATE FOR THE NUCLEAR HOLOCAUST TO COME EARLY, YOU KNOW.

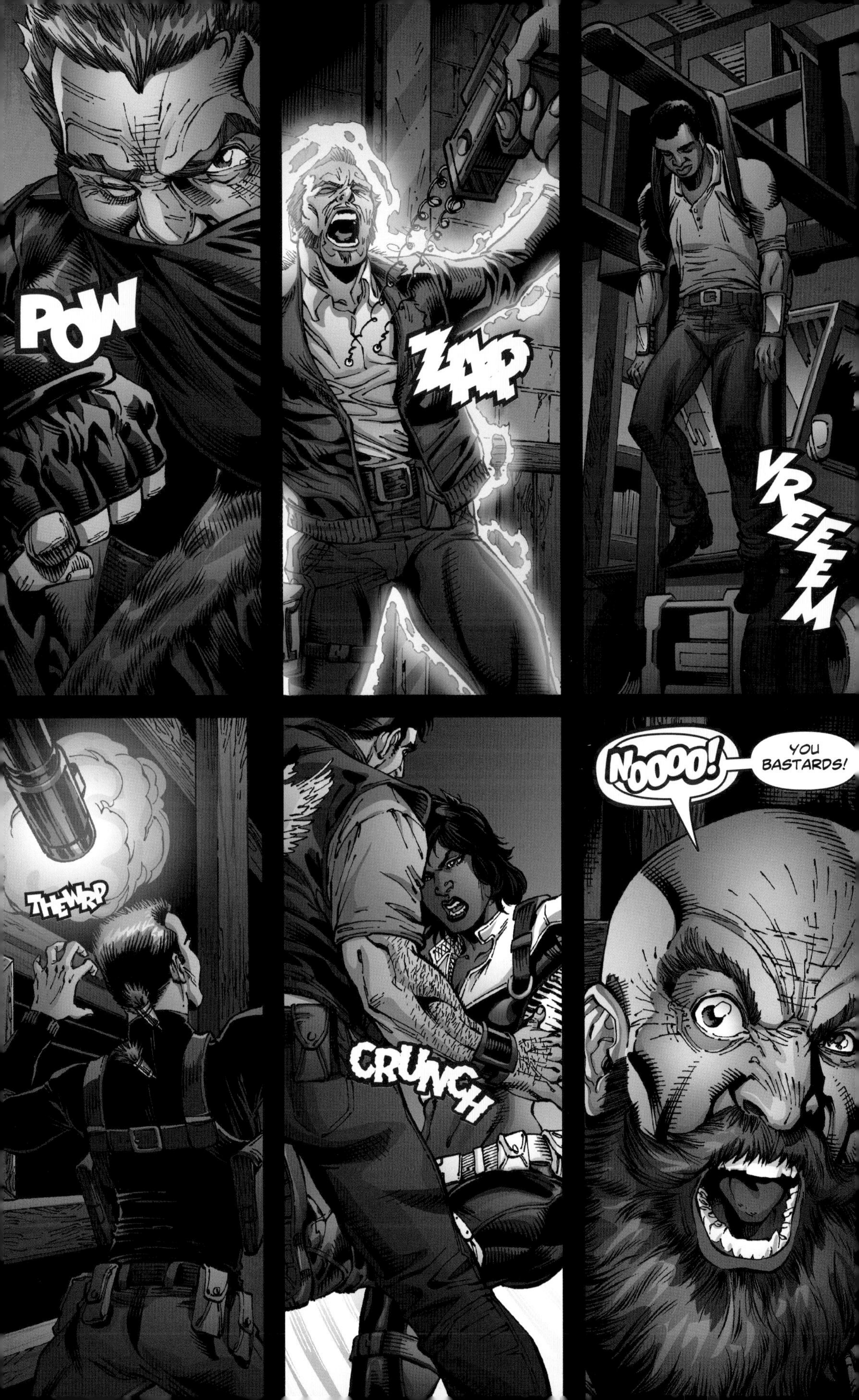
POW
ZAP
VREEEEM
THEWRP
CRUNCH
NOOOO!
YOU BASTARDS!

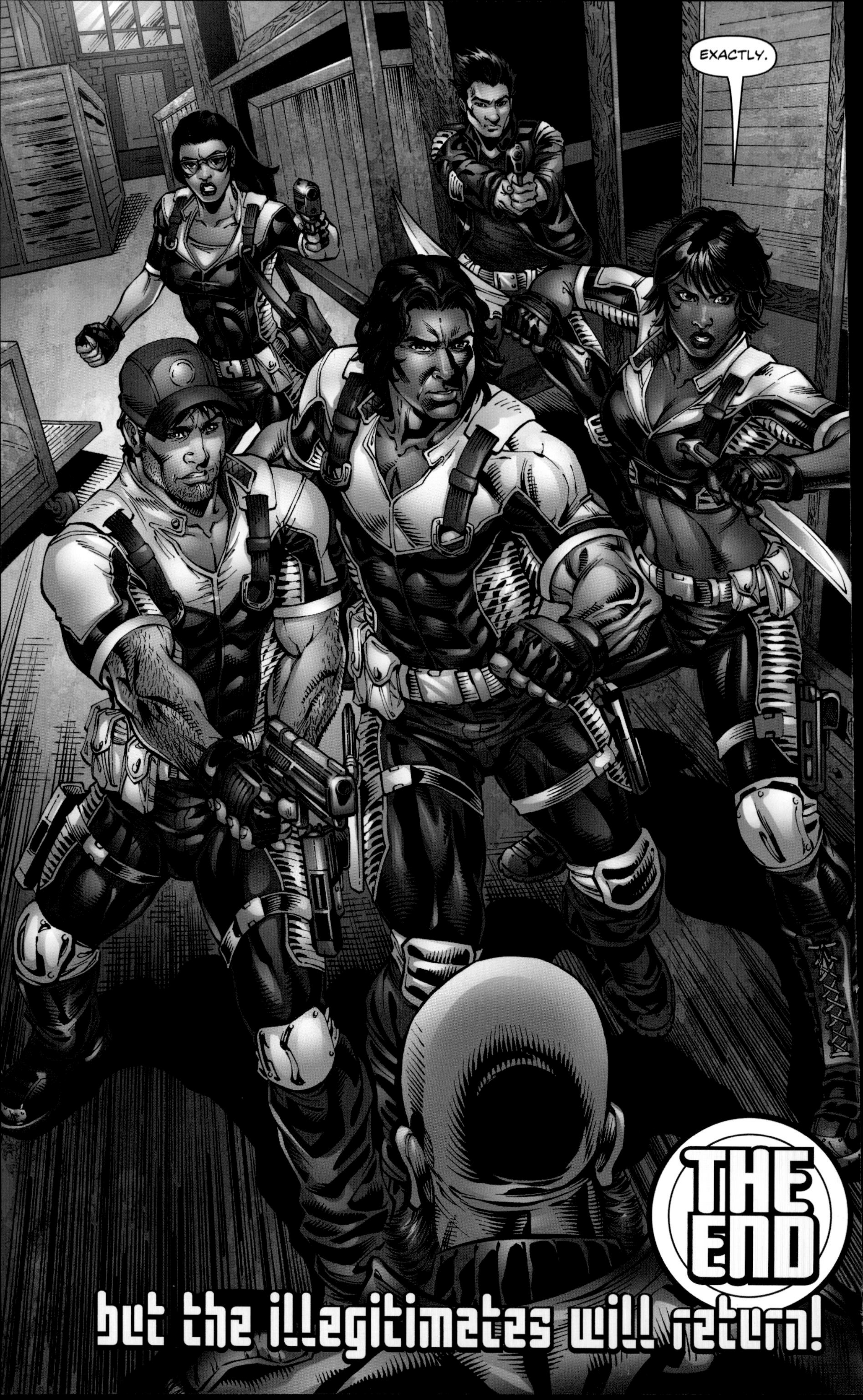
EXACTLY.
THE END
but the illegitimates will return!

ART GALLERY

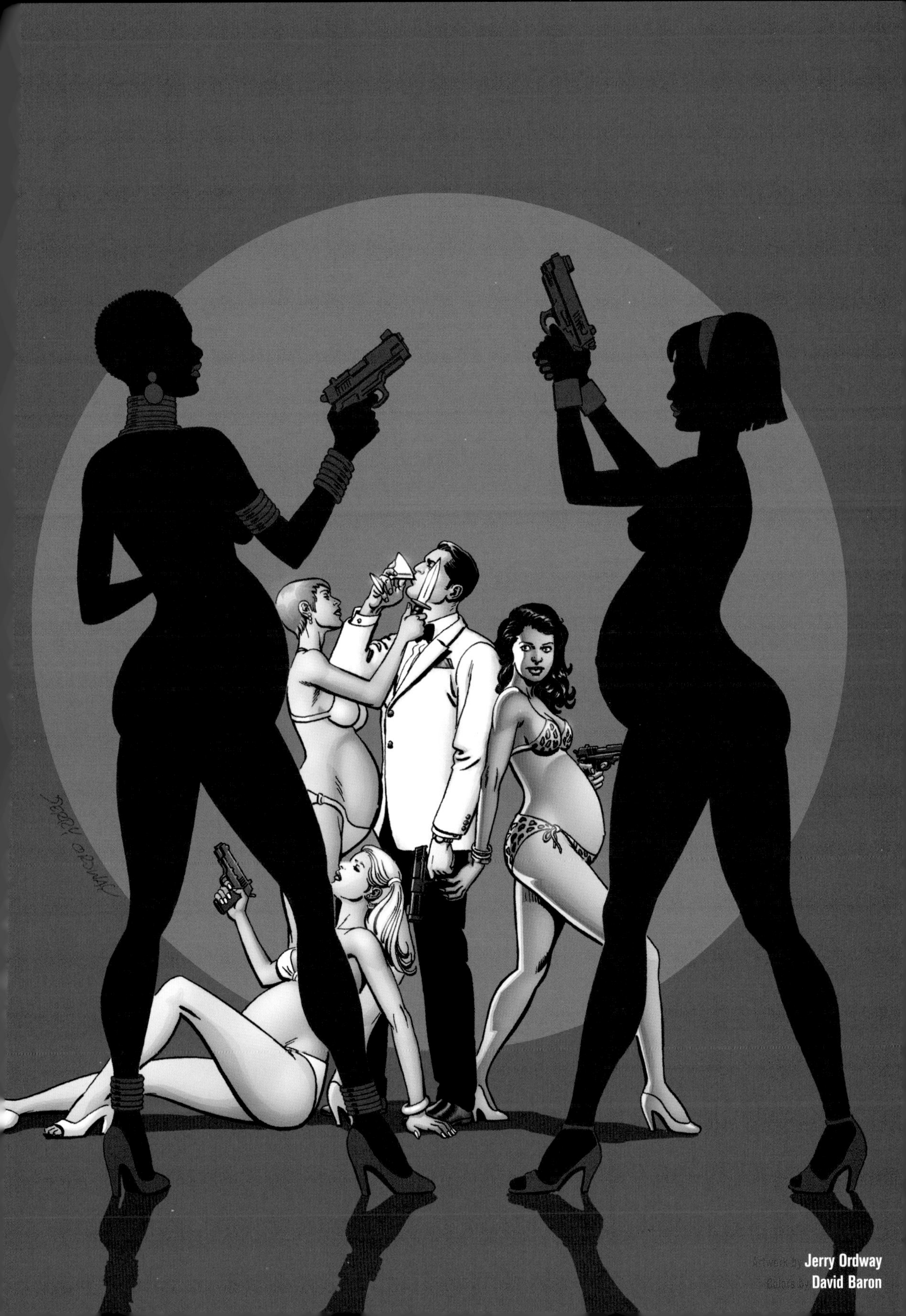

Artwork by Jerry Ordway
Colors by David Baron

Artwork by **Bill Willingham**
Colors by **Len O'Grady**

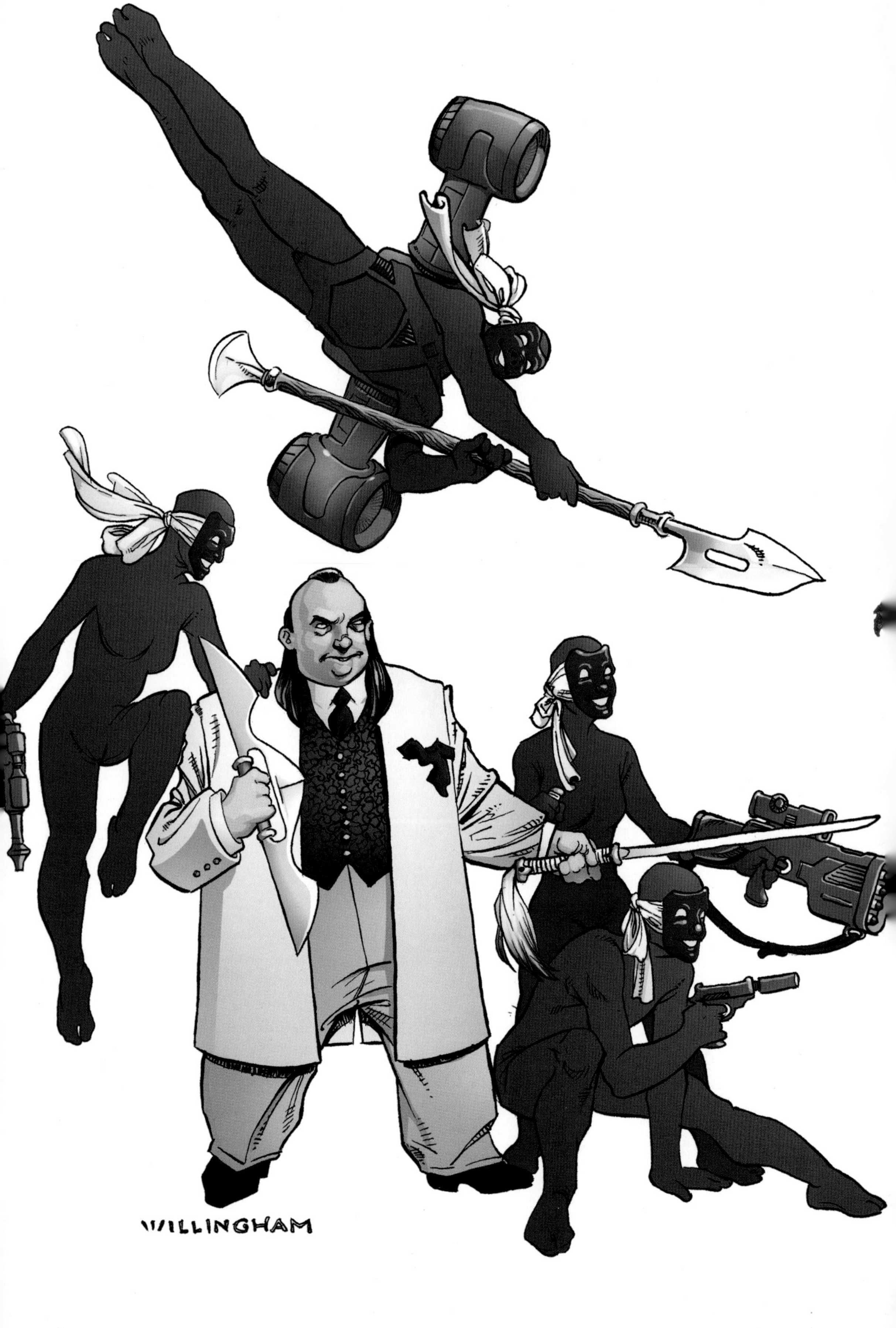
WILLINGHAM

Illegitimates™ ©

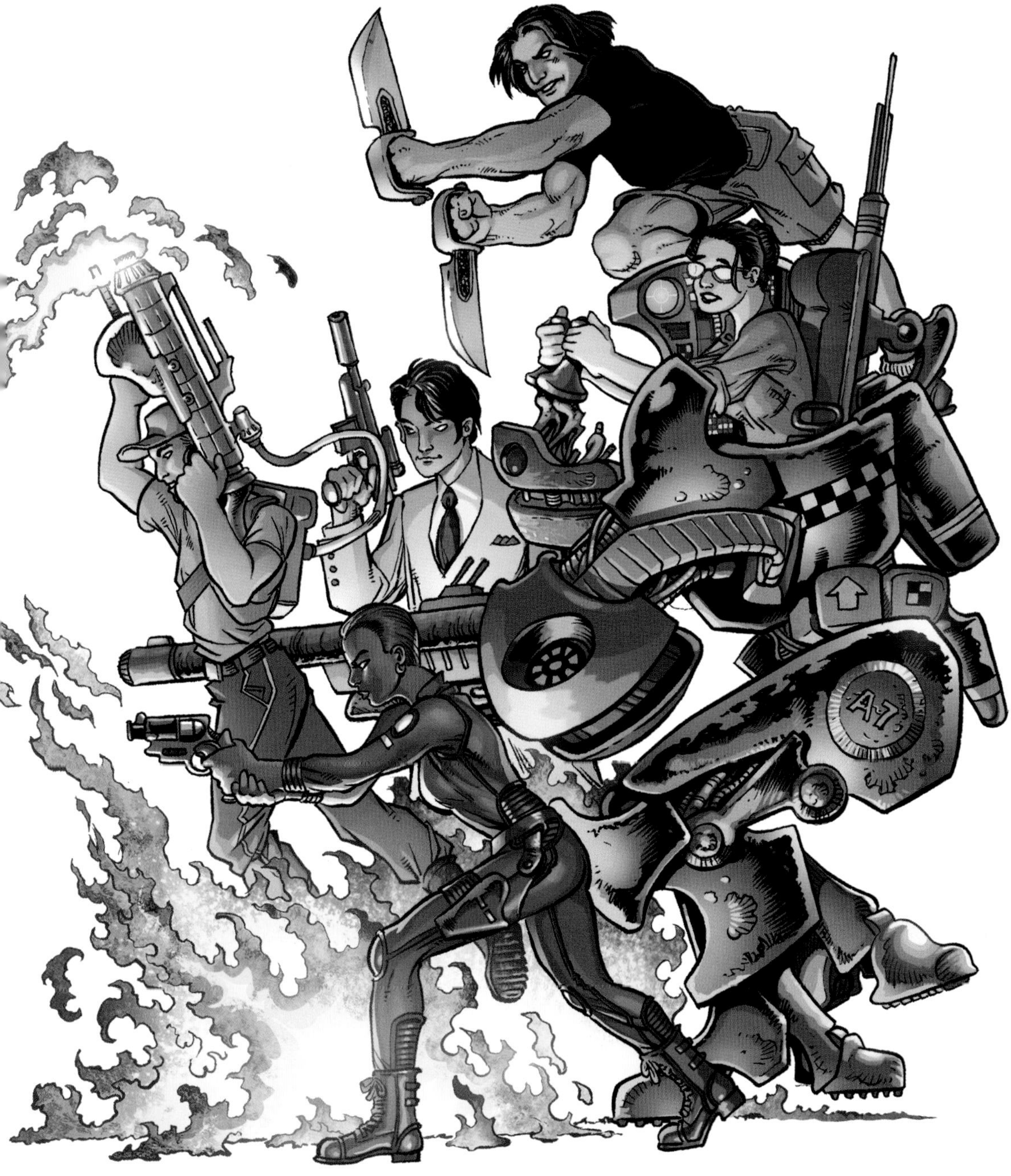
A-7

KILLAM • ANDREYKO • SHARPE

Artwork by **Paul Shipper**

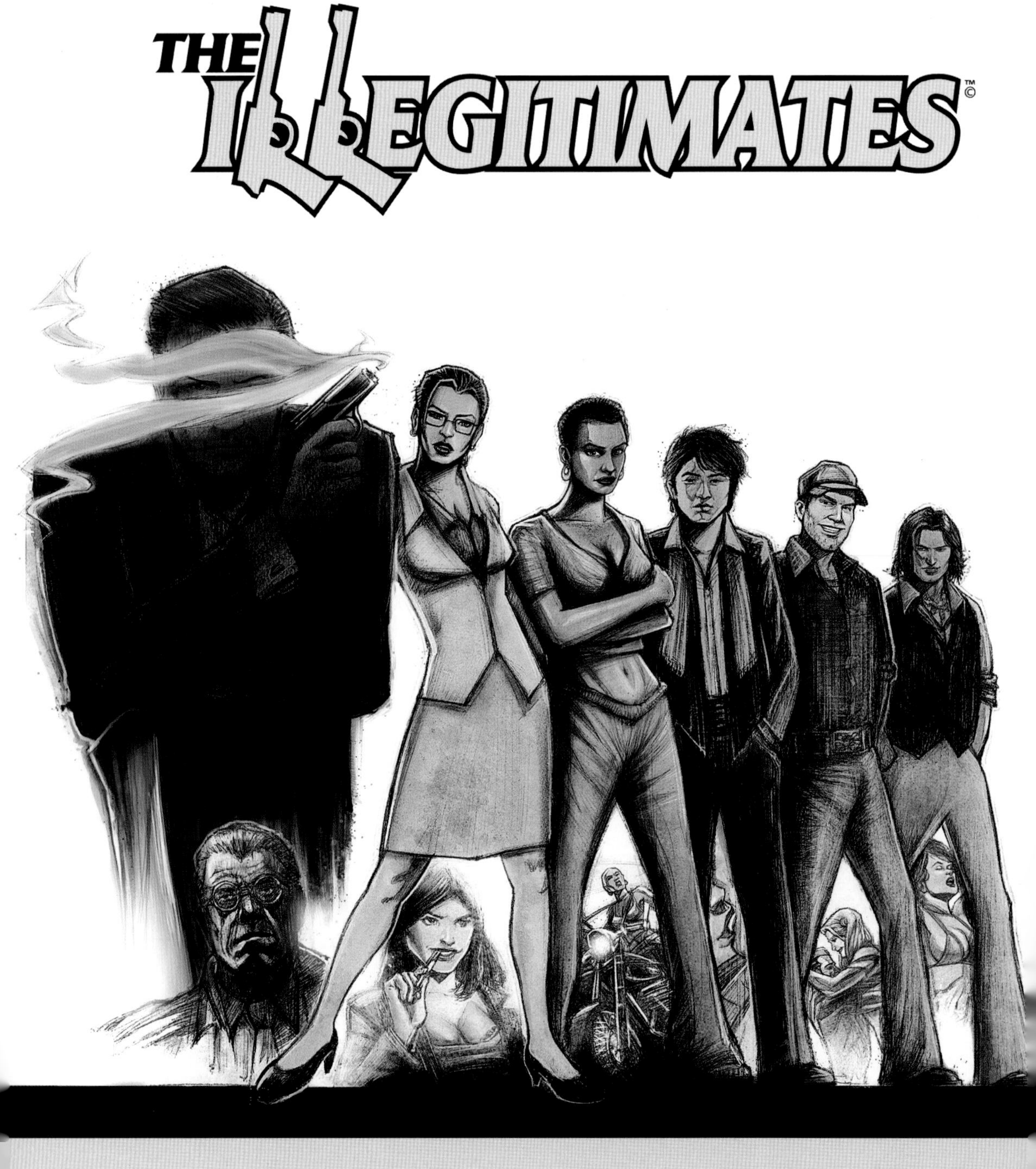
THE ILLEGITIMATES™ ©

Artwork by **Jerry Ordway**

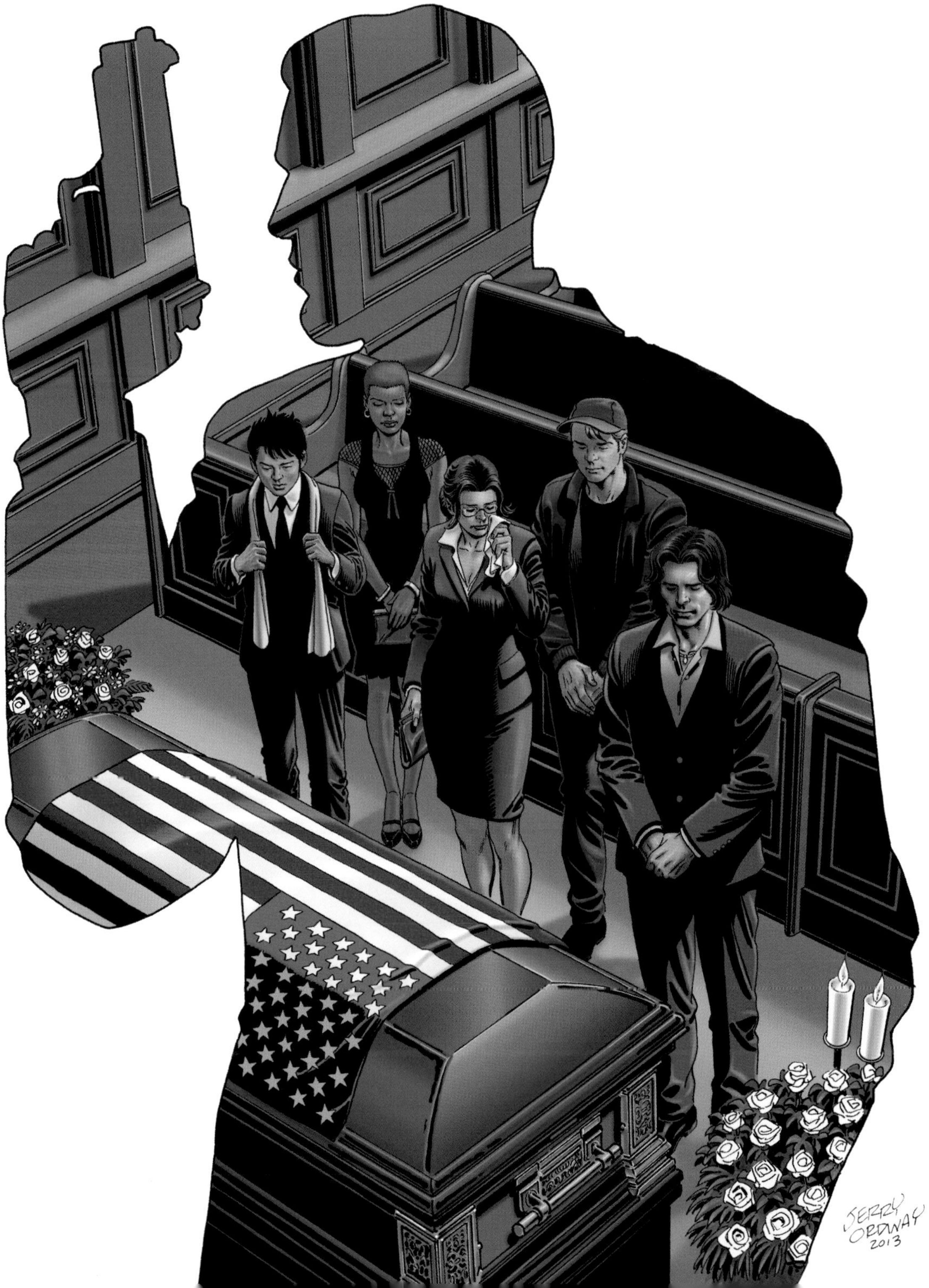
JERRY ORDWAY 2013

Artwork by Kevin Sharpe
Colors by Peter Pantazis

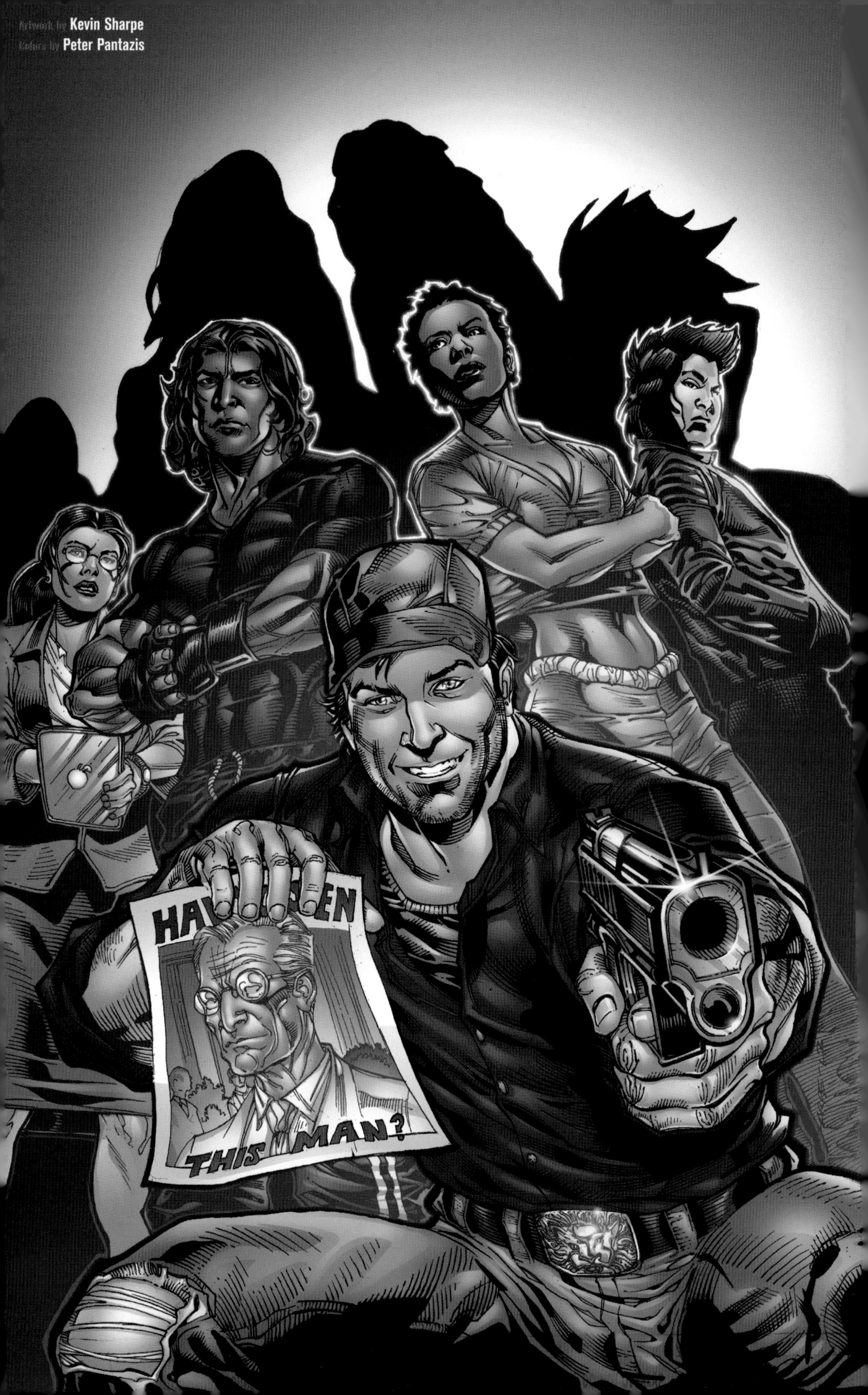
THIS MAN?

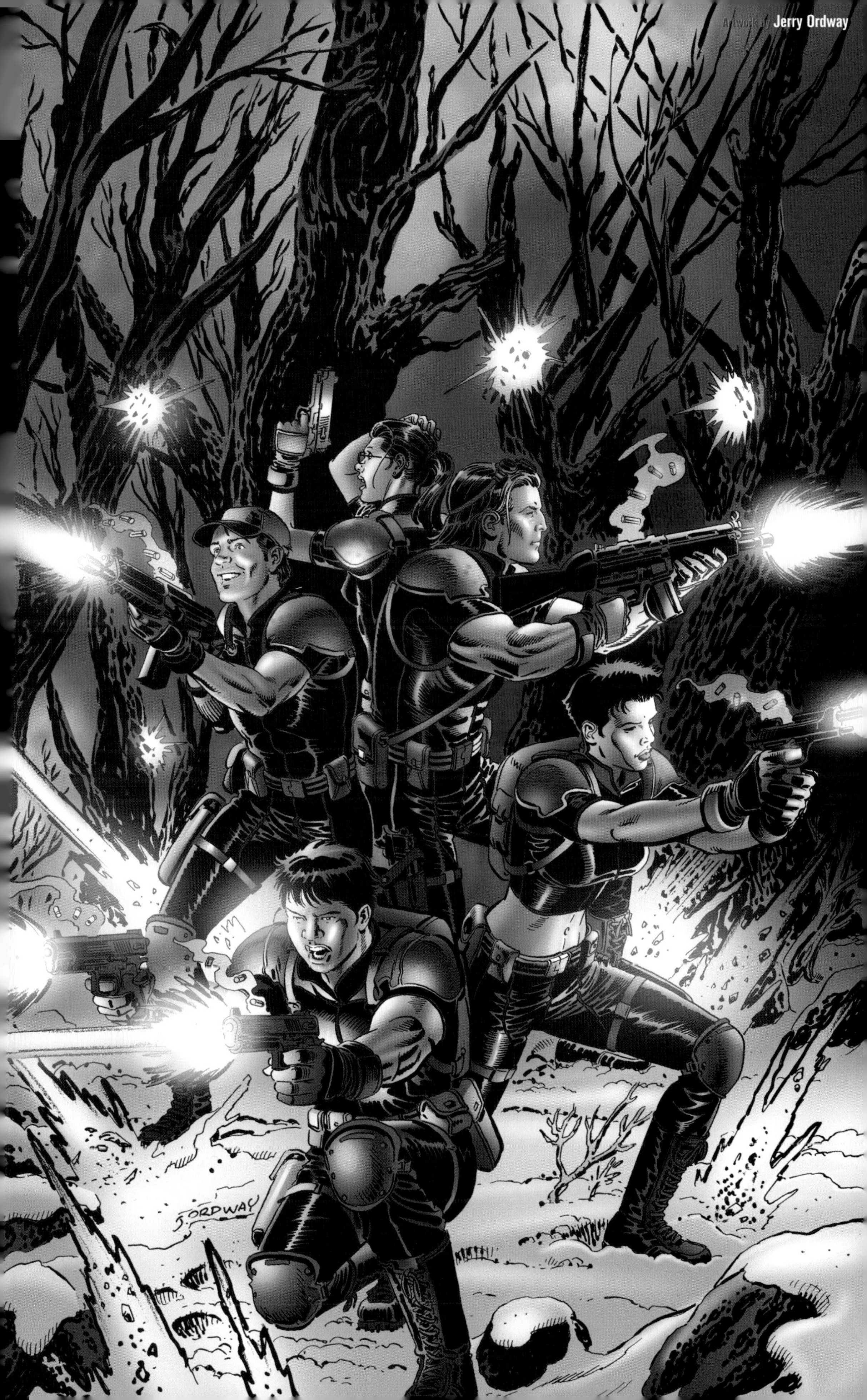
J. ORDWAY

Artwork by **Jerry Ordway**

Artwork by Kevin Sharpe
Colors by Zac Atkinson

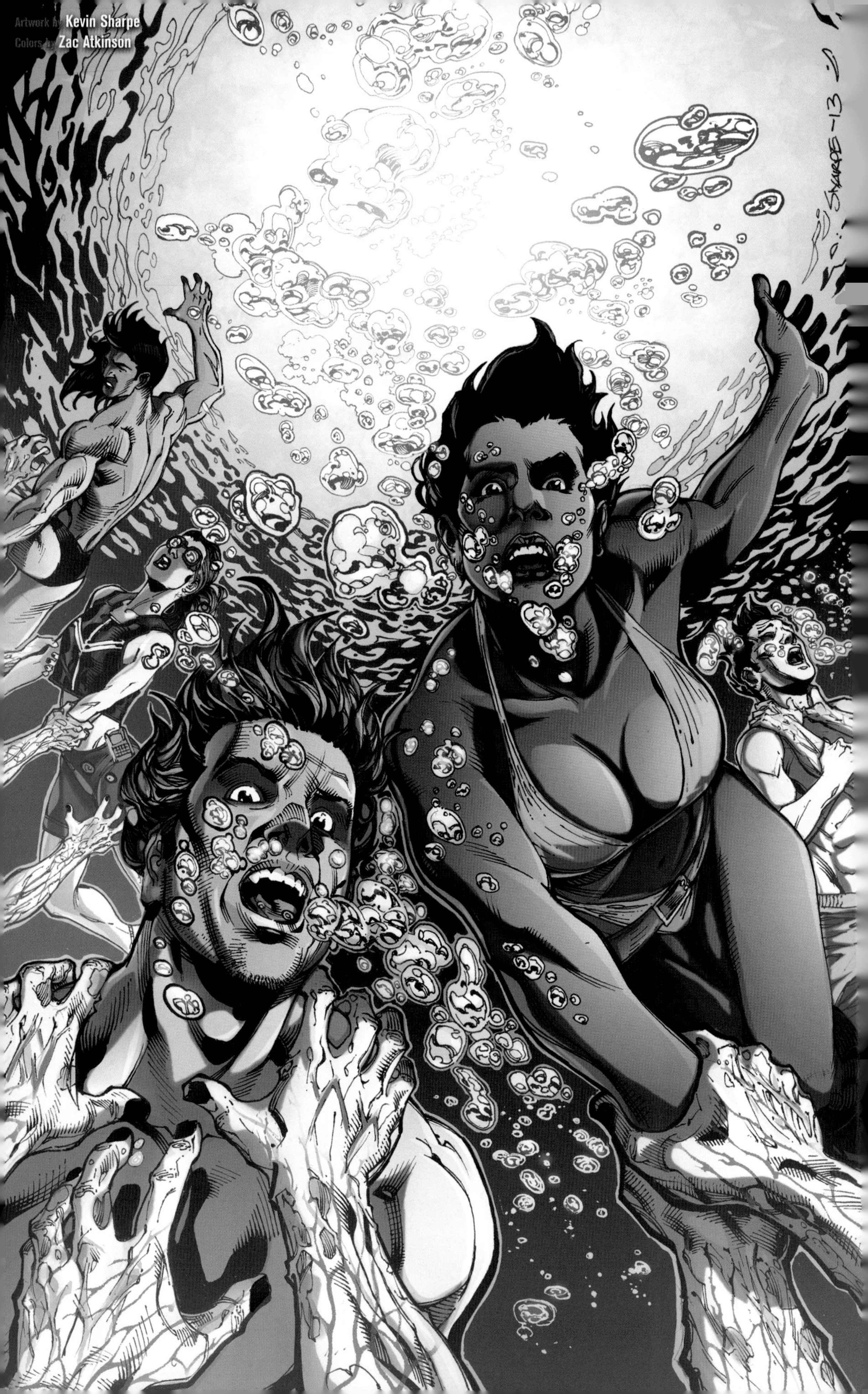
Sharpe-13

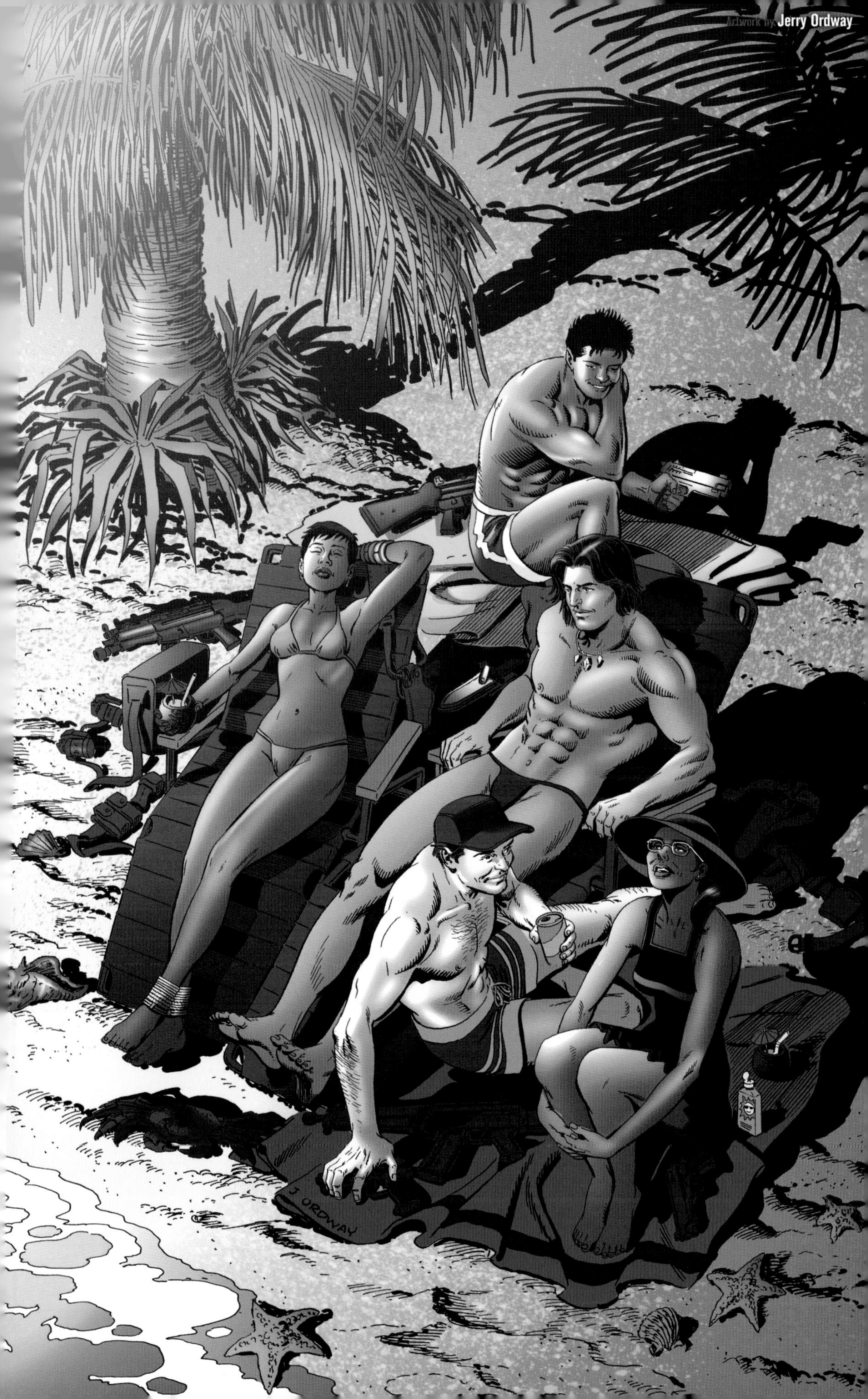
J ORDWAY
Artwork by Jerry Ordway

Artwork by Kevin Sharpe
Colors by Andrew Elder

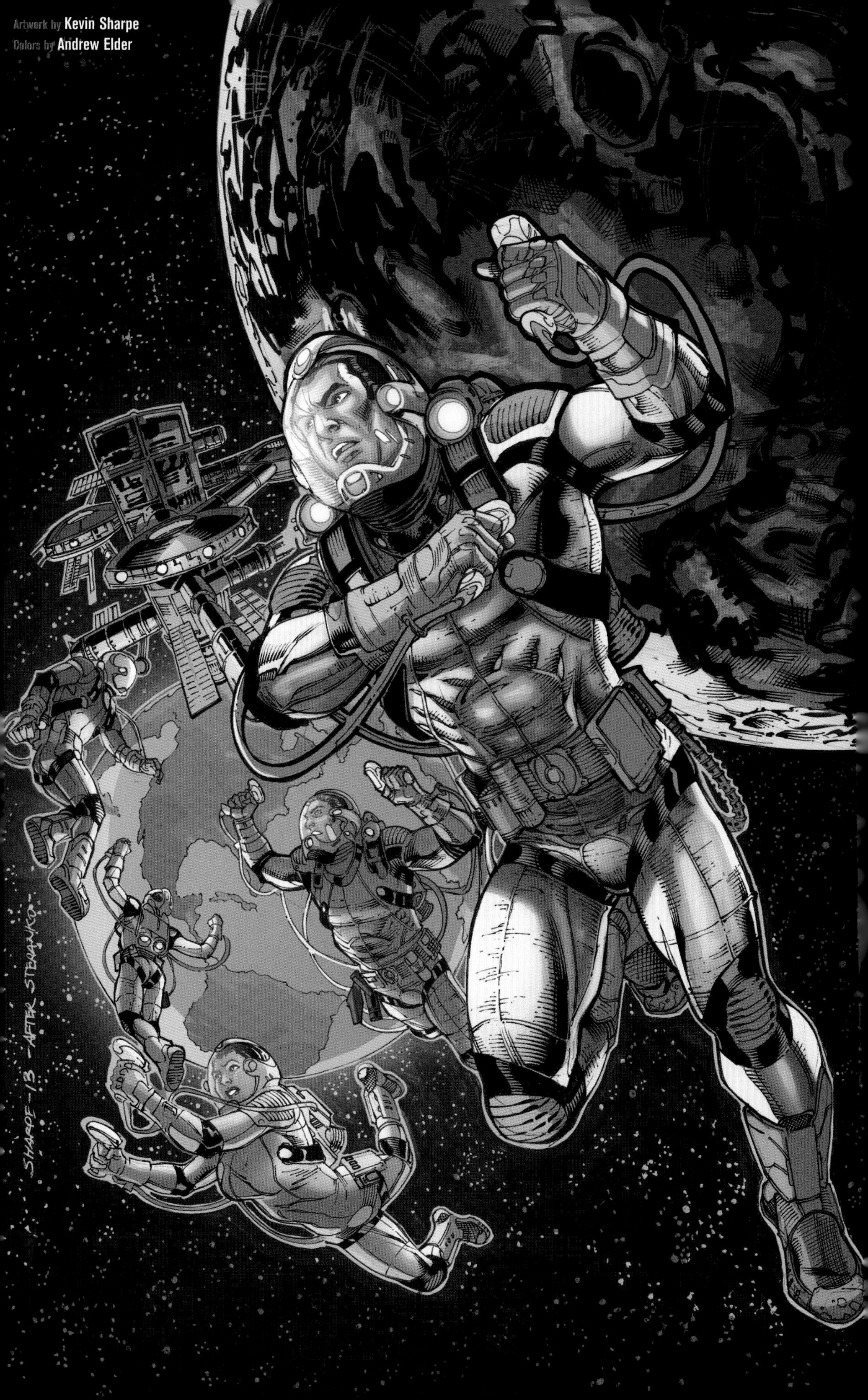
SHARPE -13 -AFTER STERANKO-

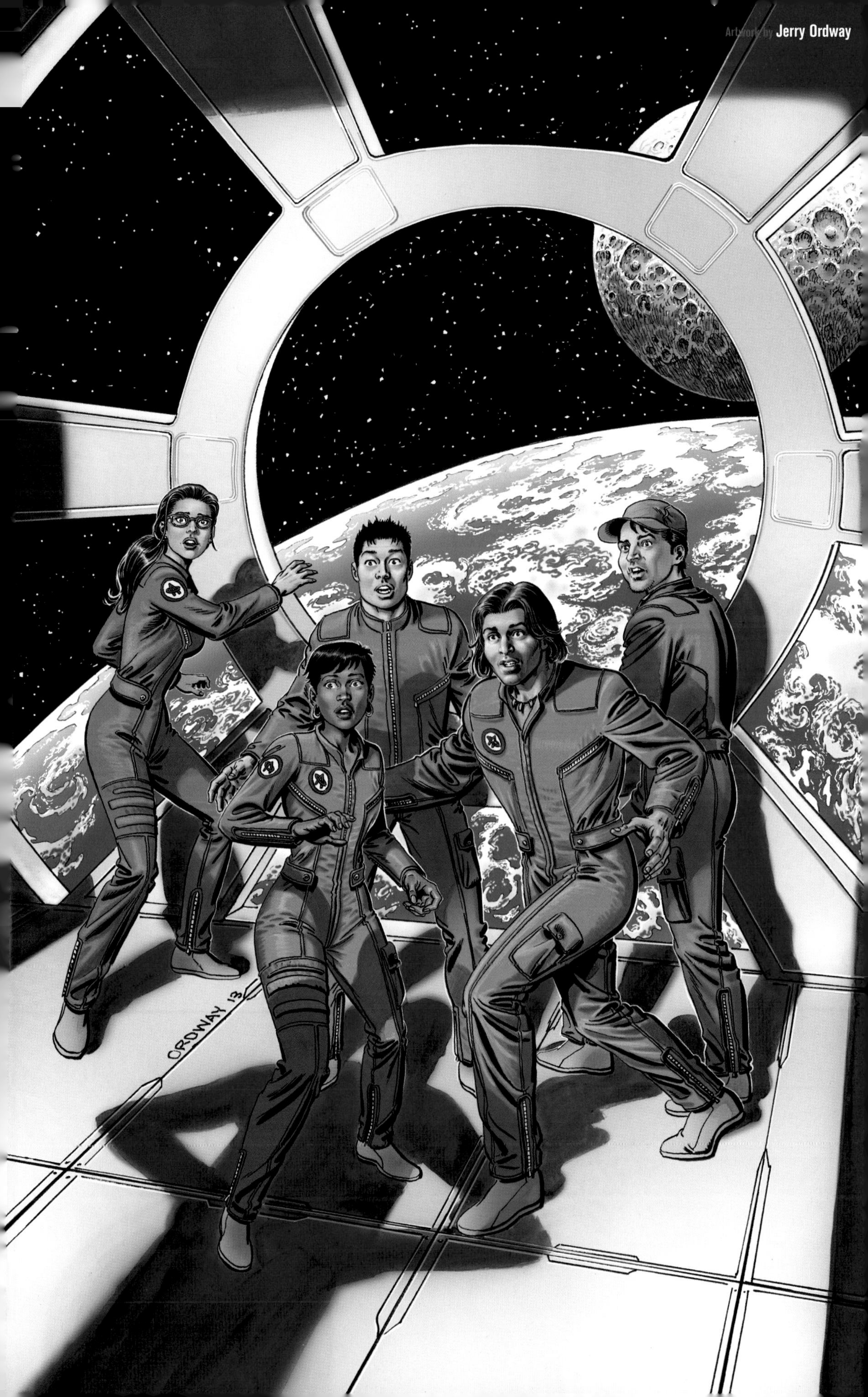
ORDWAY '13

Artwork by **Jerry Ordway**

Artwork by **Kevin Sharpe**
Colors by **Andrew Elder**

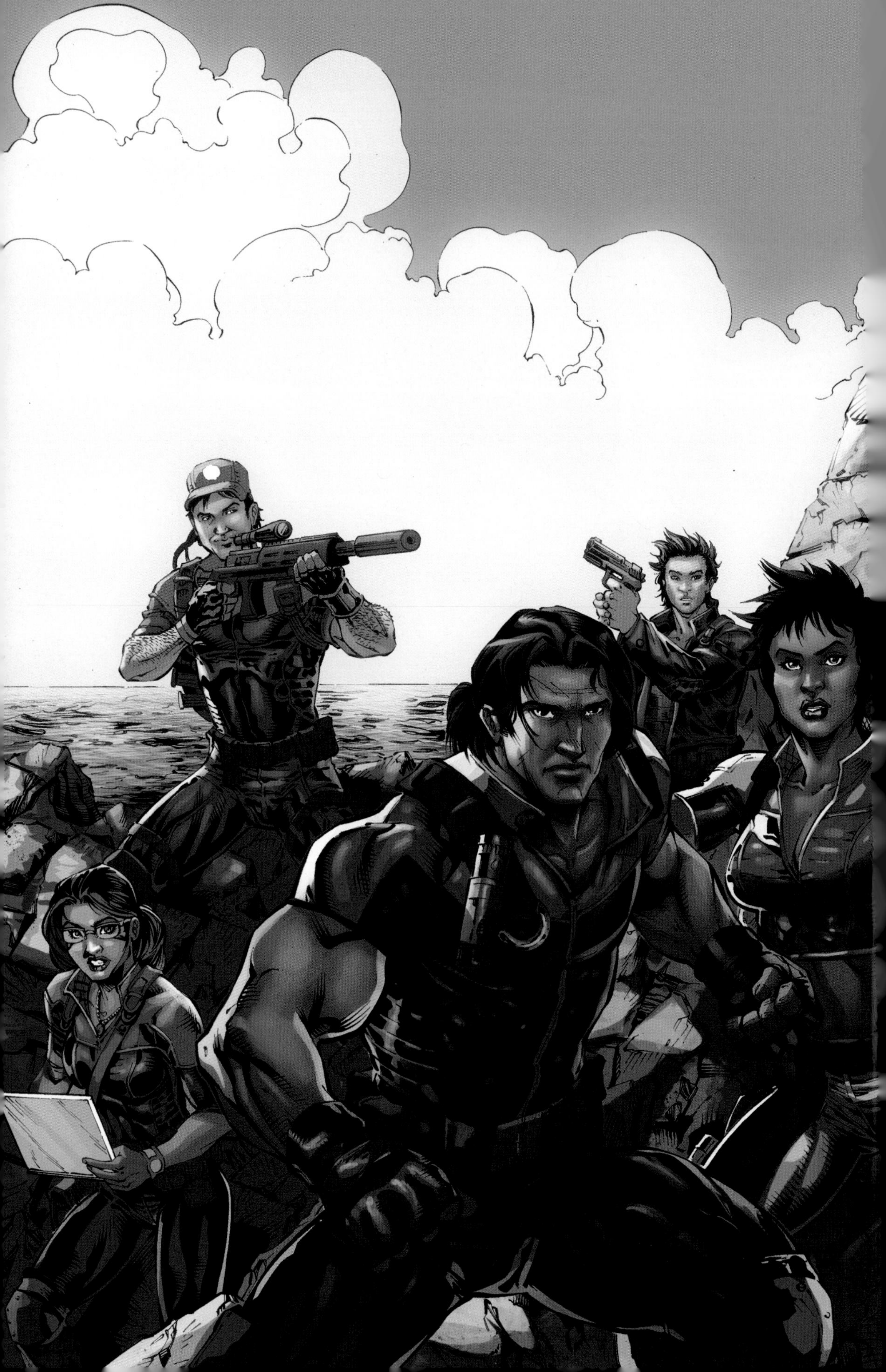

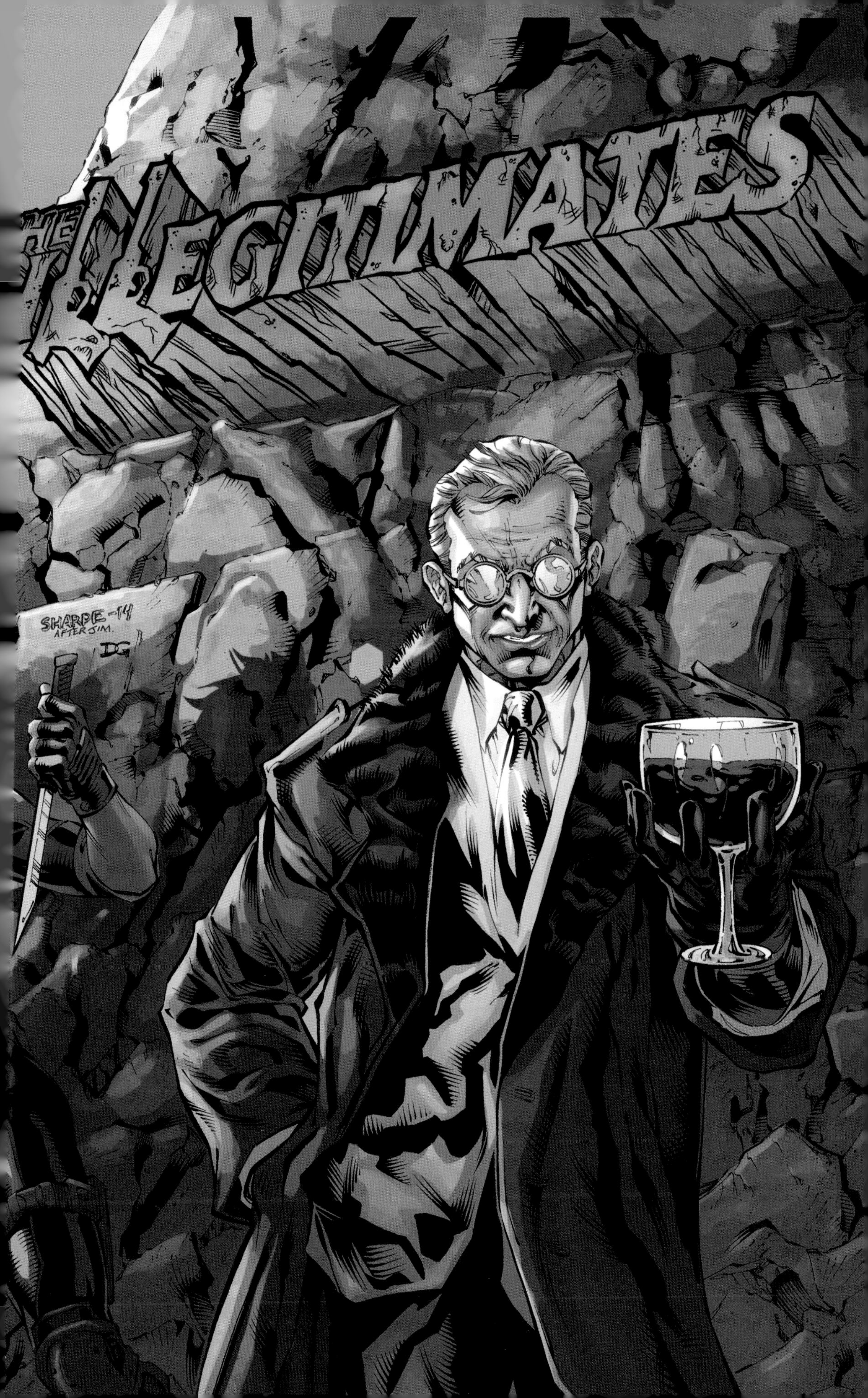
THE ILLEGITIMATES
SHARPE-14
AFTER JIM.
DG

Artwork by **Jerry Ordw**

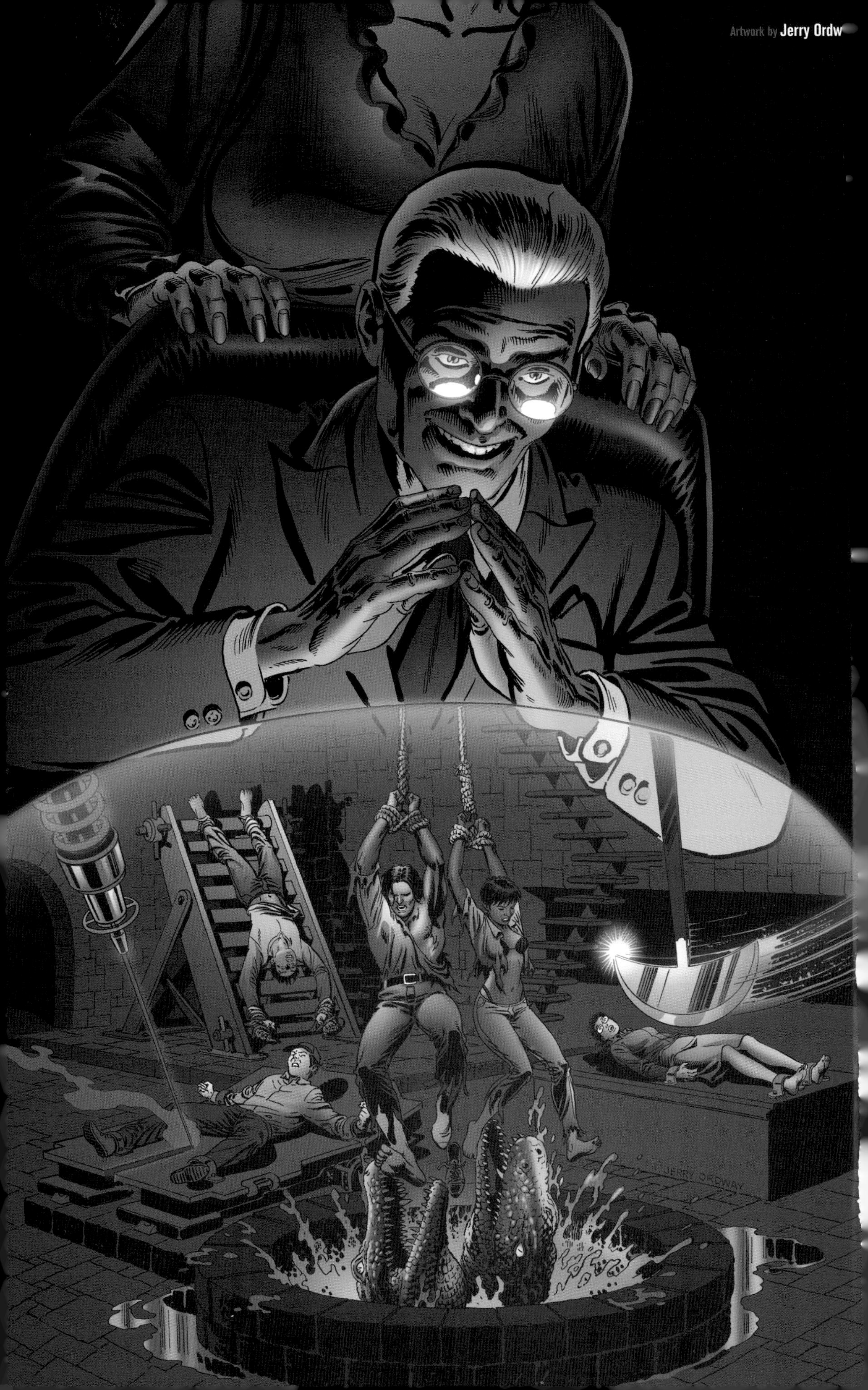
JERRY ORDWAY